# FINDING EVE

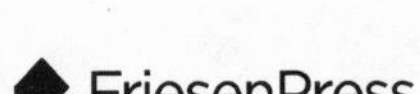


Suite 300 - 990 Fort St
Victoria, BC, V8V 3K2
Canada

www.friesenpress.com



First Edition — 2016

This is a work of fiction. Names, characters, places and incidents either are the product of the author's imagination or are used fictitiously. Any resemblance to actual persons, living or dead, events, organizations, or locales is entirely coincidental.

Author Image: Ken Dalton Photography



ISBN
978-1-4602-8359-2 (Hardcover)
978-1-4602-8360-8 (Paperback)
978-1-4602-8361-5 (eBook)

1. *FAMILY & RELATIONSHIPS, LOVE & ROMANCE*

Distributed to the trade by The Ingram Book Company

# *Finding Eve*

Stefana Mocanu

To Agnes, of course! As promised.

And to my wonderful family: husband, Vasile,
son, Marian, and wife, Alexandra,
daughter Andra and husband, Rostyslav,
daughter Oana and friend, Andrew,
my amazing grandchildren, Atticus and Sofia,
and to my beloved mother, Floarea.
With all my love for your support and understanding during this incredible journey.

In memory of my father
I know you guide me from above.

# One

February 1993

Eve was up very early. In fact, she hadn't gone back to sleep after the nightmare. Each time it occurred it was slightly different, but still seemed to maintain a pattern — as if to provide the key to some hidden secret. It had been relentless in its mission.

Nineteen months ago she had had everything a young woman could ever want. Now, after losing her husband and newborn baby, she felt rudderless and empty. Some days she felt as if she had nothing left. It took great willpower not to submit to those feelings, and at times — like now — she let herself wallow in the misery that comes with widowhood.

Eve shook her head to cast away the dreary thoughts. On second thought, she should consider herself lucky that she had had a son with the man she had loved so dearly. Anthony. Her pride, joy, and only consolation.

*Anthony!* Eve thought in a heartbeat and started up the stairs to wake him. Enveloped by her gloom, she'd forgotten about his hockey practice. It was Saturday and her ever-caring friend Crista was due to pick him up within thirty minutes.

"Are you ready, darling?" she asked her son, ten minutes later from the bottom of the staircase. "Breakfast is ready." Eve was taken aback by her son's sullen face. *He's not feeling well,* was her first thought. As she bent to kiss his forehead, she noticed with satisfaction that he was not feverish.

"Mommy, my tummy hurts."

"Maybe if you eat your breakfast?"

"I'm not hungry."

"But you need to eat something."

He moved his food around the plate and finally pushed it away. "I can't go to practice today."

"Oh?"

As she decided how to pursue the conversation, the phone rang.

"Good morning," Eve said to Crista. "Anthony won't be coming to practice this morning. He's not feeling well."

Crista and her husband, Mike, had one child, Brandon, a year older than Anthony and a dear friend of his. Since Eve's husband died, Mike had taken Anthony under his wing. Eve was grateful for the time her son spent in the company of the Malone men.

"Sorry to hear that, darling," Crista replied, "but someone is on his way to pick him up right now."

Eve's heart skipped a beat as she took a quick glance at her clothes. She was wearing a banal housecoat pulled over an equally banal nightgown. *Why didn't you let me know sooner?*

"You remember Ryan? The boy who plays with Brandon?" Crista asked. "His father picked up Brandon and is on his way to pick up Anthony." She then apologized for not letting Eve know when the plans had changed the night before.

The ringing of the doorbell suddenly echoed through the house. Eve brought the conversation with her forgetful friend to an abrupt end, and started towards the door.

Taking a deep breath, she opened the door and then stepped aside to let the youthful "forces" in. The two boys hardly looked at her, their answer to her greeting echoing behind them. She couldn't help but admire their exuberance as she watched them.

As she turned to face the man who accompanied the boys, she was shocked to see that he was giving her the once over. In spite of her usual, composed disposition, Eve found herself flustered by the man's brazen stares.

"Hello!" he said, extending a hand toward Eve. "My name is Adam. Adam Carry."

She was not sure about accepting his outstretched hand, but after a short deliberation, responded, "Hi, I'm Anthony's mother." As she offered her hand to him, much to her exasperation he lifted it slowly to his mouth, kissing the back of it, his stare never leaving her eyes.

His gesture did nothing but amplify the anger she felt from this unsolicited attention.

"And…?" His eyebrows were slanted in a query, and for a split second his eyes rested on her delicate hands.

"And what?"

"Your name is? I presumed you were Anthony's mother."

"Oh, I'm sorry. I'm Eve Nelson," she said, attempting to be unaffected by the Biblical coincidence of their names.

"Enchanted!" Adam exclaimed, and Eve discerned a wicked flicker in his blue eyes. "It's not very often that I come across an Eve."

A tide of hot flashes surged through Eve's body. She realized that she had forgotten to reclaim her hand and the man before her was in no rush to let it go. She wrestled momentarily with how to extricate it without being obvious.

"My son isn't feeling well. I don't think he'll be going with the boys today. Stomach ache, I think…" Eve said, at peace now that her hand had escaped from his grasp. "He hardly ate anything."

The two adults started towards the dining room, where pleading voices were trying to convince Anthony to attend the practice.

As Adam got closer, Anthony looked up and asked him if he would stay to watch the practice. Receiving an affirmative reply, Anthony announced that he would come along, his face bright and merry.

And that was all the feisty youngsters needed to hear. They started running up and down collecting Anthony's equipment. In no time, they had scampered through the door, leaving an awkward stillness behind.

Eve was left to wonder how a "yes" from a stranger had transformed her son's disposition from one of ill humour to one ready for a new adventure.

"I guess I'll catch up with the boys," Adam Carry said, interrupting Eve's thoughts.

"Yes, yes," she said, guiding him towards the foyer. As he passed by her, the mixture of his spicy cologne and the vague scent of cigar tickled her nostrils and made her a bit giddy.

"Mr. Carry, call me if my son is not feeling well at the practice, please."

"If there are any problems, I'll call. I promise. And call me Adam, please," he said, as he departed.

She could hardly refrain from slamming the door and swearing like a trooper. She couldn't believe the guy's audacity. The whole encounter was so unnerving it left her seething. She drew in a deep breath and expelled it hotly. Still, her bitterness gathered into a well-worn saying: *Men are pigs.*

"Well, you certainly got up on the wrong side of the bed this morning," Crista said. "All I'm trying to do is to cheer you up," she added. "How was I supposed to know he's such a randy son of a beast? We aren't bosom buddies or anything like that. We know Ryan and his family from the league. We let Brandon spend time with Ryan because we assumed they're polished, well-bred, and civilized people. I guess appearances sometimes are deceiving."

Eve had been in the middle of changing the soil of a plant she had purchased a couple of weeks before when Crista paid her a visit. She decided it was Crista's fault that she felt so aggravated. Intentionally or not, Crista was the one who had sent that infuriating character to her home.

"I felt so embarrassed and humiliated," she said, taking off the rubber gloves when she noticed soil was flying off them as she talked. "The guy looked at me like I was naked. Do I look like an easy woman?" Eve's words were coming out of her mouth as fast as machine-gun fire.

Crista shook her head. She felt only slightly irked by the incident, as she suspected Eve was exaggerating a bit. In her opinion, Brad Johnson, Ryan's father — a lawyer by profession — wasn't making the womanizer list. When she first met him he had asked her jokingly if she was Halle Berry's twin. Did she think he was making a pass at her? Hell, no! They had both laughed. Crista took it as a compliment.

Eve hung the plant in its place and started cleaning up the mess she had made. Just then, the phone rang.

"Hello…Mr. Carry? Is anything wrong?" Eve asked.

Crista, who was helping herself to a cup of coffee, stopped and listened.

"I was so concerned at first…oh…oh…thank God…"

Crista carried her cup to the table, a broad smile on her face.

"Oh, she's right here, I'll ask," Eve said, and covering the mouthpiece, turned to Crista. "Mr. Carry wants to know whether you'll give Brandon permission to visit with Ryan after practice."

"Did he invite Anthony, too?"

"Yes."

"Then *they* can go," Crista said. Eve was a little piqued that Crista had made the decision on her behalf.

"But you'll go and bring them back," Eve said to Crista and then added straight into the receiver, "Yes, Mr. — err — Adam. The boys can visit with Ryan. Brandon's mother insists on picking them up, so please call her when they're ready." She hastily said goodbye and hung up. *This guy is really bold.*

Crista's laugh, which quickly became a roar, jarred her.

"What's so funny?" Eve demanded.

"Do you know who you just talked to?" Crista asked. "You never mentioned the guy's name. That man is not Ryan's father."

"He's not?"

"No! He's Ryan's uncle — God's most precious creation — Adam. Adam Carry, that is. I knew Brad Johnson, the mighty lawyer, was not *that* nice or the 'seducer' type. He is a hand-shaking type of guy. He would never kiss a woman's hand! But Adam, well...he's something else! He's a cross between Cary Grant and Clark Gable. What a *looker.* And somewhat available, by the way."

To Eve, this piece of information didn't change a thing. No matter who or what he was, he didn't impress or interest her. His conduct was rude. To kiss a woman's hand on a banal occasion is excessive and intrusive. Just then it occurred to her that her girlfriend's laugh might indicate that she had intended to fix her up with, as she put it, "God's creation." She wouldn't put anything past Crista.

"Did you arrange for this 'Grant-Gable' to pick up the boys this morning?"

"No! I didn't. I swear!" Crista replied. "Come to think of it, I don't know who called last night to announce the change. Mike was home and talked to whoever called. *I* assumed it was Ryan's father. I had no idea who picked up Brandon this morning. Brandon waited outside and I stayed inside, because I was just wearing a nightgown," Crista said. "Honestly, I didn't know it was *him* until you said his name."

Eve was not fully convinced of her friend's innocence.

"So why is he acting as his nephew's chauffeur?" Eve asked, as she poured herself some coffee and joined her friend for a cup of gossip. She hoped she didn't seem overly interested.

"I don't know. I'm not his confidante, but I can offer some juicy gossip. He is divorcing his wife — hence the pass on you." Crista winked at Eve. "It sounds as if he has the hots for you!"

"Hots or not, I could have been a married woman!" Eve snapped back.

"But you're not. You're a young, beautiful woman who happens to be a widow. Darling, if you wait until the resurrection, then I got news for you: Not even William would take you back. You would be too withered even for him."

Eve was thoughtful for a moment.

Crista added, "And I didn't insist that I would pick up the boys. Adam Carry can drop them off."

"I really don't want to see him again today!"

"Why not? What's the big deal with seeing him?"

"If you keep talking about him, I won't go shopping with you."

With shaky hands, Eve opened the manila envelope with the Edmonton Police Service logo. A man had come to the door in civilian clothing but identified himself as a police officer from the Investigations Department. He had not stayed but a moment after delivering the envelope. He didn't say much nor offer words of sympathy. But then, what could a stranger say? The contents of the letter said it all.

After her husband had died in a fierce fire, Eve made countless requests to the authorities to search for his wedding band and a gold chain he was wearing at the time of his death. She thought all her pleas had gone in vain. Until now. She ignored the trite words on the enclosed note and looked at the distorted piece of gold that was once on her husband's finger. Regretfully, the letter specified, it was the only valuable found. She sank onto the sofa and wept.

As her sobs subsided, Eve's mind was propelled back to the sweet memories of her beloved William…

In spring of 1983, Eve graduated from Julian Ashton Art School in her hometown of Sydney, Australia. Like her peers, throughout her education she had done minor art jobs. If lucky, one could grab some money on the spot. If not, they at least bolstered their credentials as "future artists." They all thought that, once they graduated, both work and money would come to them like a magnetic force. Surprise! The damn degree was worth peanuts until you made a name for yourself.

Eve realized that starting with tiny, modest offers would perhaps help her become better known and engender a 'signature'. She accepted any offers of work that came her way, from projects on school hallways to quick portraits in the mall. She even sold a few larger canvas works. Eve earned nearly enough to maintain a fair standard of living.

A few months after she finished school, she answered an ad in the local paper. It was a challenging project that piqued her professional interest.

She armed herself with her schooling credentials, references from former teachers, and a good dose of resolution.

"Considering how many renowned artists have already applied, I would say the job is as good as taken." The secretary took her application without even looking at her resume.

"I would like to leave my application here, if I may." Eve was curt with the elegant but haughty secretary.

Two weeks later, she received a letter informing her that she was invited for an interview, if she was still interested.

When a bus splashed her legs and part of her dress the afternoon of the interview, she supposed it was just not her lucky day. By the time she arrived for the interview, she was so despondent that she wished she had never applied. At least the secretary, a different one this time, was smiling. She brought Eve a damp towel to wipe off her dress. Eve was relieved when the secretary ushered her into the interview room. In her present state of mind, the demands of the position seemed insurmountable.

"Miss Davis is here, Mr. Nelson."

"Thank you, Mrs. Lee." He lifted his eyes from the paper in front of him and stood to shake her hand over his imposing desk. "Please, have a seat Miss…Eve Davis."

When he said her full name, Eve guessed he had just gleaned it from the paper before him, as he flipped it over and looked at the other side.

Eve sat down in one of the two chairs across from the impressive desk of the equally impressive man. The plaque with his name read: William J. Nelson; and underneath: Vice-President.

Having nothing better to do, as he reviewed her resume, Eve stole sideways glances at her surroundings. Her artistic eye was impressed by the decor. From the outside of the building, no one would have guessed the opulence within. The plush, dark green carpet, gigantic natural plants, expensive leather furniture, antique pieces — a huge clay pot that caught Eve's attention in particular — were all proof of the moneyed nature of the room.

She found herself weighing up the man across the desk. She guessed him to be in his early thirties. He had a strong, sculptured face, a handsomely fashioned mouth, and abundant dark hair. He was also nicely styled and tall. The subject of her study defined today's intellectual man — a bit too stern and intimidating for her liking.

As if he sensed that he was being scrutinized, he bent farther over the desk and supported his head with his left hand, creating a shield to his upper face.

Eve's mind played with a thought: Did he think she was admiring him? He was wrong. She wondered if he ever smiled or better yet, if he knew how.

When he lifted his eyes, she was caught off guard. The mouth she was just studying twisted into a grin, contradicting her initial assumption; he knew the meaning of a smile.

And, of course, *blue* eyes! Definitely, unchangeably blue. How could she ever predict the colour of his eyes would alter his appearance so drastically? She wanted to paint that blue one day.

"Sorry, Miss Davis, I just needed to review your resume quickly. How are you?"

"Good. I'm a bit nervous."

"Don't be," he recommended. "I'm nervous, too."

William J. Nelson, Vice-President, described the requirements of the job and Eve intently focused her attention. They wanted three pieces of work created. One — the biggest of all — was for the lobby. It was supposed to cover an entire wall. The others, smaller in dimension, were to reside in the President and Vice-President's offices. The procedure to be used thrilled and frightened Eve, but she didn't let it show. She found herself longing for the opportunity to create these pieces.

"When are you able to start, Miss Davis?"

"I beg your pardon?" Eve wasn't sure she heard right.

"You don't want the job?"

Not want the job? It was like asking whether she wouldn't need air. She had lived with her brother's family since their mother died. Gloria, her brother's wife, was like a sister to her and Jessie, their two-year-old daughter, was like her own. But from time to time she got the hankering to have a place of her own, no matter how small.

"Of course, I would love to take the job," Eve ventured. She would have been more prepared for a rejection than for an offer. *This must be my lucky day after all!*

She took the job and loved it. When she'd said yes to it, she didn't know that she had also said yes to love and happiness. William Nelson did his best to sweep her off her feet, just like in those too-good-to-be-true romance stories. The spark was there from the first minute and grew until they both were enveloped in an immeasurable flame.

"You never told me why you chose me to do this job," Eve asked her former boss and current fiancé, four months later.

"You were the most presentable of all candidates. Correction: You were the most beautiful. Actually, you're the only one I interviewed. I surprised my secretary as she was discarding your application. So I decided to give the unlucky candidate a chance," he said. "I normally don't do interviews. And never just by myself."

"You risked the job on me?"

"Not at all. Before the interview I called one of your teachers, and when I got the most praiseworthy evaluation, I wanted to interview you. And, here we are, happily engaged and soon to be married."

"Soon? Says who?" inquired Eve. It bothered her that she couldn't get a straight answer. She still didn't know whether she got the job because she deserved it and was good at it or because he liked her appearance. And then she gave up, not knowing which one she would like it to be. She was too happy and didn't want to waste time wrestling with unnecessary deliberation. *You got it for both: beauty and talent.*

"Come on darling, what's to wait for? It seems we've known each other forever." William tried his best to hide his frustration.

"But it's only been four months since we met."

"Haven't you got it into your beautiful but stubborn head that it was predestined by some supreme being? If it's destiny, why wait?"

"And you think four months is long enough for me to know you?"

He thought she was just teasing, but she was concerned about the direction of their relationship. There were no more ways to tell her thirty-six-year-old fiancé to "stay nice." She needed time. She was infatuated with him all right, but she wanted to know more about him before she made such an important decision. There were times when she could read him like a book. He was open, exuded confidence, and had a great deal of charm and intelligence. But other times he could be withdrawn — miles away. She attributed his aloofness to his past. Orphaned at seventeen, an uncle took it upon himself to guide him through his further education. By the time he finished university, his inheritance was gone. His uncle said that his parents didn't leave much behind, but he knew better. Angry and frustrated, he left England for Australia without regrets. "One piece of luggage and this," he once told Eve, pointing one finger towards his head.

Eve estimated that a great deal of grey matter resided in that handsome head. It was no wonder he was about to reach the paramount position in his career. He was reaching his goal, and he wanted Eve to join him in his refined world.

Compelled to make a decision, Eve sought her brother Garry's advice. After all, he was a lawyer.

"For heaven's sake, Eve," Garry said, "you just met this man! Wait and get to know each other better. Besides, don't you think he's a bit old for you? He's older than I am. Twenty years down the road, you'll find him dull and unremarkable. You don't realize it now, but there will be vast differences between you."

"Never," Eve countered.

Garry cursed his sister's unyielding resolve, and conducted an off-the-record investigation on Mr. William Nelson. The result was impressive: Nelson possessed a rare intelligence and ambition, and a flawless reputation. Who could object to that? After a tête-à-tête meeting between the two men, Garry blessed the marriage.

Eve and William lived happily until death drew them apart, eight and a half years later…

Eve was waiting for the Salvation Army truck to arrive. Someone from the charity had called the day before to say that it would be there around 8:00 a.m. She checked the time again and hoped it wouldn't be too much longer. She needed to drive Anthony to school and the thought of a delay made her uneasy. Anthony hated being late.

She was moving some smaller boxes up front to the pile when she heard a vehicle on the street. She opened one side of the garage door to see a man stepping out of a fancy-looking car in front of her house.

*Oh no*. Not him again! She had not seen Adam Carry since Saturday. She had spent most of that day miffed by the unpleasant encounter.

"Good morning," he said, as he walked up the sidewalk with a broad smile on his face. "Are you moving?"

"Ah, no!" she replied, breaking into a faint smile. "I'm giving these away to a charitable organization."

Against her will, Eve gave Adam a cursory glance, just long enough to register that he looked taller than the first time their paths had crossed. *Even more handsome*, she thought, which infuriated her. He was wearing a navy, mid-calf length winter coat that made its owner appear executive and elegant at the same time. *Obviously, he works in an office*. Her mind went further, imagining a high-priced suit underneath the coat. And further underneath…

"Um?"

"I said you maybe should close the door. It's a shame to waste the heat."

As Adam spoke, billows of breath were rolling toward her and Eve detected the same heady scent of their first encounter.

"It won't be too long until a truck arrives to pick this stuff up. I actually thought you were them," she explained.

"You have a lot of baby furniture here."

"Yes."

"Don't you need it anymore?"

"Most of it I acquired from a baby shower," Eve said. "My baby lived only two weeks. But, no, I don't think I will ever use it. I feel like it would be a sort of bad omen. And wicker is more to my liking."

"I knew about your husband but nothing about your baby's death," Adam said. "I'm sorry for your loss."

Eve held her breath for a short while and then swallowed hard, words and all.

"Thanks," she said. In spite of the nostalgia the conversation stirred, she found herself wondering how he knew she was a widow. And what in the world could be the reason for today's visit? Her curiosity was left unanswered as a truck pulled up.

Adam placed the white plastic bag he was carrying against the garage wall and put on leather gloves, readying himself to lend a hand.

Eve exchanged a few words with the truck driver, and then excused herself.

"I have to check on Anthony and see if he's ready for school," she said, and ran through the connecting door to the house.

When Eve returned, the truck was departing down the snow-covered street. She quickly opened the other garage door and got into her car just as Adam stepped inside. In the process, he pressed the button to the first door and it started rolling down with the usual, annoying drone.

"What are you doing?"

"I'm driving my son to school. It's eight twenty and I don't want him to be late."

"I can drive Anthony to school. My car is already warm."

"That won't be necessary," Eve said.

"Adam!" A young, crystalline voice echoed through the garage. "I didn't know you were here."

Adam's sideways glance met Eve's guilty one.

Eve hadn't mentioned Adam's unexpected visit to her son when she went inside, as she was hoping he'd have vanished before they left.

"Anthony, I came to see you. I heard you were a good boy, so I brought you something."

The boy's eyes became bright with anticipation as they followed the man striding toward the back of the garage.

"If it's okay with your mom..."

Eve damned him and stepped out of the car, irritation written all over her face. She drew in a cold breath. "What do you think you're doing?"

Anthony shifted his eyes from one adult to the other, not fully understanding the intricacies of the situation.

"I noticed the other day at my nephew's that Anthony likes this game. Ryan got two for his birthday. My sister suggested that Anthony could have one…that is, if you agree, of course."

Eve bit her lower lip. If Anthony were not present, the answer would have been simpler. "I guess he can have it."

A wide grin split the boy's face.

"Darling, go fast and get your coat and backpack. It's getting late."

The boy disappeared, plastic bag in hand.

Eve opened her mouth to voice her irritation, but the garage wall phone interrupted.

"Excuse me," she said stiffly as she headed for the telephone. "Eve Nelson speaking…Oh, hi Garry. How are you, darling? What's going on down there? I called and called…I had this feeling…not really, but only a minute. I was just taking Anthony to school. Oh, no…hold on a second." Anthony had just returned. She covered the mouthpiece as she said, "Darling, Mr. Carry says he can drive you to school…that is, if he's still willing?"

As soon as Adam nodded his approval, she resumed her phone conversation, catching a glimpse of her boy as he cheerfully followed his new "personal driver."

The events that transpired in the garage were still on her mind half an hour later when she was working on her art project — "the city view" as Crista dubbed it. It was an oil painting covering a complete wall in her sitting room, depicting the high-rise buildings in the heart of Edmonton. She made the unwise decision to let Anthony choose the theme of the painting.

"Mom, it would be nice to see those tall buildings from the couch," he had suggested one day when they were driving to the dentist. She fancied a wooded trail with a weathered wood bench — a tranquil scene. She was halfway through the painting and was already tired of the "tall buildings."

She was mixing a few shades of blue to reach a desired hue for the sky when the doorbell rang.

*Who could that be?* Eve asked herself on her way to the door, a thick brush still in her hand. A shudder ripped down her spine at the sight of Adam Carry standing at her door. *Again!*

She stepped back and he stepped inside. *Is this guy audacious or what?*

"I know you must think I'm crazy," he said with a crooked grin, "but there's a serious reason for my coming back."

"Oh, is there? Let me hear it then." She was determined to be in total control this time.

He was casting amused glances at her, examining her from head to toe. "What were you doing?"

"I beg your pardon?"

"Are you painting?" he said, looking at her brush and the painting shirt that covered half her tall body.

Finally, Eve understood what he was asking, but it irked her that he had replaced his answer with a question of his own, the answer to which was none of his damn business.

"You may call it painting, if you like," Eve said.

"Anthony forgot his lunch," Adam said. "And he was not late for school."

*Darn.* Eve was surprised to realize he had a legitimate reason to return. Adam had driven her son to school because of the phone call she received, which was important, unexpected, and somewhat unsettling. Her brother Garry told her that his daughter, Jessie, was still battling the sinus infection she'd had since January.

"Thank you very much for driving Anthony. I wasn't expecting that phone call, but it was important…" Her faint smile completed the sentence.

"Glad to be of use."

"And thank you for letting me know about his lunch. I'll take it to school later." Then she remembered. "As for the game you brought Anthony earlier, you really shouldn't do that. I was ticked that you didn't ask me beforehand."

"I should have called to discuss it with you first. Will you accept my humble apology?"

His face exuded sincerity and Eve acceded that perhaps she misunderstood some of this man's intentions. Some. Not the bold, ineffable ones. She nodded.

"So what were you doing with that brush?" Adam asked again.

"I'm working on an oil painting in the sitting room — a project inspired by Anthony." Eve explained, "I'm an artist. Not well known like da Vinci." Eve laughed and Adam laughed with her. A lock of curly reddish-gold hair had escaped from her hair clip and dangled about her face. Adam appeared fascinated by it. She noticed his steady gaze and tried to think of something to divert his attention. He was quicker.

"May I see your painting?"

"Yes…you may, but not now. When it's finished."

"Promise?"

"Promise."

"Good morning, young man," his secretary greeted Adam as he walked into the office.

"It's not good; it's excellent, Miss Annette," Adam stated, as he skimmed through the mail she had just handed him. "How is Princess?"

"She's fine, don't worry," she chuckled. "She was just tipsy, that's all."

"Tipsy? How in heaven did that happen?" Adam had bought the cat for her as a Christmas present.

"It's a long story. I'll tell you another time. Now go in and see your father. *She* is in there, too. They're waiting for you." At Adam's inquisitive look, she shrugged.

"Good morning, Father, Alicia," Adam said, as he entered his father's office. Two heads turned at the sound of his voice. However, only one answered his salutation.

"Morning," George Carry replied.

Adam didn't expect anything from Alicia, the woman he was in the process of divorcing. Good manners dictated he maintain a cool — if not normal — professional relationship at the corporation, especially in his father's presence. George was becoming increasingly annoyed by the "whole, damn divorce business."

"Son," George demanded, settling into his favourite leather chair, "I want to hear your reason for not seeing the marriage counsellor anymore."

The old man's patience seemed to have run out. His face was beet red, Adam noticed, which raised a major concern in his mind.

"What the hell got into you?" his father demanded, knocking the desk with his fist.

At that moment, both Alicia and Adam realized the seriousness of George's mood. Nine months ago, he had suffered a heart attack. Stubborn by nature, he came back to the helm of Carstone International Oil Corporation prematurely. Everyone was concerned for his health. To shield him from stress was simply impossible, no thanks to the domestic friction between the young Carry couple.

"Light a cigar for me, Alicia," George demanded, then looked at his son. "And I'm still waiting for your explanation, son." He paused long enough to take possession of the soothing device, as he called his cigar, and then continued. "Give me a really good reason this time."

"I decided to quit marriage counselling because it was a waste of my time and energy, and as far as I'm concerned, *she* was not making any effort to show up for most of the appointments or behave amicably when she did." Adam took a seat across from his father.

"Don't you *dare* say such a thing!" Alicia yelled. "Measure your own efforts."

"It's true. I only missed two sessions — one being the last, when I decided that I had enough. How many times did you show up or even follow Carol's advice?" Adam countered. Many times he was on his way, or had arrived, only to learn that Alicia had cancelled their session. And now she brazenly tells his father that *he* was the guilty party?

"That's because she's a crummy and brainless counsellor. I never liked her," Alicia shouted back. "I want to see a different therapist."

Adam slouched down in his chair and tilted his head to one side and then the other, closing his eyes all the while. *So much for the excellent start to my day*, he thought.

Carry senior looked rather disgusted but followed the heated discussion in earnest.

"*You* picked Carol Gardner! Just like the countless ones before—"

"I thought she was different. But then she started to put a load of shit on my back because of you—"

"*Stop it.* Both of you!" The old man's words came out in a shout. "I'm sick and tired of the way you talk to each other. Two fourth-graders behave better than you. What more do you want? What more do you two need? I really don't understand." He shook his head.

The wall of smoke from his father's cigar reached Adam's nostrils, and for a fleeting instant, he wanted to snatch the dreadful thing and scream at his father, *Stay out of my life!* But the words never came out. His father's precarious health stood in the way.

Alicia fetched a glass of spring water and placed it in front of the old man. The divorce. The thought of the divorce made her mad. There ought to be another alternative! She had to think harder, that's all. Foremost in her mind now was the business. The business meant money. And that spelled happiness in her book.

Just before Adam walked in, the 'brains' of the Corporation — aka Carry senior and Alicia — were discussing a new investment prospect. The oval table was scattered with blueprints and all sorts of informative material.

George Carry rose from his chair and approached the oval table. Calmness descended upon his face as his glance rested upon the papers.

"Come and look at this, son. Alicia and I acquired some info about marketing in Italy. It's a great opportunity!"

Adam knew his father's philosophy of life and money. It deeply saddened and angered him. Saddened, because Adam knew that no amount of money could ever buy happiness, and angered, because he blindly let himself get carried away by his father's self-ruling. But that would stop, and soon. Right now, he could almost guess what was expected of him in this new business prospect. He thought about how ridiculous his father sounded with the sudden change in his manners.

"Son, I want you to go there. I trust your competence and experience as a corporate diplomat. I'm sure you can—"

"Acquire the contract? Is that it?"

George and Alicia looked at each other. Adam had previously refused to make trips they assigned to him without consulting with him beforehand. Their trepidation was justified; Adam was unsettled by the earlier argument about divorce and he might refuse to go just to spite them. They needed him to be on board with this *colossal* moneymaking plan. The truth was that they couldn't make him go. Unlike both of them, Adam was only an *employee*. A highly paid one, but free to take his capacity and experience elsewhere.

Adam had the feeling he had just walked into the middle of a well-rehearsed play. Alicia abandoned her hysterics and assumed an aloof, almost civilized manner that a blind person could see through. His father was no less of an actor. He didn't explode as he typically would, and as he had done when discussing marriage counselling. *Yes, this is just another one of their plays*, Adam thought. *So let them play.*

"I meant…get the first step going…" Carry senior said.

"I'll go to Rome."

"You'll go?" Two voices echoed each other.

"When?"

"Tomorrow."

"Tomorrow?"

"The idea is, the sooner the better," the father confirmed, pleased with his son's cooperation.

After George gave Alicia a few instructions, she retreated to her office to complete them. As part of the play.

As father and son remained in the room, an acute silence descended. Apparently, neither of them wanted to be the first to break it. Adam decided he had nothing to say and began to rise from his chair. He was brought up short by his father's words.

"About your marriage, are you going to give it another try? I mean, at least you could resume getting professional advice."

Adam met his father's pleading glance. He needed his father's undivided attention for what he had to say.

"I'd appreciate it if you don't intrude into my private life from now on, Father." He left the room, and behind him, a perplexed, old man.

Carstone International Oil Corporation (CIOC) was established in 1934, under its original name — A.C. Oil Ltd. — named after its founder, Adam Edward Carry. As a new company, A.C. Oil Ltd. struggled to break into the market of established oil companies. It took Adam Carry more than courage to keep his young company afloat. His wits, intuition, honesty, and respect for his workers were qualities of the gracious man he was, and what held his company together during the Great Depression.

Adam Carry was a widower in his mid-fifties, raising his nine-year-old daughter, Janet. His forty-three-year-old wife, Sabrina, had died in childbirth. Janet was their only child.

Being a workaholic all his life, Adam Carry couldn't find time or space to bring another woman into his life. His widowed mother, Kathleen, had raised the child in Adam's stead.

As a child, Janet saw her father very seldom. Although he came home every night after putting in many hours at work, she was normally in bed. Janet was in high school before she started seeing her father more often. Kathleen died when Janet was in her last year of high school.

Adam sensed that his daughter was devastated by the disappearance of her only female idol, so he bought a car for her to compensate for the loss, which in his inexperienced opinion, was the most appropriate thing to do.

Janet was delighted with the gift as it served to create a special bond between father and daughter. From then on, more often than not, Janet could be found at her father's company, by his side. She made herself useful, circulating papers between the main office and the so-called workshop.

With her tall and slender body, long dark hair, and blue eyes, it was impossible for her not to attract attention. But only one young man held sway over her heart: George Miles.

George was an engineer and a very skilled young man. Adam Carry himself hired George as a foreman, but in less than a year, he requested that George work beside him and act as an adviser. Adam Carry knew the "real stuff" when he saw it, and George Miles possessed all the right qualities: He was gifted, and he had a lot of gumption.

George Miles was reckoned a rare and precious asset to the company. He had ideas that, when put into practice, helped the company prosper immeasurably.

In 1943, Janet started college, but after her freshman year, books were not the only thing on her mind. When not at school, she was beside George and both of them were beside her father. Their relationship evolved gradually, to the point that Adam Carry started paying more attention to the two young people. He was increasingly concerned and didn't know what to do about his daughter's attachment to George. As it turned out, the issue suddenly came to a head before he had made up his mind.

One Sunday afternoon, Janet and George announced that they wanted to get married.

"Married?" Adam had asked, dumbfounded.

"Yes, sir. That is, with your consent," George replied with all the courage he could muster.

Adam Carry frowned. He signalled Janet to leave the room.

"Have you compromised my daughter?" Adam asked. From the look on the young man's face, he could tell that George Miles had not.

"No, sir. I've never thought of dishonouring Janet. I admire and respect her. I love her and I want to share my life with her."

Adam Carry paced the room. From time to time, he stopped to look at George. A couple of times he attempted to open his mouth but changed his mind and started his pacing again. All he could think was, *Oh, God. If Sabrina was alive, she would know what to do*. And then his conscience encouraged him. He recalled that he had made good decisions before where Janet was concerned. He called Janet in.

With his arms clasped at his back, he inquired about the course of her education.

"I want to quit college, Dad. I know now that I don't want to be a teacher. I…" She trailed off intimidated by the penetrating look in her father's eyes.

"Go on," he prodded.

"I want to work at the company," Janet said. "You need to hire more clerical staff for the office anyway."

Adam weighed the pros and cons of the marriage proposal. There was truth in her words. He was not getting any younger; that was a fact. By acquiring a son-in-law like George Miles, he could be assured the company would be in competent hands later on. He also wanted to see his daughter happily settled.

"You may marry," he finally said.

Along with his blessing though, he had a special request. As he had no boys to carry on his name, George was to change his last name to Carry. Marrying Janet Carry in 1944, George Miles took the name of George Carry.

The company bore Carry's name until 1979 when, merging with H.P. Stone Oil Industry, it became Carstone International Oil Corporation — CIOC.

Adam stared at the impressive portrait occupying the best place on the wall. Many people said he resembled his grandfather, Adam Edward Carry. He remembered the day his mother gave him a small black and white picture — no bigger than the kind used for passports — the day he settled in his office years before.

"I want you to have this, darling." Janet had said.

"Thanks Mom, I've never seen this picture of my grandfather before!" He knew that his grandpa had died just before he was born, and that Janet had promised him that, if she gave birth to a baby boy, he would be named after him.

"Yes, dear. This is one of the few pictures I have of your grandfather. I found it the other day when I was going through some books in the library."

Adam had taken the picture, ordered a huge colour reproduction of it, and hung it there for his private appreciation. From time to time, he got caught up in a game of "conversing and consulting" with his namesake.

It was hard to believe he was only a few years shy of his grandfather's age when the picture was taken. The resemblance was becoming undeniable, as his mother was fond of reminding him. He often wondered if he inherited his wits and acumen.

Adam was so immersed in his thoughts that he didn't notice the door open behind him.

"Visiting with your grandpa again?" Miss Annette asked.

Adam turned to face his sweet grandma-bear secretary. "You know something, Miss Annette? I never get enough of visiting with my grandpa."

"I know." And of course she did. She had worked with him for too long not to know it. This particular phenomenon, "the grandpa visit," happened when things weren't going the way they should be. She saw him happy this morning, and now downhearted. He was like a son to her, and they shared an understanding, solid friendship in spite of the age difference. She cared enough to know not to intervene, but rather to extend a hand, if she could. She wanted to show camaraderie rather than sympathy, knowing it was all Adam could handle for the time being.

"You'll get over this hurdle; I know it," she said.

"What?"

"About the divorce, of course. Don't you think I know what's bothering you? I'll pray for you, my boy. God will help you make a decision you can live with, and whatever you decide, I'll be happy for you."

He smiled. "It's going to be all right, Miss Annette, but thanks for praying. I probably need as many prayers as you can spare. And a lot of luck." Adam's face was brighter. His enigmatic smile piqued the older woman's curiosity.

"Okay, what's really going on here, young man?" Miss Annette asked, as she sat in an empty chair, the stack of papers she had brought in for the next day's trip on her lap.

Adam chuckled. “It’s not likely you won’t sleep tonight if I don’t tell you about it.”

“You can bet I won’t sleep!”

“I bet you won’t sleep if I *tell* you either.”

“So, what the heck? Hit me with it.”

Adam smiled and went around the desk to claim his chair. He looked into Miss Annette’s eyes and paused.

“I met someone. A very special woman,” he said finally. “I know she’s special. Don’t look at me like I’m crazy.”

Miss Annette’s mouth gaped, “I don’t find this crazy. I’d say it’s rather spontaneous though. You want my opinion? I think it’s about time you have some fun. I want you to be happy. Wait a minute — what exactly do you mean by ‘special?’”

“It’s an assumption I’m making, of course. When I get to know her better, she may be even more special. I’ll introduce the two of you, so you’ll see for yourself,” Adam said.

“For goodness’ sake just don’t rush into proposing,” Miss Annette said with a smile.

“Proposing? Who’s proposing?”

Alicia’s interruption not only stunted the conversation, it shifted the atmosphere. Adam didn’t welcome her presence and didn’t want to satisfy her curiosity. It was Miss Annette who enlightened her.

“*I* am. Supposedly. Provided that Adam — Mr. Carry — brings me a hunk from Italy,” she claimed, ending with a gruff laugh.

Alicia didn’t buy the old secretary’s story. If anything, she was vexed by it. She never warmed up to the old woman and vice versa. She had tried many times to sabotage Miss Annette’s position. She would have succeeded were it not for Adam’s loyal and devoted support.

“Well, I have to go,” Miss Annette placed the paperwork from her lap on Adam’s desk. “Have a good trip, Mr. Carry.”

“And what can I do for you?” Adam asked, after Miss Annette had slipped out the door. It was 8:30 p.m. and their paths hadn’t crossed all day. *Why now?* They typically saw each other in his father’s office or elsewhere on the premises, but — as if in silent mutual agreement — they never intruded into each other’s private office, unless there was an emergency. He wondered what kind of emergency this was going to be.

"I was wondering if you'd reconsider the divorce. I mean...no pressure." She folded her arms. "Just give it some consideration while you're gone." She stopped long enough to adjust her voice. She decided that a more pleading tone was necessary. "There must be something left that we could save."

For a moment Adam was thoughtful. If he had not known her better, he might have taken her speech as genuine. As it was, he knew he was the spectator at a pristine play starring Alicia Carry.

"Could you take some time to think about our marriage while you're away?" Alicia asked. The anger too long cloaked finally surfaced. "What the *hell* is the matter with you? I can see I'm talking to myself. And you have the guts to blame me for not meeting you halfway."

"Calm down, I heard every word you said. I was only trying to figure out what the hell is to be saved in this sham of a marriage. In fact, it's crystal clear to me that our marriage is beyond retrieval."

"Oh puhleeese—"

"I'd be really impressed if we could find a single thing we agree on," Adam replied.

She threw her arms in the air. "Very well!" she said. "We'll adopt the child you want. We can start a family."

"Shall I remind you that you trapped me once before with this lie? You can't even bring yourself to say, 'adopt a child for *us*,'" Adam said, almost shouting the last word. "Let's not resurrect old ghosts, all right? You can't wheedle me with such nonsense anymore. And frankly, my dear 'wife', you have never been the maternal type. I doubt you ever touched a baby or talked to a child in your entire life."

His remark did nothing but infuriate her more. Discarding her last shred of etiquette, she snapped, "You arrogant son-of-a-bitch! Shall I refresh your memory about your *family fantasy?* You're such a coward to place the blame on me. Blame yourself or your frigging mother for making you sterile, but don't dump that shit on me."

Adam recognized this outburst as one of her frequent rages. To fight back would be a waste of time. But her scathing remark dug deeply. He felt disappointment beginning to engulf his thoughts, but with a force of will, he squelched it. He needed his sanity, he reminded himself, and methodically started to pack his briefcase.

However, it wasn't like Alicia to give up easily. Adam felt the air become charged again. *At least it's the end of the day and I can handle it.* He started towards the door.

"Since we don't see each other at home, I'll wish you a good trip now."

He stopped his stride but didn't turn to face her. Not until after she said, "Or should I say have a therapeutic trip?"

"What did you say?" he demanded.

"Do you really think I'm stupid to buy that shit about fetching a 'hunk' for that hag? I assume you were talking about finding someone for yourself or even taking some woman with you."

Adam rolled his eyes, his patience wearing thin. To think that Alicia was jealous was absurd. Never before during their separations had she questioned his fidelity. But then — their previous separations never lasted that long. Odd thing. When together, she wanted him afar; when separated, she wanted him back.

"Just tell me the truth, dear husband. Has my successor been picked out already?"

Her question, Adam realized, was not based on idle curiosity. There was something else, something he had never seen before. Her narrowed eyes confirmed as much.

"If you think I'd marry someone just because I want…need..." Adam started saying but changed his mind. He did not need to give her an account of what he wanted or needed any longer.

"Sex? Isn't that the word you are looking for?" Alicia offered.

Adam wanted to laugh. *Something left to save.* Yeah, right! "This conversation is finished. As far as I'm concerned, our marriage is over. The divorce is going through this time, and you'd be insane to believe otherwise." Adam dashed out the door, almost expecting to be attacked from behind.

Eve was sitting on her bed. Throngs of photos scattered around her were waiting their turn to take her back down memory lane. Her intention had been to find a picture — a particular one she took of her niece Jessica. Jessica's birthday was in a couple of months and she wanted to make a portrait to send her. She was so engrossed with her fond memories that she jumped when the phone rang.

"Hello?"

"Hi, Eve. How are you?"

Silence.

"I'm sorry, it's an ungodly hour to call."

"Adam?" Eve asked, even though she had recognized his voice.

"If you were sleeping, I can call—"

"No, no. I wasn't sleeping," she said, recovering from her surprise, "really."

"I'll be away for some time, so I thought I'd give you a call before I go." A pregnant pause followed. "I'm leaving for Italy tomorrow."

"Italy?"

"Rome, precisely."

"That's wonderful. On a vacation?" Eve said, and instantly regretted her question.

"Oh, no. It's business." He wasn't pleased to go. Especially, that he detested flying. It was here he wanted to be, where he'd have a chance to see *her*.

"Rome is sublime...enchanting. It is a venerable place to visit, even if only for a short while. I've been there once, and as an artist, I can tell you that it's—" She broke off. "Have you been there before?"

"Yes, a few times," he said softly.

"Oh, my!" Eve said. A warm sensation rose from the pit of her stomach. "I imagine you know what Rome holds for tourists then," she said, and decided to shut her mouth to avoid further embarrassment. Her impressions of a one-week visit in Rome, as part of her honeymoon, could hardly compare with his informed opinions resulting from "a few" visits.

The line suddenly filled with Adam's waves of laughter, which helped alleviate her uneasiness.

"I'll take your word for it. I never took time to enjoy the best Rome has to offer. But I will now if you can suggest some spots. Your artistic input will enhance the pleasurable part of my trip." With that invitation, Adam inveigled Eve into enthusiastic, picturesque depictions of Rome.

Her voice relaxed and transported him to a world where everything was possible. All day he had wanted to call her. Ever since he set eyes upon her, he couldn't control his urge to know her better.

To think, it had all started with him hearing the children's innocent chatter. On the way to pick up Anthony that Saturday morning, he'd overheard Ryan and Brandon talking about their friend who had no daddy. Engaging himself in their conversation, he learned that the boy's father had died. He'd met Anthony at the previous hockey practice, and now he felt such sympathy for the cute little boy with reddish hair and blue eyes. Adam's feelings hadn't gone beyond this until he faced the unexpected: Eve. It appeared that Cupid had targeted his heart. He was smitten by her appearance, the grace she presented and — yes, even the crossness with which she enforced her rules when he showed up that day with the game for Anthony.

"I hope I'm not boring you with my opinions and recommendations. I have a hunch you won't have time to see half of what I suggested."

He laughed. "True, but I appreciate every word you said. I'm not sure how much time I'll have to tour. Next time I'm in Rome, I'll hire an erudite guide like yourself to take with me on a da Vinci tour. Could you be tempted by such a job offer?"

"You forget — I'm not a tourist guide. I'm an artist, and you may not be able to afford to pay me," Eve said and laughed.

Adam joined her in laughter. "True," he lied. No use telling her that he could afford to meet any of her financial demands. "Eve?"

"Yes?"

He hesitated. "I was wondering if we could have dinner when I return. What I mean is that I would like for us to be friends...if that's all right with you. That is, if you're not seeing anyone. Let me back up a bit by adding that I'm in the process of divorce now, but it should be concluded in a few months." He thought that it was honest to get all his cards on the table. However, it seemed an eternity until Eve responded.

"I don't know what to say. You took me by surprise. Actually, I have a bit of a problem dating someone with such an unconfirmed relationship status. I'm not cut out for gambling, even for something as unassuming as a dinner date. Forgive me for asking, but don't you think you might still have a chance to sort out your marital problems?"

Adam understood Eve's concern about the possibility of reconciliation with Alicia. But by God, he was fed up with Alicia's talk about reconciliation. Why did the woman he wanted to date have to talk about it too? His annoyance came out with a sigh.

Eve heard it. She didn't know when she became so intrigued with this man. She questioned herself: *Am I ready for such a significant change in my life?*

"Eve, my marriage is past the point of recovery. I'm telling you the truth. We tried to reconcile, but it didn't work. Honest to God. We've been separated for months. This is the end of it. My divorce is a god-awful muddle, even though we didn't have children, but eventually it will end. It's just a matter of time."

*Probably as much time as I need to know you better, and for you to be unmarried,* Eve completed silently. Another thought crossed her mind: *Why are they divorcing?* She wondered if another woman had interfered in their marriage. And then, if that were the case, wouldn't he supposedly be with that woman now? Or maybe his wife was the one...

"So, this is my present status, and coming back to my initial question, will you be my lady friend?"

"Give me some time to think about it, Adam. I might need to look up the definition of *friendship*."

Adam laughed a pleasant, comforting laugh. "You're overly cautious."

"A woman can never be too cautious, can she?"

"I guess you're right. Nevertheless, I'd love to have an answer from you when I'm back from Rome."

"I'll think about it. But I warn you, it could be either way."

"Hmm. Well, I'll take 50-50 for now. What can I bring you from Rome?"

"Don't push it, Adam. You won't tip the balance in your favour by buying me presents."

He pretended to take offence. "I'm not trying to do any such thing. I meant something small like postcards or stamps — I know Anthony collects them. Or do you simply want regards from da Vinci?"

"You're an incorrigible fantasist."

"I know."

"Have a good trip."

"Good night."

Eve stepped inside the office that had once been her husband's. She had been at the bank after William's death, but had not been ready to face the raw memories, so she had asked for a different office to meet Victor Knight, the current manager. And he understood. Now, however, she felt strong enough to face the past, the reality, and the memories above all.

Her late husband's successor welcomed her at the door with a broad smile and arms opened for an embrace.

"How are you my dear friend, Eve?"

"I'm fine, Victor. I really am."

He led her to a chair across from his desk and she sat and looked around. Just then, the phone rang and Victor excused himself to take the call. She realized she felt a sense of peace she had not felt on her last visit. Perhaps it was due to the fact that, on that visit, she had to deliver very upsetting news to her husband...

"What is it, honey?" William had asked when Eve stepped into the office, after she nervously waited at the door for his meeting to end.

"It's the baby. Dr. Summer called and wants to see us both as soon as possible. There's something wrong," Eve said, unable to control her composure any longer. Through wet eyelashes and the half-opened blinds she saw the world going on as usual. And across from her, William as cold as stone. In that moment, she felt alone and guilty.

A half hour later, in the doctor's office, they both were shocked with the devastating news.

"It's possible the baby has Down syndrome," Eve's obstetrician had said. "I don't quite understand how this was not picked up at the previous ultrasound, but the one you had yesterday clearly shows the characteristics of this particular abnormality." He went on to explain, "In a case of Down syndrome, there is a larger amount of fluid than normal in the baby's kidneys. This diagnostic is evident in ninety per cent of the cases. The other ten per cent represent major kidney malfunction."

"How is this possible?" Eve asked. "I thought Down syndrome appeared in babies of older mothers. I don't understand. Are there any more tests we could run?"

"I'm sorry, Eve," Dr. Summer said. "Amniocentesis is too risky at this stage of your pregnancy."

"This is not fair!" William moaned.

His distressed state made Eve feel guiltier. She knew he had wanted Anthony but not *this* baby, and she had gone against his wishes.

"It's not that I don't want another baby, darling, but it is not the right time." He was new in a high-pressure job and increasing his family responsibilities was not the smartest move. But she yearned to have another baby — maybe a little girl to spoil with her love. Eve had miscarried twin boys at twelve weeks shortly after they arrived in Canada, in the fall of 1984, but then on January 14, 1986, Anthony was born and with that, her life became complete. Now Eve wanted more. One more. "A little brother or sister for Anthony would be perfect," she had pleaded with her husband, when she shared the big news. "He won't be alone in this world, darling."

After Eve told William about the pregnancy, he was quiet, subdued. As Eve counted the weeks passing by and preparing for the baby's arrival, he grew more distant.

If William accepted her decision to bring another baby into their lives, she knew now, in the doctor's office, that it wasn't wholehearted.

"There must be something that can be done in such cases—"

The doctor shook his head. "I'm sorry, William. If you're thinking of aborting, it's too late now that Eve has passed the twenty-seventh week."

"Abortion? How can you think of such an evil doing? This is not a 'case' we are talking about. This is a child — our child!" Eve's rage was growing. She turned to face William. "Are you ashamed to face the world with a handicapped son or daughter? Is that too unfair for the 'big shot' you are?"

"Darling, I'm sorry," William said. "I'm upset and confused."

Dr. Summer was a sad witness to the couple's conversation. In almost twenty years of practice, he'd seen it all: the denial, the disappointment, the blame, the bitterness, and the anger that follows such dreadful news. He knew there were no words to console a couple hit by such cruel fate. When Eve's first pregnancy ended in miscarriage, he had assured her that she would become pregnant again and have another baby. "I promise you that," he had said then. And she did. There were no promises he could make now that could rectify the warped reality.

The last time Eve saw her husband was in a hospital room later that day, after Dr. Summer had checked her in as a precautionary measure when the news about the baby caused Eve such stress that her blood pressure increased dangerously.

They both seemed calm. Slightly sedated, Eve struggled to stay awake. She took William's hand and pressed it against her cheek. "I'm very sorry, darling. I behaved selfishly earlier...I know you're in pain, too...We'll face whatever comes together, won't we? I love you very much...Will you forgive me?" Eve uttered her words softly in short sentences with long pauses. And, finally, her eyelids drooped.

For the longest time, William stood rooted by the bed, with a blank, faraway look in his eyes. Yanking himself out of the trance, he took her hand and rested it on her chest, then pulled the covers up to her chin. *Soon she will sleep and feel nothing for a while,* he thought, *but nothing will sedate my pain.* He kissed her forehead lightly and started for the door.

"You're leaving?"

"Oh, you're awake?" William asked. Back to the bed, he asked if she needed anything.

"Yes..."

"What do you need, darling?"

"Your forgiveness."

"Of course honey, I forgive you. But you didn't do anything wrong. I love you, too. We'll have the baby and take each day one at a time." While talking, he stroked her hair gently, lulling her into a deep sleep.

Their lives changed forever when William returned to work that afternoon.

He had been awaiting an overseas phone call when the telephone panel flickered, indicating an inside call. He answered the phone, listened to the frightened voice, and complied with the caller's request. No second thoughts. No heroic deeds. With his arms above his head, he stepped into the bank working area. A masked, armed man had taken control of the bank. William quickly evaluated the situation: All his personnel and a few customers were lying on the floor.

Steven Morrison, the security guard, had been ordered to lock the entrance door and turn the sign to read "closed" from outside. He was then motioned to lie down beside the others. Lucille Fleming from the welcome desk, who had just phoned William, was lying next to Steven.

The robber had chosen Emma Dailey, an accountant and single mother of two, as his hostage. At first, she was as brave as she could be with a gun pressed against her temple. But then she began to falter.

William Nelson just couldn't stand there saying and doing nothing. "Take it easy, man."

"Don't move!" the gunman snapped. "Shut your mouth or I'll shoot her. I swear."

There was no need. Emma Dailey's body crumpled in a merciful faint.

It took only a second for the situation to shift dramatically. The security guard used the diversion and ran for the alarm button but was gunned down en route.

Everybody froze.

"Please don't do any more harm," William pleaded. "Let's talk. I'm the branch manager. I'm sure we can reach a deal. I promise you no one is going to repeat *that* mistake," William said, glancing toward Morrison's lifeless body. Establishing a dialogue of any sort with the gunman, he knew, would bring some comfort and reassurance to his terrified subordinates. He also hoped to buy some precious time to think.

"Take the cash and leave in peace—"

"Shut your fucking mouth," the thunderous voice said. "Hey you, the blonde in blue, come here."

Linda Briggs lifted her head and looked around.

"Yeah, you bitch. Come here."

Linda assumed Emma's role. One of her jacket sleeves was wet with a dark-red, thick fluid, and for a moment she panicked, thinking she was hurt. She didn't know what situation was worse: lying in close proximity to Morrison's bloody body or having the gunman pointing a gun at her temple with one hand and holding her by the hair with the other. In that moment, she envied Emma.

The minutes dragged by. It seemed hours since the nightmare began, and worse, like it would never end.

The gunman saw Brook Reed squirming on the floor. She was seven months pregnant. He summoned her.

"You! The black woman. Come here!"

Brook complied, but as she got up, she could scarcely sustain herself in a standing position.

"Don't dare fuck with me, woman! No fainting!" The gunman's huffy bark came. From inside his bulky jacket, he produced a large jute sack and threw it to Brook.

"Start from that end," he shouted.

Brook's shaking hands failed to toss the money into the sack. Fifties and twenties scattered on the floor. That infuriated the gunman.

"If you drop any more money, I'll shoot *you* and this bitch," he said, his hand tightening in Linda's hair. "I'm not fooling around."

Brook was shaking uncontrollably. It was evident she wouldn't be able to carry out the task. To empty the last drawer, she would have to cross over Morrison's body.

"Let me help her," William offered. He attempted to establish an agreement with the thief. "Look, there's over a million dollars in the safe room. Take it and go."

For the first time, the gunman seemed to pay attention to William. His neck was glowing with fine droplets of perspiration, and his eyes shone nervously. For a couple of seconds, they stared at each other.

"Go back on the floor, woman. Your boss will do the rest," the robber ordered, pointing toward the safe room with his gun.

William took the jute sack from Brook's shaky hands and started to the safe room, followed by the gunman, who was handling Linda even more roughly.

One stack after another, William deposited the money from all compartments of the safe into the jute bag, with a mechanical cadence matching the rhythmical orders: "Next one. Next one."

Although the operation was performed quickly, the gunman grew edgy. William glanced at him quickly. He realized that $1.7 million was going down the drain. The new recording camera installed in the safe room would catch the eyes of the robber, but it wouldn't be enough to identify him.

"Listen to me everyone! Listen very carefully. Your boss's life is in your hands. He's coming with me," the robber said. Pushing Linda to the floor, he switched the gun to William's head. "Nobody move until you hear back from your boss. Don't play with the alarm button. Don't make a call. Don't take a call. Understand? One mistake and your boss will pay for it."

Later that day, Crista and Mike Malone came to the hospital where their friend Eve was sleeping peacefully, unaware of the tragic event that had unfolded at the bank. As they waited for her to wake up, Mike checked repeatedly for any news about William.

"It doesn't look good," Mike said to his wife, when they met outside Eve's room. "Four hours have passed and Will is not back. Nor has he called. I have a bad feeling. I better go back to the bank and call you from there."

Crista shuddered at the thought of delivering the shocking news to her friend. She was still trying to comprehend the mind-boggling tragedy. She had been at work when Mike had called her and had been shaking ever since.

When Mike called the hospital later, both Eve and Crista were hysterical.

"Where is my husband, Mike? What happened? Is he back?"

As he listened to Eve's outcry, his heart sank. He knew something had gone drastically wrong, even though they obeyed the gunman's conditions. In those three hours, not a single soul ever brought up the suggestion of summoning the police. They agreed to the terms the robber had imposed on them. Mike recollected William's last words: "Mike, watch out for my wife and son if—" The robber pushed him violently out the back door.

"Eve, he'll be back. You'll see. Everyone thinks the robber took Will out of the city and now he's stranded some place without a phone."

Mike didn't share his ominous premonition.

That night on TV, news of the event was released. The police refrained from making too many comments. But the next morning, the robbery at the downtown CIBC branch made the headlines. Reporters from the *Edmonton Sun* and *Edmonton Journal,* as well as the local and national television stations, were there. They were buzzing with news: "One security guard dead, one woman suffered a heart attack as a result of the hold up and is listed in stable condition. An employee gave birth to a stillborn during the night. The manager of the branch was taken hostage and there is no word on him yet. Just in. Information connected to the branch incident: The bank manager's wife just gave birth to a premature baby."

Police Chief Peter J. Jackson issued a statement offering his sympathies to "those families affected by the tragedy" and committed his police force to doing all they could to apprehend the criminal.

Four days later, new evidence proved that William Nelson was, indeed, dead. The burned-out remains of William's car had been found about 500 kilometres south of Edmonton. They were unable to "identify a body" but there were ashes of human remains.

Eve was in denial. Her brother, Garry, and his wife, Gloria, came from Australia after Crista called and informed them of the devastating news. They became increasingly concerned about Eve's mental health as each day passed. She seemed somewhere far away from reality, locked in an illusory world where her beloved husband was *not* dead; it was only a matter of time until he came back safe and sound. Garry didn't know what was worse: a screaming and kicking Eve or this delusional version. She was focusing all her attention on her tiny baby boy Jacob, whose little body was buried under tubes and wires.

As the tests had foreseen, the baby had Down syndrome. The fact that he was born prematurely made matters worse; the immune system of his tiny body was seriously compromised, and when he developed a respiratory infection the chance of survival plummeted.

Eve denied that reality, too.

One morning, while Eve was in the shower, a police officer came and talked to Garry. He was told the ashes of the deceased would be released for burial.

Garry tried to talk to Eve that morning, but she was in a hurry to leave because a neonatologist was coming from the University of Alberta Hospital, and she had some questions for him about her baby. Garry stopped her halfway out the door.

"I want to talk to you, sis. *Now.*"

She glanced at her watch, annoyance evident on her pale, tired face. "We can talk on the way. I thought you were coming too."

"Darling, we must talk now and here. Let's have a seat. While you were in the shower, a police officer came and said that they are going to release William's ashes for burial. You are going to stop a moment and give some serious thought to this matter. We must make arrangements." He stopped there to give her time to absorb his words. Over the table, he clasped her hands in his.

"It's time to accept the loss, darling. There is no other way to move through this tragedy. We'll help you and stay with you for as long as you need us. Crista and Mike want to offer their support, too. You're not alone in this, and you have Anthony to think about. In your sorrow, you've completely left him out. You're shutting us all out just like Mum did and destroyed herself when our brother died."

Eve started crying, and Garry was quickly on his feet to embrace her.

"I don't want that to happen. I love Anthony too much to do that to him. Please help me to be strong again. I need you."

Garry held her tight to his chest, wanting to shield her forever.

"Hush, baby sister. I'm here. I'm here." Hot tears rolled down their cheeks.

Baby Jacob died two days after his father was buried. Once again, Garry and his wife helped her overcome the painful parting of a loved one.

"Did I startle you?" Victor Knight said, smiling. "You seemed far away."

"*Time* stole me away. But I'm back now," Eve said.

"Sorry to keep you waiting. That was a very important call I had to take. Nothing will disturb us now. I gave Lucille instructions to hold all my calls."

Curiosity had piqued her ever since he had called her earlier that morning, saying he wanted to see her "regarding a matter of great importance."

It was nothing bad, he had assured her.

"This morning, a donation of $25,000 came from a Canadian source for Anthony's education fund. Twenty-five thousand dollars!"

Eve's eyes went round. "I can't believe it, Victor."

When Victor told her he wanted to set up an education fund for Anthony, she was reluctant to accept. Eve was astounded to learn how many institutions and civilians responded to the cause. Because of the ongoing media coverage of William Nelson's disappearance and death, the fund continued to increase. Victor also proposed to the bank that it forgive the remaining mortgage on Eve's home in honour of William's heroic actions. And now, twenty-five thousand dollars!

"I can't believe it!" Eve repeated, "Are you sure you didn't miscount the zeros?"

Victor laughed. "Count them yourself," he said, showing the bank draft to her. "A lawyer delivered it this morning."

"Who made this impressive donation?"

"I honestly don't know. All I know is that he was carrying it on behalf of a Canadian source."

"Victor, you have to pass a letter of gratitude to Anthony's supporter through this lawyer. I'll write one and get it to you tomorrow."

Victor agreed. "All business aside now, Gina and I want to invite you for dinner on Sunday. We brought Anthony something from Hawaii, but don't tell him, please."

"Oh, Victor!" Eve smiled. "You shouldn't buy him anything; he's a 'rich' kid already, as you see," she said, pointing towards the bank draft, "Do you want him to be a spoiled brat?"

"That won't happen. Besides, we love the little guy and love is something we can share with friends."

"Thanks for everything. We'll see you Sunday then."

Eve tossed and turned long after she went to bed. Although her day had started on such a positive note, it ended like most of them: lifelessly flat. Did she want to lead such a lonely life or was she longing for the taste of real life again? She hated the loneliness — she admitted it — but she was scared to death to think about loving again. Part of her was content that God had sustained her through the irretrievable losses, but the other half (the lower half namely) longed for human affection: a man's tender, loving touch, and ultimately a warm body she could snuggle up next to during the long nights. Involuntarily, her mind wandered to Adam.

Eve sipped the cup of coffee she bought at the arena snack bar. She had brought Anthony and Brandon to the hockey practice and regretted her decision not to go shopping with Crista during the boys' practice. She wanted to be here just in case she ran into *him*.

"Hi!"

"Adam!" His name gushed out so fast that Eve mentally kicked herself. With some effort, she kept breathing at an even pace, but excitement was written on her face. From Adam's smile, she knew it pleased him to see her. A lot.

"When did you get back?" Eve asked, cheeks burning.

"I came in last night," he said, slipping into the only other chair around the small, quaint iron table. "I wanted to call you, but by the time I got home, it was after midnight. I was hoping I'd see you here today."

"How was your trip? Did you find time to wander through Rome? Were my reference points useful?"

"Is it a habit of yours to ask so many questions at once?"

"No!" She studied him for a moment. His face was radiant; the laughter lines that were etched on both sides of his mouth emphasized his charm. It seemed that everything about him was totally different than she had initially thought.

"I suppose Rome is nice and all that, but I'm glad to be back."

Eve blushed at his words; she knew they carried special meaning. Still, she wondered why she was unable to completely enjoy him when he was so engaging. Was it because he was still legally married? She was attracted to him, no doubt. She vacillated between what was the right and wrong thing to do. *If only I'd met him three months later…*

"Your insights were quite useful. As a matter of fact, I could have become an intrepid art explorer. But, of course, I didn't. Not enough time. However, thanks to your advice about using public transportation, I managed to stay safe while wandering the streets of Rome, seeking out your ancient friends Michelangelo and da Vinci. They are well, by the way, and send their regards."

They both laughed. For the moment, they enjoyed themselves and each other's company. At one point, their eyes locked for a couple of seconds and Adam wondered what chance he might be given now, after two weeks.

"Oh Adam, your laughter is contagious," Eve said, still laughing.

"I'm a comedian in training. I enhance my skills when I see that my services are needed." Adam studied Eve for a long moment.

Eve noticed.

"That bad, hmm?"

"What?"

"Do I look that bad that I need a little amusement?"

"You look fantastic, but 'a little' doesn't describe the amount of amusement you need. I'd say I better put the clown costume on."

"What did you say you do for a living? Are you sure you aren't a social worker? Because if you are, your employer won't be so happy to hear that you give free consultations," Eve quipped.

"No, I'm not a social worker," Adam grinned. "I work for my father and my soon-to-be ex-wife. They run the business together. It's related to the oil industry. However, it doesn't interest me now and never has."

"Really?"

"I studied Structural Architecture and hope to go back to it once I'm divorced. I have never done it full-time, but I think I'll be good at it. Ever since I was a child, building design has captivated me. I was about nine or ten years old when the twenty-seven story CN Tower here in Edmonton was built. On my way home from school, I used to stop and watch people with hard hats, checking on large papers — blueprints, as I learned they were called. And then, one day, something cool happened. A construction worker — probably a father who had a boy like me — beckoned me to approach the restricted work area and 'introduced' me to what, until then, was a mystifying operation. It was the translation of ideas into reality. I believe *that* moment originated my love for structural design. It got into my blood."

For a moment, Adam's facial expression hardened and the glimmer in his eyes faded away to reveal a great deal of pain. She saw another side of him. One with much depth and sadness, which intrigued her. Was he sad because he was not doing what he most desired to or was it something else? Perhaps it was a mixture of things, including the ugly business of divorce. Eve couldn't help but wonder how a successful man with great ambitions had such little control over his destiny.

Eve looked up for a moment and watched the boys practicing on the ice.

"What do you fancy yourself building?" Eve asked.

"I'd like to focus on a different type of building. Like removing the debris of a poorly constructed dwelling and building a new one, which I'd simply call *friendship*," Adam said.

"Are you referring to the friendship you offered before you left for Rome?"

"Exactly. Have you looked up the definition yet?

Eve gnawed on her lower lip. "No. And I haven't made up my mind yet."

"You know, you're a lucky soul because I am a generous man. I'll give you some more time. The question is, how much?"

"Three, four months…?" Her answer came softly, but she knew from his gaping mouth that she was pushing her luck. She tried again. "Three, four weeks…?"

Business-like, he pretended to ponder her request and then counter offered.

"Three days."

"Five."

"Four."

"Deal."

"Not one day longer," Adam warned.

They didn't shake hands, but their smiles said that the deal was sealed. Irrevocably. Undeniably. That established, there was time left for more relaxing topics.

"God strike me if I didn't think I was in the Garden of Eden," Crista said, her voice coming out of thin air. "Oh, my God! Is that an engagement ring?"

Eve gave her friend a reproachful look. She knew Crista had a bad habit of surprising people, but this time she had caught Adam and Eve completely off guard.

Eve's hand shot out of Adam's hold.

Moments before, he had noticed her new ring — the only jewellery she was wearing. "Nice ring!" Then he took her hand in his for a closer look. The diamond was mounted in a twisted-leaves setting on what seemed an ordinary wedding band. Plain and simple, yet elegant. "What happened with your wedding band? I'm sure I saw you wearing one last time."

"This is it. Enhanced. It's my wedding band and what was left of my late husband's wedding band. I had them melted together to make this ring. It took more time to coax the jeweller into doing it than it took designing it, but in the end, it came out just the way I wanted it."

It was at that moment that Crista appeared.

Eve's displeasure at Crista's immature remarks was obvious. There were a number of occasions when her friend's blabbering mouth embarrassed her and this was one of them. She was mortified: *engagement ring!* She flushed slightly, hoping that Adam realized by now that Crista was, well…Crista.

"Crista! What a surprise! I thought you were shopping."

March arrived with spring aplomb. A few more weeks and the city would be ready for its post-hibernal spring cleaning, but for now the gentle breezes were irresistible.

Eve and Crista noted the beautiful weather through the window of a restaurant, where they had retreated for a late lunch.

As their food arrived, Crista dominated the conversation. "It's a sort of belated wedding anniversary present. We've never been on a cruise before. It's going to be a dream come true. I can't wait until summer vacation!"

"If someone deserves a lovely vacation, it's you my dear friend," Eve said but was only half listening to her friend's story. She was thinking about the fact that today was Adam's deadline. She had to give Adam an answer.

"I don't know why, but I get the impression you're not here with me. There's an ocean between us, not just a glass of water."

"I ran all over town with you this morning, and what do I get instead of being thanked? Reproaches."

"Now, don't act offended — or innocent, for that matter. You can't deceive me. Did it ever cross your mind that I know when something is bothering you?" Crista nodded to reaffirm her point. "You'd better come clean with it."

"Crista, what do you want to know?"

"Well, not every morsel. You can spare the one I had the pleasure of witnessing on Saturday morning," Crista said, eyeing Eve.

Her steady look said more than Eve could put into words. She had practically done everything she could to avoid conversations with Crista in the past three days, so as not to give her a chance to broach the subject. And Crista had pretended not to want to meddle in her life. But she should know Crista by now. Patience wasn't one of her best traits.

Eve's irascibility breached the surface. "Are you trying to give me a bigger headache than I already have?"

"You know something? It may bring you a bit of relief if you spilled your guts more often. There is quite a connection between the brain and body. But you don't have to confide in me about your love issues…"

Eve decided she might as well share her troubled heart and 'spill some guts.'

"Adam asked me out and…I don't feel at ease with accepting."

"Don't be silly, Eve. What's wrong with Adam? He looks marvellous to me. He's definitely not in the same category as Paul Marrek."

Eve wiped her hands on a table napkin. "I don't know Crista. Maybe I'm scared of getting involved. My experience with men is limited. I only need two fingers to keep track of all my relationships: Brian — the man I regret that I met, and William — the one I regret that I lost. That's all. Marrek was a fiasco I don't even count."

A few months back, Crista and Mike decided to introduce Eve to Paul Marrek, a relatively new Loan Representative at the branch. The Malones staged a meeting at their place that was too well put together to fool Eve, but she agreed to see him again.

One day, Mike overheard snippets of a telephone conversation. Marrek was planning on opening some business with one of his buddies, and was counting on convincing Eve to "invest". A few key words were enough for Mike to realize Marrek was eager that she would "lose" the money due to a "bad investment."

*Thank goodness that's history*, Crista thought.

"Does your indecision have anything to do with the fact that Adam was sort of cheeky when you first met him? *Something* must have happened in between with you two or else you wouldn't be sitting at the same table hand in hand."

"It happens that I misjudged his actions when I first met him — if it pleases you to hear me confess — and 'in between,' as you say, we became lovers!" Eve joked.

Crista started laughing.

"I always suspected you let your sexual prowess take over too easily."

Eve's smile disappeared. Crista's quip, harmless as it was, reminded her how petrified she was to let herself fall in love.

"Here are the issues. First, I don't know him very well. Secondly, the fact remains that he is—"

"—without a woman momentarily, and he might opt for intimacy sooner than you may be comfortable with. Throws you off balance," Crista said and continued, "There is nothing wrong with having sex, Eve. You're a woman, and he's a man and you both are entitled to some kicks. Come out of your bubble about love and marriage. What year are you living in?" Crista took a sip of her Diet Pepsi, "Hey, who knows? Maybe sexual incompatibility broke up his marriage. You have to check it out for yourself."

Eve was speechless. She had known Crista for close to ten years, yet obviously that was not long enough if her friend thought she would consider her advice on sex. Though, perhaps, she had lived in a bubble for too long. Apparently her firm guidelines, which she was not willing to revise, conflicted with those of the rest of the world.

"What if I got pregnant, even if we took precautions?" Eve said, almost whispering.

"Double them."

"It's not that simple," Eve said. Even though they were a safe listening distance from other tables, Eve feared that everyone knew what their argument was about.

"Unless my guess is incorrect, we're not talking about *just* sex here, are we?"

"No. It's my guilty conscience about dating him while he's still legally married."

Crista intended to hail the hovering waiter, to ask for another Diet Pepsi, when she abruptly changed her mind.

"Need to go to the washroom," Crista said, as she looked up past Eve and left the table.

Eve played with the last piece of lamb on the plate.

"Good afternoon," a voice said from behind her chair.

"Oh, Adam! How are you?"

"Optimistic." Adam said, nodding slowly.

The hint was too obvious not to affect Eve. A glance by Adam told her that the group right behind him was with him. Against her wish, she blushed.

"Do you own an answering machine?" Adam asked.

"Yes. Why?"

"It must not be on then. I tried to leave a message earlier...I'll call you tonight."

"Oh, yes, call later," Eve said with relief. For a moment, she feared he would reveal more private details.

"I'm looking forward to it," Adam said and returned to his group.

Crista reappeared as fast as she disappeared, and had the grace to refrain from making any comments.

Anthony was in his room doing his homework. Eve was going through his closet, plucking out dirty clothes from amongst the clean ones, when the telephone rang.

It was Adam. "I'm afraid I have only a few moments. I just wanted to know if we can talk after I'm finished for the day. I'll probably be here until nine, so if you have some time after that…"

Silence.

"Eve, are you there?

"Yes."

"I mean in person if you don't mind. I could stop by."

"Yes, that would be all right. See you then," Eve said, but as soon as she hung up, she had misgivings. If only she had asked him for a daylight meeting in some coffee shop. As much as she felt guilty about it, she realized she would have to put Anthony to bed promptly so he wouldn't question Adam's visit.

Trembling and feeling like a schoolgirl, she went to open the door before the bell had the chance to ring twice.

"I'm very sorry about coming over so late," Adam said, once he was seated on the sofa.

Eve sat stiffly in the armchair. "One might say you don't sound too sorry."

He laughed. "Okay, I'm not a bit sorry."

Eve felt warm under his gaze, and before her senses could catch up with her, she asked him if he wanted a cup of tea.

"Tea would be great."

Five minutes later, as Adam was sipping his tea, Eve was restless. It was ridiculous to think that all this time and formality was being invested just to determine if they could be friends. Simply, the man was begging for a 'yes' and she was deferring her answer. Under normal circumstances, there would be no need for an answer at all. But then again, these were no ordinary circumstances.

"What are you thinking?" Adam asked.

Eve placed her cup and saucer on the coffee table and worked up her courage.

"I guess we can be friends."

Simple as that.

After his initial surprise, Adam recovered but felt that she had more to say.

"But…?"

"But, on my terms."

"And those would be…?"

Eve clasped her hands together, not wanting to look him in the eyes. If he just stopped looking at her for a moment, maybe she could formulate her thoughts.

"Adam, I don't want to seem difficult, but I don't have this kind of discussion on a daily basis, so please, bear with me until I make some sense of it. There are some things that I need to make you aware of. I know you haven't asked for anything outrageous, but I have to take into consideration all the facts that affect our lives."

"You're right. About your sense, though—"

"Let me finish, please. In all fairness, I want you to know that I hold my son's well-being as a great responsibility. He comes before anything. *Anything*. I don't want to expose him to immorality or neglect." She took a small sip of tea.

"Secondly, about your situation — if at any time down the road, you wish to reconcile with your wife, please let me know right away. I'll honestly be very understanding and back off without any fuss. Let me finish," Eve said, sensing that Adam was ready to take up the issue. "And finally, I don't want to be rushed into something I'm not ready for yet. I'm not trying to complicate this, but I like to set things straight right from the beginning. It's just the way I am. Now, you are free to make a decision about whether this would work for you."

To her surprise, Adam's facial expression relaxed. His smile was warm and genuine, and his handsomeness never more evident.

"You're sure you didn't leave anything out of your conditions?"

"Mmm...no! That's all."

"Just checking. You know what they say: *Always check the small print*. As for my answer, I think your friendship is too big an opportunity to pass in spite of the strict conditions you set. I do wish you were more flexible with some of the conditions."

"Oh? Which ones?" Eve asked.

"Well, I do agree with what you said about your son and his entitlement to a decent environment, and that he comes first — no objections there. Thoroughly admirable. What I hoped you would be more flexible about though, is your last condition, around intimacy."

Eve's composure slipped. She was made of flesh and blood like anybody else. She yearned for intimacy, but as long as an impediment was in the way, she couldn't bring herself to think of that freely.

"Oh, Adam I wish you wouldn't go into—"

"Just let me finish," Adam said. 'It's my turn. I want to assure you that there is no pressure into intimacy. I also want to make it clear that there won't be any reconciliation between *her* and me. I'm through with wasting time in marriage counselling. I tried my best and I have a guilt-free conscience, and I advise you not to consume yourself with it. That being said, I propose we close the 'terms' chapter and proceed with our brand-new relationship."

"Very business-like!" Eve smiled.

Adam chuckled. "I'm beginning to like your sense of humour. I must confess I once doubted you had one, and I'm delighted to be proven wrong," Adam said, a mischievous gleam dancing in his eyes.

"Many things seemed different at the beginning," Eve said, thinking of her first impression of him. And to think, they say you never get a second chance to make a good first impression!

One hour later, Adam looked at his watch. "I have to go. I don't want to wear out my welcome." He started slowly to the door.

Eve followed him, not knowing if bidding a simple "goodnight" was appropriate enough to part with for the time being, or what to do if he had something else in mind. She swallowed hard as her thoughts clouded.

"Goodnight, Adam," she finally said, with a semblance of control.

# Two

GARTH STEWART WAVED HIS HAND TO CAPTURE ADAM'S ATTENtion. When Adam finally noticed his friend across the food court, he made halting progress through the throng of people having lunch in the humming hive of the Edmonton Centre Mall.

"Thank God you're on the hamburger diet again," Adam observed and pulled a chair across from the corpulent man. "I've been wondering how you're planning to get to the next life. It's obvious you plan to eat your way there."

"Cut it out, buddy. I'm not in the mood for taking crap from anyone today — even you. Especially, when we both know that your life isn't a bed of roses," Garth said, between two bites of an enormous cheeseburger.

"I know my life is no bed of roses, but I don't go to such extremes as to worry my friends with it. Every time I see you, you're bigger and bigger. Grow a beard and you'll be the most sought after Santa Claus next Christmas season. Provided, your heart lasts until then."

"Thanks for noticing my weight," Garth retorted. "Why are you so worried about my freaking health? Am I the last lawyer in town?" His words contained no trace of malice. They could discuss anything, disagree with each other's opinion and still remain the best of friends. That's the way their friendship has been since Grade 10 when Adam joined Garth's school. He gobbled down the last of his French fries. "Don't worry. I won't die until I divorce you. I brought this for you,"

Garth said and produced an envelope from a pocket of his once-roomier jacket.

"I assume it's a little thank you note, from you know who, for your munificent philanthropic act. And please don't worry about my heart, blood pressure, any of that shit." Garth added, "I actually lost three pounds. I met someone I'm trying to make a good impression on." He watched Adam engrossed in reading the card. The satisfied gleam in his eyes and the soft, almost imperceptible smile were evidence that his earlier assumption was correct.

When Adam lifted his eyes, he had to ask Garth to repeat his last statement.

"…And I guess I'm a bit nervous about it." Garth added.

"I see…so you're satisfying your nerves with food. Three pounds you say? I have to go now. Tell me next time how it went with your date."

"All right. I get the hint. Your tricks always work," Garth retorted. "Her name is Betty Coughlin. She's a teacher, a colleague of my sister Val, who introduced us. She is a couple years younger than I am and has a six-year-old daughter."

"Are you sure you're up to the challenge of this relationship?"

"Well, I'll give it a try. I think it's worth taking the chance."

Yes. How well Adam knew about taking chances.

Adam began flipping through the myriad of paperwork on his desk, and soon determined he was too distracted to bother with it. Alec Coulter's resignation was on his desk. Adam had a hard time comprehending it. George had come into his office, hurled the resignation at him and demanded to know what was going on and why was he leaving. He expected Adam to have answers, as if he were responsible for other people's decisions! "Why ask me?" he wanted to say, but was dumbfounded by Alec's sudden decision.

He looked at the resignation. All he knew was that Alec had asked for a few days off. And, now this. One month prior, Alec's brother, John, also resigned. At least Adam knew a little bit more about *that* decision: John was gay and was following someone to Toronto. But what was Alec's reason? He had a family, a wife, and three young children to support, and Carstone paid him a very good wage, with benefits that only the best companies could offer. Adam doubted Alec had found a more tempting job opportunity. *If* he found some other job, he would have told Adam. After all, Adam considered him a true friend.

He couldn't help but wonder if Alicia had a hand in this. The more he thought about it, the more convinced he was that Alicia had, somehow, influenced the Coulter brothers' hasty and mystifying departures. He would get to the bottom of it, but for now his mind shifted to a personal matter.

He had called Eve before lunch only to be disappointed that she had no time for him. She answered his call but politely excused herself and ended the conversation with a promise to talk to him later on. He was sure he'd heard a male voice in the background, addressing Eve by her first name, and he found the incident disturbing. In the conversation, Eve had not used his name, as if to keep it a secret from her company.

He wondered if he should call her again or just drop by. And then he thought, *God, I'm jealous. I must go and see her.*

One hour later, he was more than pleased with his decision to show up at Eve's door.

"Adam!" Eve opened the door with a wide smile. "I'm so pleased you stopped by. Come in. I have something to show you."

Eve took his hand and motioned him through the hallway towards the family room, where Crista, Mike, Anthony, and Brandon were chatting.

"How do you like it?" Eve asked, after her guests exchanged greetings, gesturing towards the *Downtown* scene on the wall with her left hand while with the other she clasped Adam's upper arm.

Adam just stood there, silently enjoying the artwork. He was spellbound and realized he had never seen anything quite like it. An entire wall was divided into five parts by wood panels — simulating the existence of a real window — and in between the panels was a panoramic view of downtown Edmonton. A set of lights, smartly installed in the ceiling, projected a bright light on the upper side of it, giving the picture the ambiance of a sunny day, slightly stirred by a gentle breeze.

"It's breathtaking! Outstanding. Congratulations!" Adam added. "Same to you Anthony, for this wonderful idea."

Anthony jumped happily at the compliment but soon ran upstairs after his friend Brandon.

"Placing the scenery between the wood frames is ingenious, Eve. It makes you think everything is real and within your reach."

"Well, time for us to get going or else Reba will start her concert without us," Crista interrupted.

"Did you want to see Reba's concert?" Adam asked Eve later, as both of them sat on the couch in the family room, cups of tea in their hands.

Eve laughed. "No. I'm happier to stay home babysitting the boys. I'm a country music illiterate, and so is Mike. I bet he's bored to death by now," Eve said laughing. "Crista is a country music fanatic and would do anything to go to a show like this. I bought the tickets for them. Poor Mike. I guess I didn't do him a favour by sending him along, especially when I owe him one."

Adam looked at her.

"Mike is responsible for finding the greatest crew to create and install the wood panels. He even helped finalize the configuration of the lights today," Eve said.

As Eve was talking, Adam realized his error, and chided himself for being jealous of Mike, although, truly when he called he didn't know who was with Eve.

"I wish you'd asked me to come and stay with you, while the crew was here," Adam said, breaking a long ardent look into her eyes.

"So I can owe you, eh?"

"Well, I would've settled for a less expensive kind of compensation." As soon as the words were uttered, he realized the double entendre. He smiled as he tried to mend it. "Just a cup of tea, and a couple of hours in this delightful 'downtown' ambiance, would have been more than sufficient. Fact is, I got all this for doing virtually nothing, and you have no idea what it means to me after the tough day I had."

"I'm sorry to hear that. I mean, about your day."

"Did I tell you I brought something for you and Anthony from Italy?

"Adam, you shouldn't have," Eve protested, but Adam was already on his feet.

"Stay put. I'll fetch it from the car," he said, and disappeared through the hallway.

When he returned, Eve looked somewhat incredulous at the bag he was carrying, with the graphic design on it: *Galleria Borghese*. His "little surprise" looked heavy in that plastic bag.

"I only hope you don't have them already," Adam said, as the bag changed hands.

Eve took out a huge tome, eyed it, and then pulled the second one. Her mouth dropped open.

"Do you have them?"

"Are you kidding me? *Complete Arts* and *All About Da Vinci* are new releases, in Europe only, right now. I read about them in one of the art magazines I subscribe to. Adam, these books cost a fortune! I must pay you for them."

Eve was resolute, but Adam couldn't say that it surprised him. When he saw the books and decided to purchase them, he envisioned this reaction.

As she went flipping through the pages of the fascinating books, he said, "No need to pay me, I got a good deal on them. It was next to nothing."

"I'm afraid I could live royally for a month on that 'nothing,'" Eve said, and pulled the last object from the bag. "Plus two more weeks for this!" Eve added, as she discovered a frame encasing a large amount of Italian collectible currency. "Really, Adam!" She positioned the case on her knees. "You are lying nicely, sir, but ineffectively. I've seen those books advertised in the art magazine, remember? I know how much they're worth. You either take the money or take the books back."

"I'd figured you would be this stubborn. Let's make a deal," Adam offered. "You can make a portrait for me."

"Yours?"

"Nope. Yours."

"Are you serious?" Eve asked and studied his facial expression for signs that he was teasing. He wasn't, she concluded. "I have never done a self-portrait, never mind given one away. I think of a portrait as a farewell gift when you break up with someone," Eve said. "I know it sounds old fashioned, but it's a superstition I grew up with."

Adam was forced to think fast.

"I have another idea. How about doing my nephew's portrait?"

"That, I could do. Consider it a deal."

It was well past midnight when Adam turned off his night-table lamp. If it weren't for the unsettling feelings in the lower part of his body, he could actually be sleeping and dreaming about Eve. He'd planned to push a step ahead in the brand-new and challenging relationship with Eve earlier, but he wasn't quick enough. Besides, as if Eve had read his mind, she didn't make it easier for him. He was about to kiss her goodnight when the doorbell rang announcing the Malones' return. Guessing Eve's uncomfortable position, Adam left her house at the same time they did. Amid the vortex of chaos created by noisy goodbyes and goodnights, Adam managed to squeeze Eve's hand and catch a tender look that had awakened all of him: body, mind, and spirit.

The next morning, he was still thinking about the time he spent with Eve when Miss Annette poked her head through his office door.

"Your father wants the D.S. account," she said.

"Why are you asking me for it? Dean has it. He was working on it this morning," Adam said and returned his attention to a document he was studying.

"Dean is not in his office."

"Could you please find him?"

"I'm afraid I'm too old to be taking up a detective job, dear."

"What do you mean by 'taking up a detective job', Miss Annette?"

"I don't know where to begin looking for him. He left in a hurry before lunch and hasn't returned. His pager and cell phone are on his desk. To make matters worse, his filing cabinet is locked, and George is going to have a fit if the D.S. account is not ready on time."

Adam strode out of the room and over to Dean's office with Miss Annette close behind.

"Are you two looking for this?"

They were in Dean Blaine's office trying to pry open his filing cabinet when Alicia walked in, waving a red file in the air, a triumphant smile on her face.

"Where did you get the D.S. file from?" Adam asked, irritation evident in his voice.

"From that cabinet," Alicia said pointing at the filing cabinet behind them. "*I* have an extra key." Alicia was just about to turn and leave, when she added, "By the way, there is an emergency meeting in ten minutes — at 3:30 to be exact — in the Blue conference room."

"Why didn't you tell someone you had it?" Adam asked, slamming the screwdriver down on Dean's desk. "Miss Annette, please send Dean to my office as soon as he returns. God help him."

"We call it a boomerang mistake—"

"I don't care how you call it," Alicia retorted. "You're paid to assist legalizing contracts. George and I decide if it's a mistake or not."

"But it is a mistake, and you knew it from the beginning," Thomas Morgan, the representative lawyer, said. In the past three years at Carstone, he had experienced similar situations but none this bad: George and Alicia went against his advice and then blamed him when the results weren't as they expected.

Five months ago, Carstone Corporation attracted a new customer, a wealthy plastic consortium in Spain. Alicia was in charge of the new contract. She followed business protocol, but when the contract was signed, she'd had everything charged in U.S. currency instead of Canadian. The contract was signed and celebrated. When Alicia came back and told George what she had done, he didn't rush to congratulate her, but he didn't slap her wrists either. Legally, the deal was correct; nobody forced the client's hand to sign. Recently, the client discovered the change. George was inclined to take Tom's advice. After all, it was under very similar circumstances that his son-in-law, Brad Johnson, had quit his position as representative lawyer three years ago. George hadn't taken his counsel, and they paid for it — trying to keep the corporation at the top of the market. George decided they wouldn't take the same path.

"George, you must realize I'm right," Tom said.

"I say we rewrite the contract before anything slips out and we attract media attention," George responded.

Alicia jumped to her feet. "Hold on, George. You sound as if you're the one and only master around here. Convince me that you're right or fight me like a lion!"

"I'll certainly do both, young lady, if that's what it takes for us to find a way out of this. Your conniving schemes got us into this mess, and I refuse to immerse the company in it this time around — not with the *LJ* downfall fresh in mind."

The biting remark about her previous error didn't go unnoticed. It unleashed a sequence of fiery words just as Adam's pager started buzzing. He feigned some irritation as he checked who the disturbing caller was, and as if with some regret, left the room.

His only real regret was that he had been truly enjoying himself, watching Alicia fight like a cat when she was in the wrong.

Adam needed to know what happened with Dean. Whatever Dean was up against had something in common with other employees who had recently left the company.

Adam went around his desk and slumped into his chair. "Where have you been?" he started. "By the way, that tie is a no-no with that suit. Did Silvia approve it this morning?" Adam thought he was being casual, and tactful in his approach. His voice was relaxed, more akin to one inviting his buddy out for a nightcap.

In one swift gesture, Dean placed his hand on the tie. It was the only one he could find in his office. His crimson face and shaky fingers immediately alarmed Adam.

The gesture indicated that Dean was in some kind of trouble, which came as a surprise. He met Dean four years ago on a flight from Toronto and learned that Dean was trying his luck in the west. Adam was impressed with his verbal resume, and had given Dean his private phone number. Three months had passed when he found a message on his answering machine. Dean was putting in long hours doing the accounting for a large dental office, underpaid, and hardly able to spend time with his family. Adam hired him, and Dean had never given Adam any reason to doubt his capability or his loyalty to Carstone.

The two men established a solid friendship — a friendship that, unfortunately, wasn't shared by their spouses. Alicia had been haughty and unappreciative, never warming up to Dean or his wife. It was his fault, Adam supposed, for sharing confidential information with Alicia about Dean's past. He uprooted his family from its native east coast to prove to his wife that he had ended an extramarital affair. After hearing this, Alicia hadn't even bothered to show up at her own house when the two couples planned to spend time together.

Perhaps the past was rearing its ugly head, Adam thought.

"I guess the right thing to do is to resign," Dean said, and got to his feet.

"No, my friend. Sit down. I believe the right thing to do is to tell me what's going on," Adam said, as he left his chair and went to lock the door.

"Look Adam, it's a private matter and—"

"Come on, I thought we were friends!"

Dean averted his eyes, "I can't talk about it. I have to leave Carstone and no one can change my mind."

It must be the old business, Adam decided. "If that's how you feel I don't want to pry. I am disappointed though, as I suspect this is about you cheating on Silvia again!"

"No. That's not it," Dean started. "Well not really…I mean…not in a conventional way. Oh man, don't make me say more. I don't want to see anybody else here hurt."

"What the heck are you talking about?" Adam asked. "Wait a minute. What do you mean anyone else from *here* being hurt by this?"

"Oh, man," Dean sighed. How could he explain that *he* was not the one who played dirty? He shook his head as the memory of the day before played in his mind...

It began innocently enough, the day before, when he met *her* by coincidence, or so he thought, at the Fairmont Hotel Macdonald restaurant. He was meeting an old friend and former colleague who was job hunting in the west. Dean talked to Adam about his friend's job search and was quite excited to give him promising news. At around one o'clock, it was obvious that his friend was not showing up.

As Dean was heading towards the door, he saw Alicia coming in. As soon as she eyed him, she insisted on having lunch together. He knew she went out for lunch with subordinate males so he harboured no suspicions about the gesture.

However, earlier today, Alicia called and asked him to bring her briefcase to her from the same hotel. "The key for Room 512 is at reception. It's urgent," she had stressed. Half an hour later, entering the hotel room, he had been shocked to find Alicia in a see-through negligee. He quickly realized he was being set up.

"I thought you called me from your office…" He was so surprised that he couldn't find any more words.

"I love surprises. Don't you?" Alicia's lazy voice was suggestive enough, as was the negligee that fell to the floor. She edged forward seductively and removed Dean's tie. She went on and removed his jacket before he even realized it. It was when Alicia pushed him on the bed and straddled him that he regained his full mental capacity. With a mighty push, he extricated himself from beneath her body and seductive spell. He retrieved his jacket and ran out of the room. Her hysterical laughter and the menacing threats were still echoing in his ears: "You better resign or I'll destroy your marriage." *Boy, what a sick bitch,* Dean thought, disgusted. *This*, certainly, he could not tell Adam.

"My office door is not going to open unless you start talking," Adam intoned.

"Adam, please try to understand that my resignation is the only way to solve this problem without causing collateral damage. I can't risk my marriage, man. You don't want that to happen to Silvia and me."

"Does your wife have any inkling about this?"

"No. Well, I hope not," he said, the last shred of confidence disintegrating. "I don't know that, as of yet," he said, remembering Alicia's threats.

It crossed Adam's mind that two resignations in a very short time — and now this happening — must have something in common. But what?

"You said that you didn't cheat on Silvia in a 'conventional way'. What did you mean by that?" Adam asked. He had done Dean a favour, been his friend, and now he received a "none of your business" attitude in return. "Look, if you really didn't screw around at all, how can someone *here* get hurt? It doesn't make any sense. *I*, personally, would be livid *if* you picked up your behind and vanished after all the time we've invested in our friendship."

With an audible sigh, Dean said, "Besides risking my marriage, I'll hurt *yours* if I don't leave."

Adam's sudden burst of laughter confused Dean.

"*My* marriage?"

"Man, I can't believe I said that."

"I'm surprised there's anyone left around here who isn't aware of the status of my marriage, although Alicia and I have been trying to keep the news of our separation quiet. Don't be concerned about something that doesn't exist anymore, my friend."

It took some time until Dean found the fortitude to expose the truth, and he certainly didn't enjoy summoning up the recollection.

"I would lie if I said that, as a man, I was not tempted, but God is my witness, I didn't take advantage of the situation. I didn't sleep with Alicia. I couldn't," Dean tried to assure Adam again, as he ended his story.

Adam was quiet for a moment. How could a person like Alicia have such harmful intentions towards another human being without pangs of remorse?

"My friend, I'm glad you opened up to me. No need to leave the company. I'm on your side," Adam assured him. "Now it occurs to me what really must have happened with the Coulter brothers. Alicia did it before and again."

Adam's life outside Carstone felt like living in a wonderland. He felt like a young man experiencing the thrill of first love. Visiting Eve after work became the highlight of his day, and the fact that his calls and visits were accepted and anticipated was most encouraging. He was definitely making progress in bringing her level of warmth and affection closer to his own. Yes, she liked him. That was clear. Not that she was gushy with her words, but the way her face stayed bright and focused when he was around gave away a lot.

"How is Ryan's portrait coming along?" Adam had asked one morning on the phone.

"It'll be ready soon," Eve said.

"Have lunch with me!"

"Oh, I have to go to the art gallery soon. I don't know if I could..."

In her floundering response, Adam suspected the real reason for her hesitation.

He laughed. "Eve, it's not a date. We won't be alone, if that's what bothers you," he offered in an attempt to keep the prospect open. "I'll bring my favourite secretary. She's dying to meet you."

Because Eve already knew a bit about Miss Annette, she agreed to meet with them.

"Miss Annette, you never told me how Princess got tipsy," Adam said, after their meals arrived. He explained to Eve that Princess was a cat he had given to Miss Annette last Christmas to replace her beloved, departed tomcat. As he anticipated, the two women warmed up to each other, a fact that pleased him enormously.

"I didn't tell you, dear, did I? Well, one day I had a terrible headache when I got home from work. So, I 'administered' myself a dose of brandy, and lay down on the sofa. I had drunk it in a few gulps — maybe too fast — and I poured another one, from which I must have taken only a small sip because the first one had already made me sleepy. When I woke up, Princess was lying flat, motionless on the floor. At first I was convinced she was dead! It was only after I rushed her to the vet, and he ran some tests, that her 'sudden death phenomena' was cleared up! She must have tipped the glass and licked the liquor off the floor!"

Eve and Adam couldn't stop laughing.

"One day, shortly after this happened, I pretended to doze off on the sofa with a glass of brandy close by, to see what 'Her Highness' might do. She must have had the hangover fresh in mind, because she did not so much as take a curious sniff."

As the older woman finished her tipsy-cat tale, she sensed that she had lost her audience when Adam quickly excused himself and left the table, saying, "I must attend to some business for a second." It took only a split second for Miss Annette to register everything, as she discretely watched the scenario unfolding at the bar. She was thankful for the fuss someone was making about their soup at the next table, which prevented Eve from becoming aware of the scandal Adam and Alicia were creating right behind her back. Hastily, Miss Annette fabricated a story to keep Eve captivated. She was extremely relieved when Adam returned to the table, sporting a calm expression that, to her, looked artificial. With dexterity, Adam coaxed Eve to "divulge" her next art project.

"I'm doing a number of paintings for an exhibit at The Edmonton Art Gallery in the summer," Eve started. "I'm very excited about it, because Nora Murray is exhibiting with me — well, not to tell lies, I am exhibiting with her," she said. "Murray is an international celebrity, an art veteran, and I'm grateful she chose me, a foreigner with no name as a partner," Eve added.

Adam caught the puzzled expression on Miss Annette's face. "Eve is from Sydney, Australia." And to Eve: "But I don't see any relevance between art and the artist's origin." With the exception of the art project in her house, he had not seen any of her work, but his instincts told him that Murray's choice must reflect her appreciation for Eve's artistic talent.

"Oh, but there is," Eve replied, a wistful look in her eyes. "You see, art is a business, too — a very delicate one, I might add — in the abstract and subjective way. For example, if you wanted to buy a piece of art, an oil painting for instance, and have two exhibited before your eyes. Two different artists. You like them both, both are about the same price. Which one would you pick?"

"The one whose works are better known," Adam and Miss Annette said in unison.

"Exactly!"

There was a shadow of concern in Adam's eyes. Technically, he knew Eve was right — in business, there is no place for sentimentalism. However, he wondered if Eve was not a bit downcast about being stranded in a foreign land that had adopted her but was not willing wholeheartedly to accept her work. For a second, he wondered if Eve ever thought of returning to her native country.

Alicia had done some investigating and concluded that Adam was seeing a long-legged Barbie, using a more colourful description when she told George about it. Alicia expected that, from now on, when they needed Adam to go out of town on business, he would put up a fight. She still couldn't comprehend why he hadn't confronted her about the scene she created at the restaurant the day he was having lunch with *that* woman and the old secretary.

She talked to her lawyer about Adam's "silence" and his reluctance to fight back. She wished he would have at least hit or slapped her so she could have gotten the upper hand in the divorce proceedings. "It's a calculated silence," her lawyer said. Adam was following his lawyer's advice, no doubt. He advised her to do the same: to keep her mouth zipped, even if she had a hell of a time in doing so.

As for her encounter with Dean Blaine, Alicia was more puzzled than miffed. When she saw him at the office, he acted as if the incident at the Fairmont Hotel Macdonald had never happened. He didn't resign as she thought he would. Adam, it seemed to her, was unaware of the hotel episode, which somewhat irked her. She expected more damage on more levels. It crossed her mind to call Blaine's wife and "confess" their "ardent affair" but ultimately changed her mind. The bitter memories of the time she disturbed another couple's life, and the consequences, were still on her mind even after so much time.

The following Wednesday, Adam went to Calgary for business. It was not the kind of business that would necessarily demand his expertise, but he offered to go — a decision which greatly baffled Alicia.

Adam had another reason for being in Calgary: He wanted to chat with his sister and brother-in-law, Cassidy and Brad Johnson who lived there during the week and returned to their house in Edmonton on the weekends. Brad moved to Calgary three years ago after an intense argument with George and Alicia, which had ended up with him resigning from his position as representative lawyer at Carstone Corporation. He didn't waste any time feeling sorry for himself or regretting his exit. He pulled some strings, and with his excellent experience, landed a position in the Calgary courthouse. The change in his family's life was meant to be temporary, but Cassidy followed him after a year, and the likelihood of them returning diminished.

In Edmonton, Cassidy had been a paediatrician who specialized in neonatal practice at the Royal Alexandra Hospital. When Dr. Timothy Spence — the director of the Neonatal Intensive Care Unit — NICU — left his chair for a finer, "warmer" opportunity in the States, it was predicted that Cassidy Johnson would be Dr. Spence's successor. But, to everyone's surprise and Cassidy's disappointment, Dr. Olivier Pelisse claimed the job. Shortly after the news became official, Cassidy Johnson resigned her position and left for Calgary, where she settled in an office of family paediatric care where she could have the weekends off, giving her and her husband time to drive or fly to Edmonton to be with their son, Ryan.

Ryan was in school and lived with his maternal grandparents, Janet and George Carry, who loved him unconditionally in spite of the rocky relationship they shared with their son-in-law. Cassidy was thankful for her mother's devotion to her son, who — after an attempt to adjust to a new life in Calgary failed — went back to live with his grandparents in Edmonton.

Cassidy was enjoying the sunshine when her brother pulled up to the sidewalk in front of Parker's Clinic to pick her up. She walked to work daily, when weather permitted.

"Are you staying with us tonight?" she asked, as soon as she was in his car.

Seven years his senior, Cassidy had been more present in her brother's life during his childhood than their mother was. She remembered that Adam was confused at the age of two over who to call "Mother." This was during a time when Janet was utterly caught up with her husband's demanding responsibility at the helm of the oil company her father had left them.

After supper, Cassidy ushered the two men into the den, cups of coffee in hand. She winked at her husband as she retreated to the kitchen to 'clean up'. From the kitchen, she could hear strains of an enthusiastic conversation about cars — a passion the two men shared. She joined them just as the subject changed.

"So how is that lady friend of yours?" Brad asked.

Adam could no longer mask his pleasure. "If you're referring to the wonderful lady I'm seeing, her name is Eve, and please, spare me the pretence that you know less than my chatty sister does."

"Sorry brother, no secrets in this household," Cassidy said.

"No apologies needed. As a matter of fact, I stayed in Calgary tonight so I could bring you up to date about my life," he joked. "Relax. I'm not talking about wedding bells or anything. She is just a really lovely lady. In fact, I would like for us to get together so you can see for yourself. That is, if she'll agree to make it a date."

"I just happen to know of an upcoming occasion," Cassidy said.

The next morning, Adam woke up well before his hosts. It was 5:20 a.m. when he opened his eyes and discovered he was alone in bed. Hands folded under his head, he recalled the past evening. "Do you like her?" Brad had asked him, and Adam knew he felt something even deeper: He was certain that he *loved* her.

Eve checked the time. She planned to start a new painting, but the way the day started, she felt the inspiration draining away. Subconsciously, she knew the reason for her mood had originated the day before. She planned to take the boys to hockey practice to be with Adam, only to be disappointed when Adam called and said he was going to Calgary. He asked her to go with him after he assured her Mike and Crista wouldn't mind missing the movie and taking the boys to hockey practice in her stead. She told him she didn't feel comfortable about the trip. Deep down in her heart, she knew the invite and trip meant a slight push towards meeting his sister and her husband. She felt lonely as she waited for the children's hockey practice to finish. *I wish he had insisted on taking me with him.*

The phone rang and interrupted her thoughts.

"Hi! Are you back?" Eve couldn't keep a note of excitement from her voice.

"I'm still on the road. I'd like to talk to you…to see you, actually. Do you have some time now, this morning?" Then he added, "If it's not a bad time for you, that is." He had calculated each step of his approach since he woke from his dream early this morning. The thought that they would be alone made his heart beat faster.

"Yes, you can stop by. You can see the portrait. I've finished it."

"Excellent! Do you think you can help me frame it? I don't know any places that would do a good job on short notice. I need it on Saturday."

Eve couldn't contain her reaction. "Oh? I mean, I can probably help with that. I know a shop called *Frame Gallery on Whyte,*" Eve said, and gave him the address.

As soon as they said goodbyes, Adam made another call, and then pressed harder on the gas pedal. He had just passed the "City of Champions" welcoming sign.

Eve stepped into the bathroom and applied a touch of makeup. Next, she removed her faded jeans and t-shirt and put on a light blue blouse that complemented her eyes. Black slacks or a black wool skirt? Her second choice won out. She was taking her leather jacket out of the closet when the doorbell rang.

"Are you going on a date?" Adam asked, mischievous smile on his face.

Eve tried to ignore the compliment. "Right, this early in the morning?"

"Then let's wait here for a while." He paused just long enough to let the suggestion sink in. "I don't think the stores are open yet," he added. He couldn't begin to guess her reaction if he had said all that was on his mind. He looked her in the eyes and hoped she would tell him how badly she missed him the evening before, but he knew she wouldn't give him the satisfaction to get "warmer."

"How was the practice last night?" Adam asked.

"It was okay. How was business in Calgary?"

Adam laughed. "Business was good. But I missed you guys," he said, looking into her eyes.

Eve blushed as she realized how vulnerable she felt under his long, steady gaze. "Follow me. I'll show you the portrait."

*If I can move,* Adam thought. Her earlier warm, responsive glances had struck him, while his mind had run amok. Then a sensitive part of his body started to function on its own will. He endeavoured to suppress the surge of testosterone that overcame him.

"Are you ready?" Eve asked Adam, who positioned himself in the doorway of the room she used as workshop. A thin layer of wax paper covered the painting.

"I'm sure it's perfect, but before you show it to me, I have something to ask you."

"Yes? What?" Eve asked, in a half-teasing tone of voice.

As Adam removed himself from the doorway, her heart started to beat violently. He moved closer to meet her face to face.

"You really enjoy tormenting me." His accusation was obvious.

All the pretence of innocence aside, Eve took the blame gracefully as she took his possessive, hungry mouth.

It was bound to happen sooner or later, this explosive passion. The fact that Adam felt Eve giving herself up to the mounting deluge of sensations was equally rewarding and excruciating. It seemed to him that all her past indecisions were obliterated as she totally, willingly followed him along into the oblivion of the moment.

Their urgent kisses were matched by responding, restless hands that touched and caressed everything that came in their way: first timidly, then probing and more educated. He splayed one hand against the small of her back, and with a mighty possessive force, pressed his hips close against hers while he slid the other hand underneath her blouse. The impact produced a chain of soft moans, which Eve had no awareness of being hers. She was thankful that from time to time she had a chance to breathe, briefly though, and only when Adam, in a ragged voice, managed to utter short words of endearment and incoherent intimate thoughts.

His mouth ravished hers again and again; his tongue plunged into the warm sweetness of her mouth with insatiable thirst. He wanted more, and she gave more. There was no tension, no boundaries imposed. She leaned against his firm body and clung to him. The more she gave, the more he took.

After a fervent but futile search for the bra clasp at her back, Adam gave up and brought his hand to the front. After a fumbling attempt, he resorted to sliding his hand beneath her bra and swiftly freed her breasts. So triumphant was the victory that he could have screamed from pleasure. He took in the feminine scent of her round breasts with hardened nipples. He repositioned his hands, securing Eve's balance, since she seemed in need of better support as her back arched acutely to offer the sweetness of her body to his mouth.

So deep were they entangled in the passionate moment that they didn't immediately hear the phone ringing. It was only when the machine started recording the caller's message, and Anthony's name was mentioned, that Eve disengaged herself and raced into the next room. She picked up the phone with a swift move.

Adam remained immobilized for what seemed a long moment. From the next room, fragments of Eve's conversation came to his attention. They served to remind him that he was in second place, after her son. The conversation ended, filling the atmosphere with overwhelming stillness, which crept into the workshop where Adam attempted to tidy up his dishevelled appearance. He ran his fingers through his hair and stuffed his shirt into his trousers, having no recollection of how on earth it came out. Unless...Oh, yes, Eve's hands were at his waist. His hands...and mouth — never mind. Just like the past night's dream, the best moment, he was certain, was over.

Eve needed a bit more time to restore her self-control and stepped into the bathroom. She realized she would have to face Adam sooner or later. Her heart threatened to burst out of her ribcage as she reviewed the moments of ecstasy spent in Adam's arms just minutes before. Just when she thought her heart couldn't beat any faster, a soft knock on the door followed by Adam's voice initiated another jolt.

"Eve, are you all right in there?"

"Yes, I'll be out in a moment." Her voice was, to her dismay, a weak imitation of her normal one.

"Was that call from Anthony's school?"

"Yes," Eve said. "By mistake they marked him as absent and they needed to verify that he had been dropped off this morning."

"I'm glad the call didn't bring bad news."

"Yes, me too. Do you mind waiting for me in the car? I'll be ready to go to the frame shop in a minute."

Adam didn't mind. He too needed the time to cool down. If it wasn't for that inopportune telephone interruption, he was not so sure if he would have been able to hold himself back. What he minded, though, was the silence in the car once she got in. They were halfway to the store without having exchanged more than two or three simple sentences. Adam feigned interest in the traffic.

Eve sat motionless, trying to determine a safe topic of discussion to break the deafening silence.

*Ah, the portrait!* At the next red light, she removed the portrait from its wrapping and showed it to Adam.

"How do you like it?"

"Whoa! It's him, all right. I almost expected it to breathe."

For one short moment their eyes locked. The honking of the car behind them reminded them that the light had changed. Soon they turned on 75th Street and Eve tried to sort out what had happened less than twenty minutes ago. Was she sorry? Was she dragged into it? And uppermost, would she have been able to stop it if the phone hadn't rung? What she felt in those moments was pure passion. Why should she be ashamed of that? She wanted it to happen. God knows, she had daydreamed of it enough lately. She felt as if her old, established theory of not rushing into intimacy had been shaken from its foundation. She had to admit, she participated with unrestrained willingness.

A swift turn brought her back to reality.

Adam had brusquely changed lanes, cutting another car off.

"Adam, you don't turn right here!" Eve shouted, swaying left and right. The car came to an abrupt halt on the shoulder of the side-road.

"I'm sure I got the right directions. What I don't get though, is why you are going to such lengths to avoid looking or talking to me, or just being your old self?"

"I don't know what you mean."

"I'm sure you know exactly what I mean. Look me in the eyes and tell me that you regret what just happened," Adam said.

"For God's sake, of course I don't regret it. I was only taken by surprise, that's all."

Blue eyes stared into blue eyes.

"No guilt about my marital status or anything?" Adam probed.

"Now that you mention it—"

"Don't even go there!" His tone had become accusing. "There is *nothing* I can do to make the time pass any faster."

To her surprise, Eve started to relax. "Time — it seems to be our enemy."

Adam laughed. He took her hands in his. "My darling, true lady! I must say I was afraid I came on too fast. Yet I won't apologize. I just want you to know that my actions are not based solely on weakness or lust. I adore you...and I have a feeling that it's mutual. I am bowled over by your charm, beauty, and character." He laughed. "I probably stepped out of bounds a bit, and you may think that we could have lost control if not for the telephone disruption, but I swear I didn't have any intention of pushing things further without *your* full cooperation."

Eve blushed profusely but never lost eye contact this time. If anything, his candid outpouring eased her uncertainty about how he felt for her. No more words were said. None were needed. Besides, his eyes said more than a thousand words could convey.

And in that moment, Eve felt an overwhelming peace about their relationship.

Eve stepped out of the car and welcomed the cool, refreshing breeze. Adam came by her side and took her hand, as if he'd done it a hundred times before. The gesture caused a surge of apprehension in Eve's stomach, but she made a quick, silent resolution not to make a big deal of it. It didn't seem to affect Adam. She was so caught up in her thoughts that she missed Adam's scrutinizing glances around the parking lot.

A short man with a kind face appeared from a side room connected to the workshop. Eve had known him for a long time. His name was Tom Chen. He was the co-owner of the establishment — an ambitious, grateful Chinese immigrant, who made no secret that he valued more the freedom he gained in Canada than his university degree from his birth country.

"Good morning Mrs. Nelson, what a coincidence! I wanted to call you today about one of the frames. I got some new material I want you to have a look at, because it may work for your *Deep Sea* abstract. I remember you had some doubts about the flat profile you originally chose for it."

"Thank you, Tom. I'll have a look at it. But first, I have a favour to ask of you. This is Mr. Carry, a friend," Eve said, and the two men shook hands. "He has a portrait that needs framing." Eve took the portrait and handed it to Tom so he could appraise the job. "Would it be possible to have it done by Saturday?"

Tom said that he was certain he would be able to frame it in time and Adam left Eve to decide on the appropriate type of framing. Tom offered a variety of new samples, which engrossed Eve as she attempted to envision the most fitting choice. When the buzzing sounds of an electronic device announced the door opening again, Adam made an effort not to turn around. Casually, he wrapped his arm around Eve's shoulder and gave his opinion on one of the two samples she seemed to favour. It seemed that Eve needed that particular insight, since she made up her mind and placed the order.

As Adam inveigled her into a professional explanation of a particular oil painting adorning one wall of the store, she was unaware that their hands were linked, fingers through fingers. He showed interest in some pieces and Eve shed some light on them. She sensed that their abstract themes made the interpretation tougher for an inexpert eye.

"Which ones are yours?"

"Mine are in the back. They are not for public view until summer."

Coaxed by Adam's discreet but watchful manoeuvre, Eve stepped backwards until she bumped into someone.

"I'm very sorry—" Eve said.

"Mother?"

"Adam, darling!"

Adam made the introductions. "Eve, this is my mother, Janet Carry. Mother, meet Eve Nelson, a friend of mine."

The two women shook hands awkwardly.

"Nice to meet you, Mrs. Carry."

"My pleasure, dear," the older woman said, a degree calmer and more composed than the other. "I had the pleasure of meeting your adorable son. He is such a nice little fellow. You must be very proud of him."

"Yes, very proud, indeed," Eve said.

As Adam rushed to kiss his mother's cheek, Eve couldn't help but observe the very regal woman. She was tall and slender for her age, around seventy, Eve guessed. She had a noble air and carried herself with the grace and surety of the well-bred. She had the same blue eyes as Adam, but that seemed to be all they had in common. She smiled a warm smile that, to an inexpert eye, would seem natural.

But Eve wasn't deceived by it. She wondered for a moment if Janet Carry shared her anger and embarrassment at their untimely, forced introduction. Her sense of self-control kept Eve from checking her burning cheeks. She wished she could disappear.

"What are you doing here, Mother?"

"Oh, I was visiting the craft store next door and I was beguiled by the lovely display in the window of this store," Janet Carry said, thankful she had noticed the type of the stores in the strip mall as she waited for her son to appear. He had called her an hour ago and gave her the address of the gallery, and a mysterious invitation to a surprise. "Meet me there," he'd said and ended the conversation. Generally, she didn't appreciate surprises, but she played along only because her son was involved. It was clear to her that it was a surprise to Eve as well.

She was too kind to let the innocent young woman stew in the charade any longer. With a warm handshake Janet left, "for another matter that needs my attention."

No sooner had Adam started the car than Eve spluttered, "Did your mother really come in there by chance?" Fury made her voice shaky. "Because if you tell me—"

"No, she didn't."

"I didn't think so," Eve said, realizing how his simple, honest answer defused her fury.

"I guess I didn't think it would be a big deal—"

"But it is to me. Please don't do anything like that again," Eve responded. She still felt uncomfortable sharing their relationship with anyone else, especially his family. Yet, when she stepped back, she could see that no permanent damage had been done. If anything, it showed her that Adam had a penchant for acting first and thinking later.

"Adam? What was it you wanted to tell me this morning at my house?"

"Ah! It almost slipped my mind. You'll meet my sister and her husband this Saturday."

"Oh, will I?"

"It's so wonderful to sleep in once in a while," Crista said, as she stretched her body in a cat-like way and then plopped down on her chair.

Mike consulted his watch. “You’re promoted to a sluggard, honey,” he said and placed her breakfast in front of her.

It was Saturday, and for the first time in months, he didn’t have to go to work. Because he was the family’s early bird, he prepared Brandon for hockey practice. After Eve and Adam picked him up, Mike returned to bed where, with gratification, he found Crista awake and willing, which suited his mood. Hence, the breakfast treats…

“Come on, Mike. This is the first Saturday I’ve slept in since the beginning of the year,” Crista said, and took a bite of a thin sausage freshly dipped in maple syrup. “I end up doing a lot of your work, because you have been putting in so much extra time at work. I should call Victor Knight and demand a special bonus — besides the annual one — for the spouses of those who work on Saturdays. They end up having to take care of all the family matters by themselves.”

“You do that honey. I bet he’ll tell you where he placed the ‘annual’ bonus this year.”

“What do you mean?”

“Well, to make a long story short, there is no money for bonuses this spring.”

“Damn Victor!” Crista blurted out.

“Darling, be reasonable. It’s not Victor’s fault that the financial world is not in good shape. Besides we’re not destitute, and are not relying on that extra money.”

Suddenly the food on Crista’s plate didn’t taste as good, maple syrup or not. She had hoped to renew her wardrobe this summer, from the best brand-name stores along the west coast of the States, during their cruise. With no bonus money, she’d come back with the same old duds in her luggage. Great.

“Do you know what kind of business Adam Carry is in?” Mike asked, eager to drop the bonus subject.

Despite her curiosity, Crista had never asked Eve about Adam’s line of work. She assumed he had some fabulous position in some fancy government office.

“Don’t tell me he’s just another jerk!” Crista said, still cranky about the missing bonus.

Mike laughed. "I wish *I* was that jerk, if my father was the head honcho of Carstone Corporation."

"What?" Although she was not familiar with big business, the name sounded familiar. "You're doing this just to divert my attention from the bonus issue. I know your strategies too well, Mike Malone."

"I'm doing no such thing." He went on with the story he had read the day before about the changes in the oil industry, the war between the most competitive companies, and the speculation about the destiny of Carstone Corporation when Adam Carry replaced his father as a business partner with his soon-to-be ex-wife.

"So, the renowned oil corporation has two shareholders: Adam's father and Alicia Stone Carry — hence 'Car' and 'stone.'" Mike explained, "Which means, their business would dissolve if either of them left to become a separate entity, and both would plummet in the market."

"Why?" Crista asked, now immersed in the conversation.

"Because apart, they would lose the top place and the power of the market they have now as a whole, that's why."

"Ah. But when Adam divorces, it doesn't mean they have to divide the business, does it?"

"Theoretically, no. There was no comment from Carstone in the paper, but I suppose the old man would want to keep things soldered together. And when Adam's old papa drops dead — which is possible sooner rather than later, since he already suffered a heart attack — there is speculation that the 'oil giant' may not survive under the son's leadership."

Dumbfounded by this juicy piece of news, Crista wondered if Eve had any inkling about Adam's line of business or how intricately it was tied to his personal life.

"Man, this is incredible news. Why the hell hasn't he told Eve who he is?" Crista wondered aloud.

"He has his reasons, I'm sure. Put yourself in his shoes. He would make an easy target. He would be surrounded by more babes than Donald Trump could gather for the next Miss Universe pageant."

"I don't see Eve being like that." Crista shook her head.

"Exactly! But we both know Eve. She won't warm up easily to someone that's way out of her element either, which would explain Adam's cautious move. He's shrewd enough to sense it, so he's moving in slow motion. Frankly, I see no harm in his approach, darling."

Mike's explanation made sense, Crista had to admit, but what if Adam was using Eve solely for personal, manly enjoyment until he found a more suitable, permanent replacement?

"Now, don't go spill it all to Eve, honey," Mike warned. "It's their affair."

"Fair enough," Crista said, between pursed lips.

Saturday came all too soon.

When Adam drove Eve home on Thursday, from the framing shop, and told her about his plans for Saturday, he had made it sound casual: "Something simple, a dinner for four." She had consented, but now she felt uncomfortable. Not that she was shy to meet people. She possessed the confidence and ability to present and represent herself with grace and dignity, but she felt the nudge of being pushed too soon into an element of the relationship she wasn't ready for.

Adam sensed her tension Saturday morning when the boys were at hockey practice and they took a walk outside. He assured her that Cassidy and Brad were going to like her just as much as his mother did.

His mother. How could she forget that encounter? "Did she say that? What did she say about me?"

"Not many words. Honestly, Eve. I suspect you enchanted my mother to the point of making her speechless."

*Perhaps women see things differently — in a more objective way, than men*, Eve thought. *Women are able to put themselves in others' shoes.* It was no surprise to Eve that Adam's mother had been speechless at her son's spontaneous mission of bringing the two of them face to face. What mother would have had words of praise for her son's new woman when he was not divorced yet? The more Eve thought of that encounter, the more uneasy she became. She would have understood better if he had shown her off to his friends. It would have made more sense and would have been easier to get over.

She was stepping out of the bathtub when the telephone rang.

*It must be Adam,* she thought, as she ran to the phone in her room wrapped only in a towel. The wicked, naughty part of her wished that the ring came from the doorbell. She had some rather sensual, erotic thoughts during the bath that were still on her mind. She picked up the receiver with trembling hands.

"Garry! What a pleasant surprise," Eve said, when she recognized her brother's voice. "I wanted to call you."

There was a short pause before her brother said, "Oh, dear sister, I'm glad you didn't."

Eve felt a chill. "Why? What's wrong?

"I wasn't totally truthful with you when I called you last month, with the news about Jessie." His voice trailed off in a choked sob.

"What is it?" Eve asked and sat down on the bed, feeling as if her legs might fail her. His words evoked a memory of another time, sixteen years ago, when their brother Jonathan died. She was in summer camp and Garry called her with the devastating news and the same tone in his voice.

"Jessie has leukemia."

*"Oh, no!* Not Jessie. Not my little doll Jessie," Eve said, as tears started rolling down her face. "Garry, tell me she's going to be all right. There is treatment now. Maybe there's hope."

The silence from the other end made her realize that hope was in scarce supply.

"I didn't want to tell you before. I didn't want to upset you. You've had enough heartache already," Garry said softly. "Jessie is having chemotherapy, but we were told that this type of leukemia can respond erratically..." He went on explaining the procedures Jessie went through, sparing her the side effects.

Garry, as Eve suspected, was consumed with pain, but she knew he would stay in one piece. It was Gloria, her sister-in-law, who she was worried about. She tried to imagine how terribly upset Gloria must be. Eve was almost afraid to inquire about Gloria's state of mind.

From the other end, the answer came as she expected.

"I'm fearful for Gloria's sanity, darling. She's in total denial...and then of course, there are some doctors that raise her — our — hopes with talk of new experimental treatments. My wife, I'm afraid, is leaning on a dream and I think she'll break into pieces if Jessie..."

Long after the conversation ended, Eve thought of her brother's plight. How could she help? She could almost see his face constricted with pain each time as he avoided uttering the horrible word: *Death*. She wished she wasn't so far away.

If she had to choose only one thing that her maternal grandma, Evelyn, impressed and inspired her with, it was a simple saying: "Smile. No matter how heavy your heart feels, put on a smile and face the world."

It took a lot of discipline for Eve to apply her grandma's old, practical, and wise counsel while she prepared for the evening ahead.

In spite of everything, Eve was determined to enjoy her evening.

There were only a few people in the restaurant lobby when Eve and Adam arrived at *La Bohème*. Eve was a bit apprehensive, as she had no idea what kind of people she was about to meet.

The woman Adam embraced tenderly and kissed on the cheek had the same blue eyes as his, but — just like with their mother — that was the only likeness they shared. Eve knew already that Cassidy was a paediatrician. As for her husband, he fitted the description Adam had given: "Brad is the best lawyer anyone could hire." The man was the epitome of the word "lawyer." Just like Crista had said — not a lady-killer, but not unpleasant to be around either.

Eve felt more relaxed than she thought she would be. Her companion was handsome and well mannered. The food was glorious as always. French cuisine — one of Eve's favourites — was the staple of the menu. She drank only champagne, which caused some teasing.

"Champagne? For the main course?" Brad asked in complete disbelief.

"It's the only drink Eve would have," Adam chimed in with a warm chuckle.

"Truth is, I can drink anything, but if I do, after a few sips, I'm under the table and miss all the fun."

They all laughed. Adam pulled her closer and squeezed her shoulder.

Brad and Cassidy were easygoing and warm. When the discussion reached the topic of children, it felt as if she were talking to any of her friends. The men, as always, embroiled themselves in discussing business, cars, and sports.

The evening glided along smoothly from one course to the next. Eve's misgivings and hesitation for coming out gradually dissipated.

Adam presented the Johnsons with the portrait, neatly wrapped in silver paper.

"Adam, this is the best present you've ever given us!" Cassidy said.

"The *best* thing is that Eve created it."

"I remember you said that Eve is an artist," Brad said, taking the portrait from his wife. He held it at arm's length for a proper viewing. "It is amazing, Cass. Look at that impish smile. And his eyes look so lively."

It was obvious that Brad's words were sincere. Cassidy also looked pleased with what she saw.

"Eve, this is priceless! An original. I assume we could make a bundle if hard times ever hit us and we needed to sell it," Brad joked. He took a closer look at the right corner of the portrait and read the signature. "Why does it say, 'J. Angel?'"

"I sign my work with a pseudonym," Eve offered.

"You do?" Cassidy and Adam said at the same time.

Eve felt compelled to give an explanation.

"It's a fad every young artist goes through at the beginning of their career, a silly thing, of course, as it can be risky to get rid of later on." Eve explained. The truth and lie concoction resurrected the memory of the time she made the decision of choosing a pseudonym for her artwork.

Shortly after they moved to Canada, the Nelsons were invited to a reception given for all the CIBC branches in the city. Eve was twenty-two years old and a beauty in bloom. Whispered questions and hypotheses about her "vocation" was the subject of gossip. Eve sensed that the talk in the room was focused on her and decided to take the matter into her own hands. “I’m an artist,” she had replied to a query. “Is that acceptable with you?”

The man winced but recovered well. “Yeah, no problem, but why in the world does a Venus like you have such an airy-fairy kind of job?”

Eve understood the guy’s true, intended question: “If you’re a good artist, why did you have to get yourself an older guy for back up?” She decided not to waste any more time among those people who thought the worst of her. She turned around and looked for her husband. He was, Eve realized, within earshot and suddenly engrossed in a conversation with a middle-aged stranger. Nearby, people pretended to ignore their colleague’s blunder and turned away.

When they returned home, she released her anger.

“Know what’s bothering me? Don’t tell me you were too engrossed in a conversation with that woman you just met to hear what was going on around you, because I won’t believe you. I had no idea I married such a weak man. You must have had a hunch that I was being preyed upon by those people, yet you didn’t have the decency to stand by me. You didn’t even defend me in front of that blockhead who thinks I’m a dense, useless creature living on your generosity. *Why?”* she demanded.

William was too stunned of Eve’s outburst to react or defend himself.

“From now on,” Eve continued, “I will use a pseudonym. That way if the critics don’t like my ‘airy-fairy’ work, it won’t impact the ‘Big’ William Nelson’s reputation.”

It had been some time since Eve had thought of William and that particular confrontation. To the group awaiting the rest of her explanation, she said: “At least my pseudonym is not a bizarre scribble like some other artists use.”

“Definitely not!” Adam concluded, intrigued.

“Ah! Is there more champagne?”

“Yes, but don’t drink too much, because I don’t want you to step on my toes on the dance floor,” Adam teased.

“Are we dancing?” Eve said, and for a moment, found herself hesitating.

"Of course," Adam said as he got up. "It's your favourite song, which I happen to like myself."

Cassidy and Brad relished some time alone.

"So, what do you think so far?" Cassidy asked.

"What do I think so far of *what*?"

"Very funny!"

"Well, is there any more champagne?"

"Brad! Stop joking. I want your opinion."

"Okay. Okay. But I must warn you, this field of expertise is not my forte. I don't really have much to say." He shrugged and tilted his head towards his wife, who inched closer, preparing to be his willing confidant, if she had understood the hint correctly. "She confirms your brother's description..."

"Yes?"

"...which, in my book, translates as 'too good to be true.'"

Cassidy looked her husband in the eye. "Have you talked to my mother recently?"

"No. Why?"

"She described Eve in the same terms when I dropped Ryan there tonight. Adam introduced the two of them the other day. It was quite a shocker, since neither had any idea they were going to be introduced. Mother was convinced that Eve wasn't deceived by his strategy either."

Brad fell silent. Adam's behaviour, which seemed somewhat childish, could be justified to a degree. Adam was like a bird too long confined to a cage. One day, it finds the door open and eagerly flies away to explore its newfound freedom. Brad had seen Adam at his best, but he had also seen him in the pits of the hell. Those close to Adam sensed that, under his pretence that everything was all right, he was in constant misery — the fight to stay sane and functional just the routine requisite of life.

"How did you know that *Love Doesn't Ask Why* is my favourite song?" Eve asked on the dance floor.

"It is?" Adam said, and Eve nodded. "It was just a guess. I saw Celine Dion's CD in your workshop on Thursday. I like this song the most. Actually, everyone seems to be in love with it."

Eve tried without success to relax. Adam was holding her close and that only increased her nervousness. And as she opened her mouth to suggest a looser grip, he surprised her with a light kiss on her parted lips.

"Adam! You're embarrassing me in front of your family. Please loosen your hold on me. Please don't lower your hand on my back."

"Eve, I'm not doing anything different than anyone else, in case you haven't noticed. We *are* supposed to dance this close." Adam looked around to highlight his point.

"Okay. If you're trying to make me feel guilty for being a spoil-sport, you've succeeded. Indeed, everyone seems to be cozy." Eve didn't want to think about how she was feeling. Under Adam's fervent gaze, she could become oblivious to her surroundings. Suddenly, Crista's "recommendation" came to her mind: "You can have a cozy night with him, if you like. Anthony can spend the night here."

Adam had to say her name twice to recapture her attention. And when he had, she had no idea what he was talking about. Eve repeated in her mind what she thought his last words were: *But no one more than me.* She kicked herself mentally but verbally pleaded for a hint.

"Sorry for being so distracted. Too much champagne, I guess. What was that?"

"You agreed that everyone looked cozy and happy, and I said that no one is happier than me. In fact, I'm delighted we're here tonight, enjoying each other's company, dancing..."

Dancing. The thought froze in Eve's mind. The song had ended some time ago, but they were still on the spot. In each other's arms. Eve looked around and her pulse regained its normal pace when she noticed other couples on the floor waiting for the next song to start.

"Eve, can I ask you something?"

"Yes." *Anything.* "I only hope I know the answer."

"I think you do. Who is J. Angel?" As soon as his words were out, he regretted them. The serenity he'd seen in her eyes just a moment ago disappeared. He was well aware that Eve had held back something about this subject earlier at the table. As he felt Eve stiffen in his arms, he tried to make amends.

"Forget I asked. I didn't realize it was that personal—"

"It's all right. Really. Jonathan Angel was my twin brother. He died sixteen years ago. He was with my father on a ship that sank in the Coral Sea. My dad survived." Eve thought about the loss of her twin for the first time without experiencing a dull pain in her heart. It seemed as if it had happened a lifetime ago.

"I'm so very sorry about your brother. I didn't know you had a twin."

"It runs in the family. With my first pregnancy, I was carrying twins, but I lost them at twelve weeks. Two boys."

Adam held her even closer in a protective embrace. He wished she would never leave it.

"I have never seen Adam so…so…"

"Happy?" Brad supplied. "Definitely. He looks like he just invented happiness…and very sure of himself, which kind of concerns me if this *goddess* has a shrivelled heart and greedy claws. Believe me, every day I see faces holier than the Virgin Mary's fighting for the last penny from their exes. I wouldn't be too shocked to see him tangled up again as soon as he gets away from the other one."

"Oh, Brad why would you say such a thing? I don't see Adam losing his head completely and so soon. Besides, he deserves to be happy no matter who the woman is. And I'm sorry if it pains you, but I truly, honestly like Eve and I'm happy for Adam. She has a lot to offer."

Brad nodded. "That's a good point. No. A perfect point, if it pleases you to hear it from me. And I must confess, they do look good together. There is something about her that makes one want to believe in her. She possesses Princess Diana's beauty, grace, and shyness, combined with the holiness of Mother Teresa."

Cassidy looked at her husband and decided that he really meant what he said. "Brad Johnson! You really are making me feel so jealous on our anniver—"

"Happy Anniversary!"

"*Alicia!"* Cassidy and Brad shrieked the name simultaneously.

"What are you doing here?" Cassidy managed to ask, although she was wondering how long Alicia had been standing behind them before she made known her presence.

"How are you?" Brad asked.

"I've been better. Thanks for asking, dear brother-in-law," Alicia replied, gazing at the dance floor. "The source of my unhappiness, you can observe for yourself. No woman can be too content watching her man in the arms of a new babe, now could she?" she asked. "But don't lose sleep over my hurt feelings. I have a good lawyer who gets paid to handle these *things*." Alicia produced a showy smile and departed with an airy wave.

"Brad, stop Adam!" Cassidy shouted, as she saw him striding towards Alicia.

Brad got up so fast his chair tumbled backwards. He grabbed and constrained Adam just before he could reach Alicia.

"Let go of me. I'll break her neck," Adam yelled, squirming.

"No! That would be really stupid, and I won't let you give *her* that satisfaction."

Adam's rage fuelled his strength and Brad barely managed to match it. One more of Adam's pushes and he thought he would sprawl on the floor. Cassidy came to her husband's aid.

"Don't be stupid, Adam. Don't you see she's provoking you? Calm down. Stop making a scene," Cassidy warned.

Alicia walked away, and once at a safe distance, looked back to admire the anarchy she incited. Gloating, she made her way to the exit, collecting her male companion on the way out.

Finally, Adam seemed to get his temper under control, and then realized he had abandoned Eve on the dance floor. He swore, damned his brother-in-law for obstructing him, and then damned himself for letting Alicia's act spoil his date.

The day was lovely and held the promise of an early, settled spring. Yet for all the enjoyment Adam got from it, it could have been overcast and ugly. He stood motionless in front of the wall of windows in his office. Despite the stillness of his posture, there was a great deal of grey matter at work. Among the questions that swirled in his head, he desperately needed to know if Eve was so upset with him that she was not returning his phone calls.

It had started out as a memorable Saturday evening, but ended on such a sour note. Adam knew he was not totally responsible for the turn of events, but also knew that when Cassidy and Brad's anniversary resumed after Alicia's nasty exit, he could kiss his romantic plans goodbye. Adam sensed the Herculean effort Eve exercised to retain her composure. He was disappointed but not a bit surprised when Eve, after a long silent drive home, told him to ask the driver to wait for him. At her door, he tried to clear things up.

"Eve, there is nothing I can do to change what happened tonight. I can only apologize for my irrational response. I'm very, very sorry that it hurt you."

"It did not."

"You don't need to pretend you're not upset, because you have every right to be." He drew in a deep breath and expelled it in rugged fragments.

Under the porch light, Eve held his painful gaze. "You didn't let me finish. All right, I'm a bit upset about *that*. But I'm heartbroken for a different reason. Before you arrived, my brother called to tell me that my niece was diagnosed with leukemia a couple of months ago." Her voice became shaky. "Adam, this illness is hopeless."

"Oh, Eve I'm so sorry. Maybe my sister could help. I mean, with her knowledge of paediatric care, she must know about any new treatments. Advancements in technology have really changed the medical field. My God, and to think that all of this time you knew—"

"Adam, I wouldn't want to burden anyone with this, let alone your sister. Help is not expected from here. My brother is consulting the best doctors in Australia and the world."

Monday morning, Adam called Eve and left a message. When she didn't return his call, he wondered if she might have gone to Australia in a rush and didn't have time to let him know. He was in a belligerent mood, which fuelled his desire to confront Alicia, only to be told she had gone to China. His mouth dropped in bewilderment.

"Since when?"

"Mrs. Carry left yesterday at noon." A new secretary, one of Alicia's protégés was occupying Miss Annette's chair. Adam couldn't remember if this trip was previously discussed. "I was told it was decided on Saturday, Mr. Carry." The secretary's voice was light, but Adam couldn't help but notice a slight gloating tone in her answer.

He gave a short, hollow laugh.

"Good. I'm sure Mrs. Carry will have a fruitful business trip," Adam said. "Where is Miss Annette?"

"Miss Annette had eye surgery on Friday and will be on sick leave for a few days."

"Oh, yes. I completely forgot about it. Did you send her a nice bouquet of flowers?"

"No. No one told me. I didn't know—"

"Now you know," Adam replied.

Adam was absorbed in his thoughts. He jumped when he heard a muffled sound coming from his pocket. His heart raced at the first thought. He grabbed his phone.

"Eve?"

"Anxious to talk to you too, *mon ami*," a high, squeaky voice replied.

"Garth!"

"Sorry to disappoint you. But that's the highest pitch my voice permits."

"Well, thanks a lot for making me smile, buddy," Adam said smiling indeed.

"You may not be smiling when you hear the reason I'm calling."

Half an hour later Garth was in Adam's office.

"I don't need to remind you that your sweet wife is a first-class bitch, but as your lawyer, I'm happy to show you more proof," Garth said. He placed a small pile of papers on Adam's desk, and then poured himself some spring water, giving his friend a moment to read them.

One glance back at his friend made him decide to fill two glasses. "Don't you keep any hard liquor in here? You might need some when you're done checking all those."

Adam did not reply. He was counting the pages. Eighteen. All were copies of credit card statements with Alicia's name on them. He knew she had all kinds of credit cards — just like he did, but had never seen her using this one. The billing statements were directed to a private mailbox.

Alicia had used that particular credit card solely to rent hotel rooms. She had rented one at the Fairmont Hotel Macdonald over a period of a year and half. On some statements, there were charges from hotels out of the country. According to one dated March 1991, the amount of $3,491 had been spent at Four Seasons Hotel George V. Adam recalled their trip to Paris at that time, but couldn't recall the name of the hotel in which they had stayed.

"This expense shouldn't be on her credit card. It was on the company account. Unless—"

"Unless Alicia took a companion along, put him in that posh hotel room, and paid for it on this card. What this implies, my friend, is plain and simple. Your darling wife was generously screwing an army of men even before the separation," Garth explained. "Proof is there on paper that she paid for hotel rooms in France, Japan, and twice in Toronto," he said, knowing the information by heart.

"I'm not surprised. Did she really think getting laid outside the nest was part of our fucking marriage vows? What a whore."

"Look on the bright side. Her numerous escapades are your colossal gain. Millions are coming your way and only because we possess this hot evidence." He tapped the papers in front of Adam. "If you'd prayed for these seven days a week for a year, you wouldn't have them in hand. I tell you, it was pure luck and intuition that we got these. Bang! We can nail her to the wall. Do you know how hard it is to procure such incriminating evidence?"

Adam, however, was not listening to his friend's talk about money as *his* gain.

"What's your plan with this 'hot' evidence?"

"I'm going to deliver it personally to Alicia's lawyer, but no earlier than June. I can amuse myself in the interim by knowing how hard Max Atkins will be working on her case and then this comes in as a surprise!" Garth clapped his hands. "Am I good or what?"

*Good? Yes,* Adam thought and wondered how many rules his friend had broken to get these statements.

"Don't look for any compliments from me, you sly fox," Adam said. "I don't know who got screwed over for you to get these and I'm not asking. I'll feel better the less I know."

"Thanks a lot. I'll take that as a compliment," Garth noted with a smug smile. "How did the double-date go the other night?"

"Alicia decided to put in an appearance at the restaurant, and Eve took it pretty hard, as you can imagine. Not that she acknowledged it, but it's obvious that she's hurt."

"I see," Garth said, and toyed with a suspicion. "Say...this woman God seemingly made for you, is she by any chance an old flame, someone you met before the legal separation?"

"I met Eve about six weeks ago, and other than a dinner and a lunch, we haven't had any dates."

Garth sighed with relief. "Ah, I almost forgot," Garth produced a business card from his pocket. "Call this number and make an appointment. It's a private clinic — very expensive but they take you in right away. Strictly confidential and to protect the innocent they let you use a 'nickname,'" he said with a wink.

The expression on Adam's face was a mixture of disbelief and irritation. "For God's sake, man, you're suggesting I see a STD specialist?" Adam asked with his eyes still on the card. *"Why?"* A clammy feeling spread across his forehead. "If you think that she could pass something on to me…it's been almost nine months since we separated."

"I know that, I'm your lawyer, remember? Some sexually transmitted diseases stay dormant for years. Don't freak out; an 'expert lover' like Alicia is seldom careless." He put his arm up to stop Adam's interjection. "Besides, the symptoms of most STDs are evident in weeks or a few months from contracting them. Just a few nasty ones are—"

"Okay, I'll make the call right away. I appreciate your concern."

"Thanks! I have to run now. I'm taking Betty out tonight, and I still have a pile of depositions to go through."

"Ah! Making any progress? I mean in your relationship?" Adam asked, as he led Garth to the door.

"Oh, yes. I discovered she's a diligent sex educator," Garth said and winked.

"You'll soon fit back into those old swanky suits you used to wear!"

At that moment the telephone rang.

Adam ambled toward his desk, where he had left his cell phone. From the corner of his eye, he saw Garth stop halfway out the door.

"Yes. Eve, how are you?"

Garth winked again, smiled at his friend, and left.

After leaving the Carstone building, Adam went to the STD clinic. Once the physical examination was over, he felt himself breathing easier, especially when told that "everything" looked fine. Blood work? Yes. Routine, you know… Adam had taken his supper leisurely and spent the rest of the evening at an electronics store to justify the "long working day" he'd told Eve he had in front of him when she called. His plan worked: Anthony was sound asleep when he arrived at Eve's house. Not that he came to see Eve with romantic intentions. Regaining territory would be rewarding enough. To that end, Eve was cooperative; he sensed she was ready to share more about her life. She also told him that she had not responded to his message right away simply because she was not home. Her car had broken down and she had to spend time going back and forth to the garage.

"I was born in 'the bush' – in the country, as you would say here in Canada — and lived there until I was around twelve," Eve started. "My great-grandparents named their farm 'Bluehay' because the land was covered in blue from the wild alfalfa blooming when they first saw it. They had an all-goods store in Castlewood, north of Sydney, but after being robbed, they moved their family and store to Orange County. The store served the neighbouring farms for decades.

"My maternal grandma, Evelyn, took over when her parents died. She and my grandpa managed it for many years, and then she continued with my mother's help after my grandfather died. A boar killed my mother's first husband when he was on a hunting trip. My grandpa went to get the truck to carry his body out, but on his way back got struck by lightning. The two widows buried their men and struggled to keep the family business afloat.

"My grandma and I were the last ones to leave Bluehay. She wanted to 'die and be buried' alongside my grandpa. She was the most complete, wonderful, and wise person I have ever known. And equally as stubborn. When she finally saw that I was determined to stay by her side, she made up her mind and told my mother to move us with the rest of the family in Sydney. Garry was just starting law school. Jonathan was in Grade 5."

Eve took a deep breath.

"I adjusted painfully slowly to life in Sydney. Children are very territorial, girls especially. The girls shut me out."

"I bet they were jealous," Adam said. "They identified you with the villain who comes to steal their beaus."

"Heavens, no!" Eve laughed. "I wasn't popular at all. I don't think boys even noticed me in Grade 5. I was the lanky redhead with hundreds of freckles, who was a head taller than any of the boys from my class. I hated school then. At Bluehay, I didn't attend school. Teaching was done through the radio."

Eve noticed the puzzled look on Adam's face and explained the Australian version of rural education of those times.

"It got boring at times, especially after Jonathan moved to Sydney in Grade 3, but I kept a sketchpad at hand and drew the landscape outside the window. When the 'radio teacher' was repeating the lesson, I could focus on something I liked doing. In the city, I shifted my theme to portraits." Eve sighed. "I was drawing my teachers' portraits on the sly. One day, a teacher caught me in the act and ordered me to go to the principal's office! I felt humiliated and left the room as fast as I could. Shortly after I got to the office, Miss Spencer came running to the principal, with the evidence in hand. It was that incident that led to my artistic career.

"If anyone ever doubts that God hears a child's prayer, they are utterly wrong. I'm living proof. I must have prayed for an intervention, because there is no other way I can explain the happy turn of events. Miss Spencer thought I was doing a hideous caricature of her. But after she inspected her portrait, she was so impressed that she asked me to sign it. She actually paraded my work in front of everyone! Fortunately, the principal's wife was an art teacher. She took me under her wing and convinced my parents I had great potential. Not to mention what that incident did for my popularity! And here I am today!"

"I suspect there is a lot more that happened in between," Adam teased.

Ever since he met Eve, he had been on a quest to learn more about her. Cassidy had shed some light on Eve's tragedy as she recalled the bank robbery was in the news for a while. She also mentioned the education fund for Anthony.

"Did you have a good relationship with your parents?" Adam asked.

She hesitated. "I would say yes. I was fortunate enough to have good parents. My father was a navy engineer. The 'story' has it that my father was stranded in the bush and came to my grandma's store for some necessities. He stayed for a week but returned one month later and married my mother. My mother was not nearly as experienced and educated as he was, but she was a very beautiful woman. She had a three-year-old son — Garry, my half-brother — who my father adopted. Jonathan and I came late into our parents' lives.

"But, yes I had a happy childhood. When my father came home from the sea, he doted on me! Unfortunately, he was longer on the sea than at home. Maybe that's why I loved him so much, because he was home only sporadically.

"In 1970, my parents sold the Bluehay General Store and moved to Sydney. They kept the small house though, which Garry and I still own and use as a retreat cottage. My mother opened a pastry shop, which she managed efficiently and with little help. Father, like always, functioned better at sea. My twin brother grew up to be a fearless boy, very much like Father. He was fourteen when Father took him to sea for the first time. At first, they went on two and three-day trips, and then the duration increased as school vacations permitted. Mother opposed those trips, calling them 'unnecessary swashbuckler bravado.'"

Eve took a deep breath. "The following year, on July 14, 1975, the *Albatross* — the ship my father and Jonathan were on — was hit by a giant oil tanker on a foggy night. Twenty-eight crew members were lost. Twenty-three people survived the collision, my father included. I was in summer camp in Tasmania. I didn't know about the tragedy until the day after, when Garry called.

"At home, Mother was half crazy. Word came that the surviving crew members were on another ship, being given aid and awaiting transportation to Sydney. She was still hoping Jonathan was among them. When my father called, she told him not to come home without my brother. He didn't come home until Jonathan's body was found three days later.

"There are no words to describe how hard it is to go on living after a tragic event like that. Nothing is the same. Mother blamed Father. Father blamed himself, and often God. He found refuge and consolation in alcohol and loathed himself until the day he died, one year later.

"After my father died, Garry and I tried coaxing my mother into re-opening the pastry shop, and for a while, we thought she might have picked herself up. In the end, she relapsed into her self-pity. She died one year after my father, two months short of my high school graduation. I used to feel such bitterness towards them. I felt they let me down, even before they died. They locked themselves in their sorrow and didn't see the pain they caused around them."

Eve stopped for a moment to compose her words.

"How can I explain this? When such a huge tragedy happens in a young person's life, you get the feeling they don't care about your existence, that they don't love you anymore. Garry was already on his own, establishing his practice. He was also preoccupied with the love of his life, Gloria — a young teacher who subsequently became his wife.

"I longed for kindness and affection, for someone to understand me and save me from the anger that engulfed me. About that time, I started dating Brian, who was two years older than me. He helped me through those stressful years. A few years later, freshly out of college, I met William. We got married, and well you know how that ended."

"Why did you break up with Brian?"

"Actually, Brian broke up with me. I think he had enough of lending his shoulder for me to cry on." She laughed. "The truth is somewhere in between. For all my problems, my relationship with Brian was mostly a good one. At some point I thought he would be the 'one'. But at the age of nineteen, I wasn't ready for intimacy. About that time, Brian found someone else. I was torn to pieces, but I survived and was glad I stuck to my principles. From what I hear, even today, he is as uncommitted as ever, neck-deep in trouble and drenched in liquor."

Alexia Chen, her best friend since high school and classmate from Julia Ashton Art School, kept her informed about "poor Brian." The updates started after William's death. Eve had never given any indication she sought any news about her former flame. Alexia conveyed the updates nevertheless. Through her, he learned about her widowhood and pleaded with Alexia to ask Eve if he could contact her. At first, Eve was revolted and didn't respond. When she finally did, she said, "No!" Was she subconsciously still angry with him or afraid to open a wound long healed? She didn't know, nor did she care.

"I suppose the guy felt sorry that he lost you, once he cooled off," Adam said.

Eve shrugged. "That I wouldn't know, first hand. We haven't spoken since. And, by then, I met William. William was different: mature, intelligent, ambitious, and utterly committed. It was only natural that I fell for him and said *yes* after four months of courtship."

"Wow! After only four months? Wasn't that rather fast? I mean, how can you know a person well enough in such a short time?"

Eve smiled. "You too? Some people said I married on the rebound. Some, that it was a shotgun wedding. Well, I can assure you, none of that was true."

"Eve, I give you full credit. You had..." he groped for the right words, "the kind of marriage that proved to all busybodies that they were wrong. But you have to agree that not many people marry after only four months of dating, even ten years ago."

"You're right about that; I'll wait longer the second time around," Eve laughed. "Meanwhile, let's turn the tables. You know, I enjoy memoirs too!"

Adam looked at Eve but did not say anything. She looked so ravishing, sensuous, and vulnerable. The memory of the passion they shared that day in her workroom invaded every cell of his brain. He was addicted to her and he knew it. It was a painful feeling, yet a welcome one. He shook his head.

"Hey, it's only fair. I want to hear your story, too."

"There's not much you don't know about my story. I'm thirty-seven years old, I have two parents and a sister, and I'm getting divorced. It's as simple as that...and did you know it's nearly midnight?"

"Adam Carry! There must be a lot more in between. The only reason you're off the hook is because of the time."

"My life details are so boring," Adam said, collecting his jacket. He gave her a chaste goodnight kiss at the door. Deep down, in their hearts, they wanted more but neither dared to say it.

"Ah, I almost forgot. I have something for you." He put his hand in his jacket and produced a small parcel, neatly wrapped in shiny gold wrapping paper.

"Adam! I told you, I can't take all these presents from you!"

"Believe me, this is more of a favour to me than a present to you." With that, he closed the door and disappeared into the night.

For a moment, Eve just stared at the parcel. *Hmm!* She quickly became curious. No watch, no bracelet, no writing pen would do him a "favour." She moved to the kitchen to find some scissors. She had it partly opened when a sound startled her. She almost dropped the box.

She pressed her hand at the base of her throat, endeavouring to calm her pounding heart. She answered the cell phone before its fourth ring.

"Adam! You scared me to death."

Laughter filled the line and then a click stole it away.

May came, bringing Alicia back from China and ending the tranquillity that had reigned over Carstone Co. in her absence. In an unspoken pact, all personnel kept out of her way. She appeared more snappish than usual. They sensed it was about to get worse.

The only one who regarded her return with any excitement was George Carry. She had faxed him information regarding a possible contract in Shanghai. He declared that all Alicia's past business errors were forgiven when he realized that this could be the biggest contract they procured in the past few years.

"You're something, girl! I've tried to wheedle that company into it since '85. I'm so proud of you! You did a more convincing job than I," George had said on the phone, his eyes glowing as he studied the fax.

Alicia couldn't believe the old man's reaction. Never before had he showed such appreciation for her efforts.

However, a week later things didn't look so good. The media had picked up the divorce story again. George and Alicia were both concerned that the hype created over the divorce issue could scare off the Chinese and the deal could disappear.

"It would be horrible to get this close and then lose the contract." George sagged against his desk.

"That won't happen if I can help it!" Alicia lit a cigar and started pacing the office. "Let me think for a moment."

George remained silent. He'd agree with anything she suggested, for he had no better ideas.

For the past three weeks, Adam had felt as if he were walking on a cloud. He kept a nine to five, Monday through Friday schedule and loved it. He loved sneaking out of the office at the end of the day without seeing his father. In the evening, he came to life.

Eve was floating on a cloud herself. Willingly responding to his attentiveness, she threw the "clandestine" nature of their relationship to the back of her mind. She was spellbound, yet cautious.

Adam thought her caution was unfair. Especially after she implemented a new rule: No more visits after Anthony's bedtime. He felt deprived of the moments he longed for most. But what do you say to a mother who wants the best for her child? Besides, her resolve was reasonable.

"It's not that I don't want you to stay late — don't take it as an open invitation either," she had said, wagging a finger at him, "but I don't want Anthony to get the wrong message, or worse, to lose respect for me." She was, regrettably, right. He couldn't insist that she do something for which she might lose respect in her son's eyes.

Time today was passing sluggishly for Adam. To bide the time, he placed his briefcase on his desk and started to fill it with "homework" — as Miss Annette called it when she brought it in. She had been given the task of force-feeding Adam his work, by his father. "Just a little bit of it for the weekend," she said, with a perceptive wink. *Ugh*. He spent the final fifteen minutes of the day removing a few files from the pile, and briefly scanning through the rest. Half of him wanted to take only a bit of it home, the other half wanted to leave it all behind.

At five, he came around the desk and closed his briefcase, ready to leave. At the door, he had to make a quick sidestep to avoid bumping into Alicia, with her ever-oppressive perfume.

"Oh, you're on your way out."

"What is it you want?"

"Nice to see you, too. Anything new around here?"

Adam shook his head. To lose his temper with Alicia could result in a fresh altercation that might complicate and delay the divorce process.

"The corporation is happy to have you back," Adam replied. "Now if you'll excuse me, I was on my way out."

"Make sure you see your father on your way out. He wants to talk to you."

"Mommy, Mommy! They're saying something about Ryan's uncle."

Crista ran from the kitchen, oven mitts still in her hands.

"About Adam Carry? What did they say, honey?"

"I dunno. Some stuff."

"'I don't know,'" his mother corrected him.

"Sorry! The man said something about 'divorce,'" Brandon said, his attention on his Monopoly game spread on the carpet.

"Oh, I know," Crista said. "He's divorcing his wife." She was just about to return to the kitchen when her son's next remark stopped her dead in her tracks.

"I think the man said that they're *not* divorcing."

So much for the child's lack of attention.

Crista's domestic preoccupations gave way to curiosity. She watched the *News at 6* until the end, hoping the information would be repeated.

Shortly after nine o'clock, Eve called in response to the two messages Crista had left on her answering machine. She sounded exhausted.

"My car broke down."

"Again?"

Eve took a sip of hot tea. "Thank God, Anthony wasn't with me. I dropped him at Mrs. Marvin's after school. I got completely drenched in that rain."

"What's wrong with the car *this* time?" Crista demanded. The car had been a source of contention since Eve bought it. When Mike heard she bought it because it was white, he was stunned. He was now by Crista, listening to her conversation with Eve.

"I don't know. The motor just died on the Dawson Bridge. AMA towed it to a garage. I'll hear from them tomorrow. Don't worry. I arranged with Ben's mom to pick up Anthony tomorrow morning for school," Eve added. "What's up, why did you call?"

"Don't worry? Eve, we're your friends. Why didn't you call us for help?" Crista said. "Have you at least called Adam? I'm sure he would be more than happy to oblige." She listened to Eve's explanation with increasing edginess. "Yes…He is very busy these days…Oh, yes…I'm sure of it." Crista was parroting Eve's words. "Let me tell you something—"

"Oh no you don't!" Mike grabbed the phone.

"Listen Eve, honey, don't worry about a thing. I'll drive you around until your car is fixed."

"All right Mike, I'll be in touch. I'm so cold. I think I'll stay in bed for three days to warm up."

"You do that, girl. And sleep tight."

It was well past midnight, but Crista was too upset to sleep. Beside her, Mike was snoring lightly. Before he fell asleep, he'd said some things that infuriated her.

"God, woman, you are so obsessed with Eve's life you forget you have your own."

"You're a jerk to call this an obsession."

"Then what would you call it?"

"This is called 'concern' for someone dear to you. But of course, you wouldn't understand that."

"Fine, have it your way. Wake me up when you're done saving the world," Mike said and turned his back on her.

*Great. Just great,* she thought. She wanted to help Eve, not the whole world. Mike had blown it out of proportion. She made up her mind. She wouldn't let Eve be duped by Adam in his swanky suits, gold cuff-links, and pretentious ties.

But damn. Mike made her promise she would not meddle in Eve's affairs right after they had watched the eleven o'clock news.

"To divorce or not to divorce? This is no longer a question," the news broadcaster had started. "The furor over whether the divorce between Adam Carry, the heir of Carstone International Oil Corporation, and his wife, Alicia Stone, who owns forty-nine per cent of the corporation, can be put to rest, as it has been affirmed by the CIOC's spokesperson that they are *not* divorcing. Carstone Oil Co. is a leader in the oil industry in Canada. In the process of acquiring a mega-deal with a foreign client, Carstone Co. is assessed as stronger than ever."

That news had sparked the first raw exchange between the Malone couple on that subject.

"You think the fucker had any intention of telling Eve?"

"Shit, honey. How do I know? I assume Adam is going to let Eve know soon enough that he reconciled with his wife. It's their business honey, not ours. Let them untangle it."

Mike's response upset Crista even more. "Your camaraderie is too fucking obvious. Don't side with the jerk now."

"I'm not. I just happen to know a thing or two about the facts of life. People separate intending to divorce, and in some cases, they bury the hatchet and pick up where they left off. Eve knew what she was getting into. It's not like he lied to her. She knew he was only separated."

He was right, Crista agreed, seized by utter weariness as she reviewed the conversation in her head. Looking at her husband she couldn't help thinking about her own concerns. She wanted another child...and sleeping back-to-back was not the best way to go about it.

Gina Knight had called Eve to invite her for lunch a few times in the past weeks, but Eve hadn't been able to make it work. The banker's wife was a good friend, and Eve felt she had neglected their friendship lately.

"Eve, I know you're very busy, no need to feel guilty, darling. You must be working so hard now with the exhibition coming up. Victor and I would be pleased to have Anthony stay with us anytime."

"Thank you. You're so considerate. I'm fortunate to have you as friends. I plan to take off the month of August to visit my family in Australia, but I'll be taking Anthony with me. That said, I can spare 'Dennis the Menace' for a couple of weekends while I prepare for the show, if you want to take him."

"Yes, yes. Of course," Gina said. "Darling, forgive me if I'm out of line, but I need to tell you this. I worry about Anthony. He needs a male influence in his life. I know Mike spends time with him, and Victor can play that role too, but Anthony deserves a permanent male influence around him. We don't have children, but you don't need to be a child psychologist to figure out that a little boy seeks and craves male attention."

Eve lowered her eyes.

"I don't mean to pry into your private life, but there has to be a limit to any grief. Your loss was huge, but you're still young." There was an earnest plea in those gentle, hazel eyes.

Eve gave a little laugh. "Gina, pretend you lectured me before, because your wish came true."

The other woman's eyes brightened and Eve continued, "I met someone. He is a nice man: well-mannered, patient, and caring with Anthony. But don't rush to any conclusions. I'm taking it one day at a time."

"Eve, this is indeed the best news of the day, and frankly, it's overdue. Victor will be thrilled. Or course, if you don't mind me sharing the news with him."

Eve nodded.

"Cautious is good," Gina continued. "Knowing you, it would surprise me if things were developing otherwise. It may wear a guy's patience down, but one with great character will find that admirable. I'm behind you dear, and not only for Anthony's well-being."

*How lucky*, Eve thought, *to have this conversation with Gina*. Her thoughts were interrupted by the buzz of her cell phone. She excused herself, and fumbling in her bag, found it.

"Hi, Adam. I'm fine, having lunch at Sorrentino's with a beloved friend." She listened to Adam's somewhat lengthy explanation, and the laugh lines on her face disappeared. "No, Adam. Not tonight if you finish that late. Yes, talk to you tomorrow."

Gina was busy checking her day-planner. "What did you say, dear?

"I said that it was *him*."

"Oh, *him*, meaning Adam, right?" Gina said and winked. "I'm not fanatical about religion, but I like to think that God indeed had a purpose in creating an Eve for each Adam, and vice versa."

*Amen,* agreed Eve. Nobody had put it that way, but if God went through all the trouble to get Eve and Adam to meet, it was reason enough to have faith in the story. Hallelujah!

# Three

Some people call it *God's will.* atheists call it pure chance. Regardless of words, it means the same thing: being in a particular place at a particular time, either for something glorious to happen, or something disastrous.

Crista called it *luck.*

Crista and Mike were on their way out of the Paradise Travel Agency at West Edmonton Mall as throngs of people moved in all directions. The noise level increased as they approached the Fantasy Grill restaurant, where a group of businessmen in three-piece suits were trying to make themselves heard.

A familiar laugh reached Crista's ear. She stopped abruptly.

"Damn."

"What?"

Before Mike understood what she was doing, he was towed over to a bench where Crista roughly advised a couple of amorous teenagers to move over.

"What's wrong, honey?" Mike asked, kneeling in front of her.

"Stay still. Don't turn around. Just massage my leg."

Mike complied. She had experienced cramps in her legs in the past, when...

"Honey, are you...?"

"Shhhh. Just keep doing that."

He kept quiet, as she stole glances at something behind him.

"All right, you can turn around now — and thank God I don't have a gun handy."

As Mike turned, what he saw left him speechless. His jaw dropped as he watched the group, mostly Asian, except for two familiar faces: Adam and Alicia Carry, who were hand in hand, laughing, seemingly having a merry outing.

Crista and Mike went to see Eve. Crista told her husband that she would tell Eve *everything*. To her surprise, Mike didn't try to dissuade her.

At Eve's house, and without much of a preamble, Crista shared the information they'd heard on the news. Then she told Eve what she and Mike had witnessed at the mall. As suspected, this was all news to Eve.

"He is handsome, rich, and a jerk," concluded Crista.

"I can't believe it. It can't be true. I really can't see Adam doing this to me," Eve repeated numerous times.

"Honey, believe what you want, but that won't change a thing. I'm so sorry to be the one to tell you. Mike made me promise last night that I wouldn't interfere, but after what we saw, I couldn't call myself a friend if I kept silent," Crista said. "The fact that Mike is here with me means I'm not overreacting."

"When you talked to Adam last, did he hint about reconciliation?" Mike asked.

"I was having lunch with Gina today when Adam called. That was the last time we spoke," Eve said. "He seemed okay. Said he was looking forward to spending some time with Anthony and me." And then, as though her mind was clear of sentimental debris, she added, "He wanted to come over tonight but was not sure what time his work engagement would end." There was a trace of hurt as she spoke the words.

"Ha! Of course, when his wife sets him free, he can visit his other honey!"

Mike shook his head to admonish her for the insensitive comment, but his signals went unheeded.

"I bet he thinks we're all idiots," Crista fumed. "I bet the fucking boor had no intention whatsoever of letting Eve know—"

"C'mon honey, that's uncalled for." Mike couldn't suppress his irritation. "There's still a chance that Adam will do the right thing and explain that he patched things up with his wife."

The impact of Mike's opinion was all over Eve's face.

"Adam called and left a message on my machine an hour ago—"

"And didn't say anything," Crista guessed.

*Welcome to the modern, moral-free world, Eve Nelson. Wake up and smell the roses. Face it, it's a new era. Open marriages. Sharing time. What seemed inappropriate yesterday is fashionable today and will be status quo tomorrow. Crista's right, I'm being screwed.* The reality left Eve feeling sick.

The ringing of her phone interrupted her thoughts. She opened with a flat "Hello."

"Eve? I need to see you as soon as—"

"Oh! You do? Why bother?" She couldn't bring herself to utter his name. "I already know what you have to say. I know everything. The media has already conveyed what you neglected to mention. Do you have something to add to it or contradict it?"

Eve's frosty tone felt like a two by four hitting Adam's head. He cursed himself for having this conversation over the phone. He knew his approach was not going to be successful.

"Eve, honey—"

"Don't call me *honey*!" Eve snorted. "Just tell me one thing…when did you plan on telling me? Or maybe you didn't plan on telling me at all. Maybe you wanted to get your kicks, hoping that I'd never hear about it."

"Eve, I know you're upset. I'm utterly furious about the news bulletin myself, but the information reported is not correct." He groped for a more convincing word, "It has no authenticity whatsoever." Sensing that Eve was about to hang up on him, Adam continued quickly. "My sister called minutes ago and told me about the news break last night. I didn't know—"

"If I choose to believe you — which I don't — would you tell me, why were you at Fantasy Grill tonight in the company of your wife?"

*"What?"*

"You heard me. I told you, I know *everything*. But don't you worry. Remember, I told you once that I wouldn't make any fuss if this happened? I've simply decided to remove myself from this. I'm no longer comfortable with being part of your life. Goodbye."

The anger within the Carry clan reached its zenith. Such fierceness and intensity eclipsed Brad's exit from Carstone Corporation a few years ago. Then, too, it had shaken the clan on all levels and divided its members. The only difference came from the normally well-balanced Janet Carry. Surprisingly, she threw her incredulous, ruby-faced husband out of their bedroom, his bottles of medication in tow.

Janet argued in a clear and loud voice. "I catered assiduously to your every single whim because of your heart condition. But not anymore!" Fury made her eyes blaze.

If George was quiet and yielding, it was not because he didn't understand the consequence of his actions or why they antagonized his wife. But she had never threatened him like this before.

"I have news for you, old fool. From now on, I don't give a damn about your heart. And in case you wonder why, it's because you don't have one. You are a heartless robot where your children are concerned. Let me be blunt. If you mess with Adam's life again, you will answer to me. You hurt that boy enough."

George couldn't keep his mouth shut any longer. He could not fathom why his wife didn't understand that whatever he and Alicia did was in the best interest of the corporation, and that personal feelings should be left aside.

"'Boy' indeed. I'm glad we agree on that score. He is a brainless boy who is far too sentimental."

"Is that so?" Janet asked, hands on her hips. "Do you say that because he is not as motivated by greed as you and that sick woman are? Or maybe because he was justifiably angry about the scheme you two orchestrated yesterday."

The TV stunt came as a surprise to him, too. Alicia came up with that idea but kept it to herself until after its broadcast. Secretly, he was still savouring the outcome. He refused to see it as detrimental to his son's privacy, as Janet implied. So what if some broad had her feathers ruffled over this?

It was as if Janet could read his mind.

"Don't dare to insult my intelligence by implying you didn't know about that stupid newsflash. I won't tolerate your lies."

"Okay. Yes, it was a scheme. I didn't know what Alicia would come up with to coax those people into sticking with the deal. But I would have approved anything. We need this deal and can't afford to forgo it. And it worked. End of discussion."

*He always does that,* Janet thought. She felt betrayed and disgusted. To think she had once held her husband in higher esteem.

"George, I don't recognize you anymore. You're the personification of Don Vito Corleone — whatever he wants, he gets — but at least he loved his family profoundly, whereas you—"

George had no more patience. He lifted his arms in the air. "Sue me if I'm wrong, but your *Godfather* — whom you admire so much — liked to shed pools of blood. What is my crime? I made a business deal like any astute businessman and acquired a huge chunk of dough for the company, in case you didn't think about that."

Janet ignored the slur at her intelligence. For the love of money and power, her husband would deceive, lie, maybe even kill, and definitely stomp all over his own family. She started towards the master bedroom, which was now hers alone.

At the door, she looked at him. "If that deal, you vulgarly call *chunk of dough*, is more important than your flesh and blood, you are out of your mind, George Carry. I gave you a family and you don't care about it at all. You care only for making money. But remember this: The day will come when you'll be a lonely man and money won't help. Money is made of paper. Not flesh or blood. Money doesn't give you love in return. When that happens, even I won't take pity on you."

Eve had every right to be upset but was determined to hide it. She realized her hurt and it crushed her ego mercilessly. However, she reminded herself that she had allowed herself to be lured into it. She fell head over heels for a man whose looks eclipsed his morals. It pained her that she trusted him so blindly. Her only excuse — a pitiful one — was that Adam played the enamoured part flawlessly. With his allure and confidence, he succeeded in getting her to fall for him and it was only her prudence that protected her from complete humiliation.

She decided she needed to spend some time alone. Shortly after she finished her conversation with Adam, she decided to go to Vancouver. She stayed there three days and two long nights. The hotel accommodations were excellent, but she lay awake until dawn each day. Only then she fell asleep, overwhelmed by sheer exhaustion. Though she loved the city, especially the art gallery and museum, she was not in the mood for such pursuits. She went out only to eat and to shop for summer clothing for Anthony.

Returning to Edmonton, she summoned all her strength to appear refreshed and relaxed. She even plastered a smile on her face, when she rang at her friends' door to pick up her son.

Crista played along. Mike kept quiet until he announced that Adam had called them inquiring about her. Eve's smile faded and her heart sank.

"What did he want? I remember perfectly well that I told him 'goodbye.'"

Mike cleared his throat. "Actually, he said that he needs to talk to you, and I promised I would relay the message."

Eve gave a shallow laugh. "I wonder what there is left that 'needs' to be talked about."

That night, Eve took more time than usual to tuck Anthony in bed. She indulged in a pleasant childlike chat with him. Just like old times. Once again, she realized how blessed she was to have *this* gift of life. There was someone who loved her unconditionally, someone who would never lie and deceive her to have his way.

She watched her son drift into deep sleep. The way he'd embraced her, she knew he missed her and she missed him even more. *He's growing up,* she thought. *Not a little boy anymore. And his talk!* His little mind was so inquisitive, filled with questions about stars, insects, wetland habitats, and more. 'Was she sick?' he'd asked. Much like her, Anthony took the indirect, roundabout course in conversation. Of course, she was not sick. She was on a trip related to the upcoming art exhibition. Did he remember about that? She shifted to the subject of the wetlands again, a safe subject. His teacher had sent home some information about the field trip the class was taking soon to Alberta Wetland World. And why was Auntie Crista so angry with Adam?

As Eve pulled the bedspread over her son, she made a solemn promise that she would never go away without him again. And she would never let her heart be broken again. She shuddered. It was at that moment that she knew she needed to get rid of everything she had that reminded her of Adam. Life should go on as if it never happened.

If Adam hoped to have an opportunity to present his part of the story, he was dead wrong. He knew Eve was out of town. He decided to park in front of her house each day until she came back. She couldn't stay away forever. On the fourth day, while watching from his car, his heart beat faster as he saw the garage door opening.

*She came home!* He sprang out of the car and reached Eve's car in seconds. His hope was fleeting, though, as Eve sped away like a startled bird.

Indeed Eve was startled by Adam's tactic. The thought of him stalking her was unsettling.

Anthony's voice brought her back to the present.

"Mommy, why are you angry with Adam?"

She couldn't ignore his questions about Adam anymore, as she had only moments before, when he cried in bewilderment, "Mommy, that's Adam. Mommy, that's Adam! Stop! Why are you driving away?"

She chewed hard on her lower lip thinking there was no gentler way to tell this to a child. "Darling, Adam and I are no longer friends. I'm sorry but that's the way things are." Eve watched, with a constricted heart, as her son's face dropped.

"Oh, Mommy, why? Adam is so nice to me…and to you. He even gave you a cell phone."

That damned thing, Eve recalled vexed. She had to return it. She wished she could have played this "closure" game in a civilized manner and with minimal impact on her son. "What?" she asked, realizing that Anthony had said something odd.

"Because he was my friend, I didn't have to tie anyone's skates' laces."

"Darling, what do you mean you didn't have to tie anyone's skates' laces?" she asked a few minutes later when they stopped in front of the school.

"Some boys were mean to me when I first started playing hockey. They made me carry their stuff on and off the ice. They made fun of me, because I came without my father. Brandon said that he was sorry but couldn't help me."

It never crossed Eve's mind that children could be so cruel. She never suspected their subtle childish disputes. *No wonder he didn't want to go to the hockey practice that morning.*

"Christopher said that, next time, I had to tie everyone's laces," Anthony added. "Adam came and said that he was with me and the mean boys backed off. They stopped calling me 'midget orphan' right away."

"Why didn't you tell me about this before?"

The boy hesitated, his eyes misted. "I was afraid you'd pull me out of hockey."

"No. I would never do that, but I would have talked to Uncle Mike or your coach…" She stopped. Anthony's face told her that that was not the practical solution for this particular problem. She was surprised at her child's keen perception.

Children were imposing their superiority upon her son because he was fatherless and unprotected. The profundity of this new revelation saddened her. It also reminded her of the lanky redhead outback girl sentenced to the desk at the back of the class.

After grocery shopping, Eve spent the morning wandering through the mall in an attempt to lose the feelings of betrayal and gloominess that seemed to be following her. She was avoiding coming face to face with Adam. She pictured him awaiting her return and infuriating her with some debased explanation. Reluctantly, she headed home.

Her heart faltered as she approached her house and saw Adam sitting on her steps. Her biggest worry was that she wouldn't be able to discuss the matter in a civilized manner. *I hope I don't turn into a vulgar-mouthed woman*, she thought, as she brought her car to a stop on the driveway.

As Adam approached, she did her best to pretend he was invisible.

Ignoring his salutation, she opened the trunk and grabbed a couple of bags of groceries. As she put the bags down to unlock the door, she eyed Adam on the sly. He was grabbing bags of groceries from her car.

He followed her into the house and through to the kitchen. After placing them on the counter, he said, "I'll bring the rest."

Eve was annoyed for not declining his offer. Robot-like, she started putting away her groceries.

"These are the last ones."

"Would you like to tell me why you're here? Didn't you understand my goodbye? Or maybe you've concocted another lie. You know, you can spare me any silly details you may have forgotten to mention." She leaned against the counter and looked at him. A few-days-old stubble gave him a sexy, rakish, pirate-like look. And those beseeching eyes! She chided herself for even thinking that and reminded herself that he was a liar.

"Eve, do you really think I went back to *her?* That I would think I could get away with maintaining our relationship while being with her?" He gave a derisive laugh and continued, "God! Life in hell would pale in comparison!"

Eve's face told him that he was not making any inroads, and that the clock was definitely ticking.

"Would I be here at all if she and I got back together? Being at that damn restaurant at West Edmonton Mall was strictly business. I never knew about the TV news release until my sister told me about it.

That was Alicia and my father's doing. I don't understand it, let alone accept it. Your lack of faith in me, and not giving me the benefit of the doubt, is extremely upsetting. I wish you would believe me when I say I'm innocent."

"Whoa! Innocent! That's a word that doesn't begin to describe you. Innocent! Really?"

Her sarcasm made Adam flinch. "You have good reason to be angry with me. About my identity, especially. I kept that hidden from you for too long. I was wrong, especially because you opened up to me about your past. For that, I humbly apologize. But for everything else, you have to hear me out—"

"Really?" The scorn on Eve's face spoke volumes. "'I humbly apologize, *but*.'"

Eve's acid tone led Adam to contemplate for a long moment.

The next thing that happened surprised them both, although for different reasons. Adam strode around the kitchen counter, grabbed her by the wrists, and brought her to the nearest chair. He placed two strong hands on her shoulders and forced her to sit.

"Listen to what I have to say," he said in a tone that didn't leave room for debate. He positioned himself in front of her in a warrior-type posture. "There are a few things I want to clarify for you, and after I do, it's up to you to discern the truth amid the rubbish. Number one: Alicia and I are two separate items just like last week, last month, and ten months ago. No reconciliation. She has expressed her wish for reconciliation on a number of occasions, but I made up my mind to avoid that trap again. Number two: I'm not responsible for that idiotic TV stunt. I was not part of it. I'm more infuriated by it than you could imagine." He paused. "I admit that not telling you more about me was a gross mistake on my part, but—"

"*But*. I'll detest this word forever," Eve was quick to interrupt. "Why is it so hard for you to acknowledge the fact that you didn't trust me? Did you think I might be a vampire that feeds on bloody wealthy guys? Tell me, have you run a security check on me?"

Adam heaved a sigh. "Honestly, at first I didn't say much about myself, because I have learned to be very cautious in relations with women. When I met you, I was pleasantly surprised to see that my name *didn't* register with you. At that point, I was motivated to start afresh in a relationship — to get credit for what I represent as a person and not as a potential bank account.

"When I started to know you better and what kind of person you are, I considered coming clean about that part of my life, but then it worried me that you might think I was a playboy looking for a casual relationship. I also worried that, with the truth out, you might consider us in different leagues, so to speak, and opt to leave the relationship just because of that. I let the time pass hoping that a solution would pop up on its own. If I considered that waiting was the right option, I certainly miscalculated the duration."

"You're right about one thing. We belong in different leagues. Thanks for bringing that up. Let me tell you something. I'm very comfortable in mine. I suppose, you feel the same in yours. Let's leave it at that. Our relationship is over. At this point, I couldn't care less if you are telling me the truth or not," Eve said, standing up.

Adam stared at her in bewilderment. He backed up.

"You don't mean that."

"Oh, yes I do! I told you I'm content where I am with my life. You were not honest with me and consequently you created a trust issue between us. I'm not convinced by your story that you're not back with your wife."

"Why wouldn't you want to hear the truth that I wouldn't take Alicia back? Why would I? It's *you* I want." Adam was not pleading; he was downright angry. Any hopes he had of being able to penetrate the brick wall Eve had built up were fading. He advanced a step, intending to grasp Eve's hand, but she shrank from his touch.

"Maybe so, but *I* don't want *you.* I can't compete with your wife. I'm not blind; she still loves you. Go back to her and forget about me. For all your money, lies, and charm, you can't have us both."

"Eve, you're impossible to talk to," Adam said. "I'm not with her, because I don't love her any more. How can I say it more clearly?"

"Really? Then why did you look like the perfect couple, holding hands and calling each other 'honey' at the restaurant? Those things indicate love, don't you think?"

A shocked expression crossed Adam's face. "Oh, yes. How did you come by that information? Were you there?"

"That's not relevant—"

"True. What is relevant though is the fact that you, or someone else, witnessed a 'production' Alicia devised for that evening. It was meant to mislead the Chinese delegation about the divorce — the same purpose as the TV clip — to make them sign the contract with Carstone. That's all. Stupidly, though, I didn't perceive all the implications."

For a moment, Eve just stood there, faced with two choices: believing his explanation or falling for a lie. For all the evidence he provided, it could have been either. If she had only exercised better judgement in the beginning, she wouldn't have gotten involved in such a relationship and wouldn't be in this situation right now. In her heart, there was a short but painful fight.

Eve darted by Adam, grabbed an object from her purse, and slipped it into his hand. "I don't need this anymore. Now, please leave my house and don't come back or try to contact me."

Dumbfounded, Adam looked at the cell phone in his palm. He had never been in such a position. Men of his class knew how to acquire the love, trust, and respect of women...but also when to end the pursuit. That, he knew, was expected of him. It was in his upbringing.

Eve held the door open for him, her eyes averted. He stopped in front of her for what she felt was a long moment.

*Please don't say something I have to reply to*, Eve thought, feeling her composure slipping.

And he didn't say anything. When he left, he didn't look back.

Tears, so long restrained, rolled down Eve's checks. As she was about to close the door, she saw a red car — one of those expensive looking ones that you don't see very often — slowing down, as if the driver were looking for a particular address. What incited her curiosity further was the fact that the driver fled as Adam approached his car. It was then Eve realized that Alicia had been looking for Adam.

*Now explain your whereabouts, Mr. Prince Charming,* Eve thought.

Cassidy decided to let it ring one more time before she gave up. Her brother was mature enough to do something foolish. Or, was he? She had talked to her mother the previous day, who said Adam seemed down in the dumps. Janet's voice had faltered, "Poor thing, it breaks my heart to see him so beaten. Talk to him. Lift up his spirits, will you, dear?" And Cassidy had promised to do just that.

As she recalled the conversation, Cassidy winced. *Poor Mother*, she thought, *her worry about Adam is causing her to look her age and more.* She also assumed that her mother's struggle to keep Adam and his father from each other's throats was taking its toll. One more spark and the Carry clan would combust.

"Hello."

"Adam?"

"Who else? Didn't you dial my number?" The grumpy voice reverberated through the line.

"Hey, don't be cheeky with me. Where have you been? Where are you hiding? I dialled your office, your home, and cell at least ten times this morning. Is it true that you haven't been to the office since Friday?" Cassidy asked.

"Well—"

"What's the matter with everyone? Does dementia run in the family? Mother has gone mad, Father's even madder, and you top both of them."

Adam's ripple of laughter delighted Cassidy's ears.

If it had been a face-to-face confrontation, she wouldn't know what to do first: dress him down or hug him. Indeed, he *was* all right.

"Oh, *doctor!*" Adam said. "Do you have any medicine to keep my head from exploding?"

"Cut it out, you big baby! Did it occur to you that I might have more important things to do at this hour of the day than checking on you?"

"Cass, relax. You waste more time when you don't let me open my mouth. I've been at your house all this time…most of the time, that is."

Cassidy responded, "Seriously? Why are you there? Did Alicia lock you out?"

"Very funny. I have my own key to that prison. I just needed a neutral place to regain my sanity."

"Listen brother, I have to assume you know what you're doing. You don't need my pep talk. I'll be home in two days, and if you're willing to talk about your predicament, I'll be happy to listen to you then—"

"Wait, don't hang up. Do you have some time?"

There was a plea in Adam's tone that couldn't be denied.

"You can start by admitting to and explaining the hangover. And what else is going on."

He started off doing so, but not in that order.

Half an hour later, Cassidy couldn't find the words to elevate her brother from his pitiable mood. She could tell he wasn't in a good place. Sadly, every suggestion she offered was quickly turned down.

*No!*

He wouldn't try to call Eve again. Not that he was afraid that she might take legal action against him for pestering her, but when a woman doesn't want to see a man anymore, there is nothing he can do to change that.

No! No!

He can't ask Eve's friends, the Malones, to intervene on his behalf. He was appalled at that idea.

It was getting late, and they were getting nowhere. If only Adam didn't fall so hard, he wouldn't suffer so deeply after a broken relationship.

"About Eve…are you sure she won't change her mind? Wouldn't listen to anyone? Maybe I can—"

"No! No! No!"

Cassidy welcomed his categorical refusal with relief. "You're right. If she only believes what she hears from conventional sources of information like TV, what can you do?"

That Adam was deeply affected was an understatement. In times like this, anything that was ugly in his past played in his mind without mercy. Ever since he was old enough to know how to use money, he'd had it in excessive amounts. He didn't remember how much money was bestowed upon him over the years for various occasions, but he did remember that his father was not present at his high school graduation. Nor at his hockey games. Nor was he there to pat him on the shoulder after taking his driving test. Or to calm his jumpiness before his first date. No wonder, even years later, money didn't have any significant meaning to him. Money, Adam learned, could precipitate an event, propel an action or transform it, but it had no power to create or give life to something significant.

And then there was his mother, Janet, whose interference and guidance followed him like a shadow, but only after he came close to a dreadful incident in high school. Her concern and remorse was genuine. With that old guilt in mind, she often sided with her son and against her husband. Their most common arguments were centred on George expecting that Adam would follow in his footsteps. Janet won the battle, but she never tasted the fruit of victory. In the end, Adam became an architect — exactly what he wanted — but the openings in that field were minimal at the time. His father never lifted a finger to ease his way up in his profession of choice.

Adam Carry was three months shy of his eighteenth birthday when he met Alexandra Radu — Sandy — a student working part-time for Carry Oil Industry Ltd., as it was known then. The young woman was as smart as she was charming. As soon as Adam discovered his own charm and hormones, they became inseparable. As often happens at that delicate and rapturous age, they believed they would be together forever.

Absorbed in their passion for one another, they ignored the world around them. For the next three years, the relationship proceeded along smoothly until, at the age of twenty-one, Adam announced he was going to marry Sandy.

"Son, you're too young to marry."

"Nope," Adam answered.

"Is there a reason to rush things?"

Adam could guess what his father meant. "Nope," he retorted.

His father lost his rare moment of patience and demanded, "Then why the hell don't you use your brain. You're still in school."

"My fiancée got a part-time position as a reporter at the *Edmonton Sun*—"

It was George's turn to cut him off. "Is that your idea of marriage, son? To be supported by your wife? Is your wife-to-be going to pay for your remaining years of school? Let's do the math. How much is she making — eight, nine hundred a month? That won't go far. You need to pursue your education and *then* think about marriage."

George was never good with mushy stuff. "I don't see why you two have to be tied together in marriage when I suspect you are already intimate."

"Father, I wish you wouldn't go that far, but since you brought it up, you might as well know that 'living in sin' is what determined us to legitimize our commitment to each other. Your reluctance in approving my marrying Sandy is not based on reason. It's her background you are not fond of, her family. Isn't that it?" Adam didn't need an answer. He only needed to look at his father's face and knew it was true.

Adam knew his father was aware of Sandy's family material and financial means. Her parents came from Romania in the mid-1960s, but Sandy and her sisters were raised as Canadians. Her parents worked hard to bring up their four daughters. All their hard-earned money was spent to further their education. It took a great deal of discipline, determination, and love for an immigrant to provide the opportunities that Georgeta and Victor Radu offered their children.

Adam was acutely aware that his father held all the cards. He had the money but wouldn't pay Adam's tuition if he married Sandy. It was big-time payback for not choosing the career his father wanted and for wanting Sandy by his side as his soul mate.

"I care about Sandy, for God's sake," his father said, still enraged. "I don't care if her family don't have two pennies to rub together...that's not related—"

"That's something new coming from you, sir. Since when have you not cared about power and money? Forgive me for being blunt, but you wouldn't have those either if it wasn't for Grandfather—"

A heavy hand landed on Adam's face.

"You're such a fool," George retorted. "Just like the foolish old man you idolize so much. I've achieved my fortune with my keen mind. If it weren't for me, the old man would have been bankrupt long before I could take over!"

Adam had rushed out of the room; half of what his father said had never reached his ears.

Two years elapsed and things didn't change dramatically. Not at first glance, anyways. Adam finished his schooling and was still unattached. That fact was based on "Adam's maturity and keen mind," George Carry had boasted.

The truth, however, was somewhere in between. Having learned his lesson, George put other tactics to work, but this time with patience. His theory now was that the more space he gave Adam, the better chance he had of achieving his goal of retaining Adam in his company. Despite his initial outburst over Adam's intention to marry Sandy, George continued to pay for his schooling expenses. He coaxed his son into taking a part-time position at his company and stepped back to wait. Of course, he compensated his son "accordingly" with money that went right through his pockets. Somehow the busyness of life kept Adam and Sandy from setting a date for their big day.

The year Adam finished his education had not exactly been a busy year in the field of architecture. In fact, it was hugely impacted, ironically, by the dry period in the oil industry. A novice architect had few options: grab any temporary work in the field, or seek work in a different field and try to keep an eye open for job opportunities in architecture.

Adam did the latter.

His "different" field was pre-determined: Daddy's business.

The next phase of George's plan started to unfold. Higher wages and a company car of his choice were only a couple of the perks designed to entice Adam to make himself at home. George Carry "empowered" his son with duties that had not been previously assigned to anyone. "You will oversee all, son," the old man said with confidence, "and report to me only."

Adam was surprised, pleasantly so. He ascribed his father's behaviour to making up for the love and affection he had deprived him of in his childhood years. For the first time in his life, Adam finally felt his dad was on his side. It appeared that George had truly changed, Adam thought with gratification and enthusiasm. It was better late than never to rekindle their father-son relationship.

The year 1979 marked a milestone for Carry Oil Industry. It marked the most major change in its existence. The competition in the oil industry was monopolized by a few corporations that grabbed the best contracts, leaving the smaller companies barely surviving. Carry Oil Industry was not among the larger ones and continued to suffer. George Carry spent many sleepless nights attempting to save the business, his lifelong work, his honour, his pride, and his sanity. He realized there was only one way to avoid bankruptcy. Salvation was only a phone call away.

Howard Stone was round, sturdy, and in his early sixties, with a face so red it seemed as if he had perpetual sunburn. At one time, he was known to be an easygoing man with a happy disposition, but he rarely smiled these days. His wife's death had left him bereft and empty. Alicia, their only child, was the only one who brightened his life. Unfortunately, he saw her so seldom that he could not count on her bringing him happiness. Relaxing had become difficult, as his once-prosperous business seemed to be falling apart.

He was at the point where he was ready to sell. However, no one was interested in a stagnant business. The oil industry was on the brink of saturation, and many competitors were feeling the threat of bankruptcy. He wouldn't be plagued by those stresses if he lived only for himself, but he was concerned for Alicia. At twenty-eight, she was still not standing on her own feet financially. It was not her fault. She tried very hard to succeed.

The year after her mother died of breast cancer, Alicia headed for Hollywood. Acting was her childhood dream. Since acting was so natural and easy for her, she hadn't thought it would be so difficult to establish a career. Reality proved different: Talent was not the only requirement. In acting, money and clout came before talent. Every step forward that Alicia made in the acting world was supported by the money her father kept pumping into her bank account.

When she finally landed a minor role in the popular soap opera, *The Young and the Restless*, her father was in seventh heaven.

"Praise the Lord!" Howard Stone voiced his gratefulness with a jump in the air, forgetting about the money he'd spent to generate the "heavenly" result. He called to congratulate her and to say he would like to fly down to celebrate her first success.

"Daddy, you're so sweet," Alicia said, interrupting his description of travel plans. "Did you like my appearance on Tuesday's show?"

Tears rolled down Howard's face, as he told her he wouldn't have missed it for all the money in the world.

"I know it was only for six minutes, but I'll work my way up from there. You'll see, Daddy."

Of course, he knew that; he was only wondering how much more it would cost him.

"By the way, Daddy, I need ten T's. I've moved into a more suitable apartment but my income is not yet covering my expenses."

He expected as much. Not long ago she used the letter "H" to denote the hundred dollar bills. Now the apple of his eye needed "T's" for thousands.

"And, Daddy, it's best if you don't come for a visit just now. I'm very busy."

Alicia vowed to acquire the leading female role and bragged about it. She decided that in order to get noticed, she needed to infuriate the actress who was playing "Nicky."

The effect was not as she expected.

There were no eyewitnesses, but there was a brawl in Alicia's dressing room on her last day on the legendary soap opera set.

In the years that followed that disquieting clash, opportunities for the coveted Oscar roles passed her by, and Alicia clung to "Dearest Daddy's" wallet. There were small parts here and there, but she claimed that they were not rewarding enough to cover the expenses of her "required" lifestyle. So Howard Stone kept replenishing her bank account with unfailing regularity.

Eventually, with a little luck and a discreet touch of influence, Alicia's acting career got back on track. She finally got another opportunity at becoming a "name" in the movie industry.

Alicia was selected for the leading role in a movie that everybody deemed an Oscar contender. The role was perfect. She didn't even need to act. She just had to be herself. The film was an adaptation of author Hector McCormack's novel, *Evil Deeds*. It was as if McCormack had written the role for Alicia. The devilish heroine, Dinah Prray, was a spitting image of her. Never before was Alicia more confident about a role. Every cell told her she was the perfect match for it.

From the start, Alicia set her sights on hunky Roger Hayes, her male lead — except Roger was married to actress Haley Moor, the daughter of powerhouse producer and director Barnes Moor.

One Friday evening, after a tedious, irritable day on the set, Hayes called his wife to announce that he was working late. Haley sounded almost relieved that he wouldn't be home. She wasn't planning on going out. The little football player changed any plans for that, she had said to her husband, as she patted her swollen belly. For a moment, a flicker of guilt crossed Roger's face. But it passed quickly, as he was paying more attention to Alicia Stone unbuttoning his shirt.

Haley Moor was a month away from making Roger Hayes a happy father for the second time — a fact that obviously had an effect on his insatiable sex drive. Hayes forgot about being married into money, clout, and (most importantly) to curvy and watchful wife, Haley Moor.

Barnes Moor was a bear when it came to dinner interruptions, especially when his wife, Sue Ellen, was present. Particularly this time, when they were celebrating their second wedding anniversary.

"It's your daughter, sir." The waiter saw the look on his face and quickly retreated.

Moor snatched the telephone. "Is it the baby, darling?" The tightness of his facial muscles relaxed in the next moment. "You scared me." He listened intently. "Sure. Shoot…that bitch? Hmm…Yeah? What's with her? Oh, no. Calm down, baby. I'm sure it's nothing." He was caught in between doting on his trophy wife and paying more attention to his daughter, now that she was about to gift him with another grandchild.

Half an hour later, Barnes Moor was unlocking Alicia Stone's dressing room.

And what a scene was playing there!

With the calmness and stoicism he was renowned for, Moor waited for Alicia to return from the bathroom, unfazed and smirking, clad in a bathrobe. His son-in-law remained on the floor, with a pillow on his lap, where only moments before Alicia and he had been making wild love.

For a while, Moor gazed about the room as though interested in the decor, but in truth, he was recalling a similar incident twenty-three years earlier. At that time it was *he* who was caught with his pants down. Unfortunately, it was his wife Julianne, Haley's mother, who had been the unexpected visitor. This memory spurred him into action. He decided that his grandchildren ought not to suffer as his little daughter Haley had when he and his wife divorced. Instead, he determined that this bitch was going to carry the burden. As for his son-in-law, Moor was adamant that he would obey his orders, if he knew what was best for him.

The night of the Oscars was a blissful one. As predicted, *Evil Deeds* was an immense success with twelve nominations and nine wins.

The Oscar festivities were well-trodden territory for Barnes Moor. He knew when to smile. And now his son-in-law, Roger, was up on the stage, publicly thanking him as he accepted the Oscar for best male actor. *He deserves it for staying away from that bitch Alicia Stone,* Moor thought. He had pulled every string to see that Hayes received an Oscar. He did it for Haley.

"And last but not least, I would like to thank my beautiful wife, Haley, and sons, Ty and Toby…" Hayes droned on.

*Yeah, sure, bastard,* chastised Moor, *if only she knew what a lecherous cad you were!*

Although she was nominated for best actress, Alicia received nothing. While Moor appreciated her artistic potential, and realized that his vengeful resolution would hurt his business to some degree, he would never hire her again. It was a price he was willing to pay.

Or so he thought.

Alicia knew she had played her role like no other actress could have and awaited the well-deserved, ultimate reward. Under different circumstances, being overlooked would have hurt her but she would have found the strength to admit that someone else was better than her, and that she was not yet an established name in Hollywood. However, she knew what really happened. She decided Moor would pay for his ruthless interference.

After the evening's award ceremony, everyone went to the post-ceremony parties. Alicia assisted her frail father into his limousine and said goodnight. She then hopped into her limousine and headed to the Miramax Studio bash in the Polo Lounge of the Beverly Hills Hotel, where all of *Evil Deeds'* cast were beckoned to rejoice "devilishly" and without restrain.

Alicia kept a watchful eye on the high-profile winners of the night. Roger was being assaulted by women, regardless of age or marital status. Emboldened by the growing rage inside her, Alicia kept on sipping but hardly tasting the contents of her glass. She was enjoying observing how jealousy was driving Haley Moor to the brink of desperation. Her rather daring crêpe de chine number showed signs of milk spots in two particular places. Alicia's instincts sharpened. She worried Haley would want to leave before she could put her plan into action.

Alicia quickly reassessed her action plan.

Moor was having a private moment with his young wife, who was acting up, a result of her fourth Kir Royale.

Roger welcomed a short moment of respite, as the last group of adoring starlets relinquished him for Kevin Costner, who had just made his entrance "unattached".

Haley emerged from the ladies' room and started across the room toward her husband.

But Alicia was quicker.

Three — two — one — *action!*

"Roger, darling! I never had a chance to congratulate you," Alicia said loudly, a dazzling smile on her face. She locked him in an embrace and pressed her body against his provocatively. "I wouldn't forgive myself if we parted without saying that it was such a pleasure to play with you. You know, side by side." In that moment, Dinah Prray and Alicia Stone were one and the same person.

Hayes hadn't seen this coming. Never had he suspected any inkling of revenge. They had continued the wild and illicit love affair after Moor caught them in the act. He tried to disengage himself from her tight, uncomfortable embrace, but he was too slow.

Alicia threw her hands around his neck and placed a passionate kiss on his open mouth.

Silence fell across the room.

Haley, too stunned to react, remained glued to the floor.

"That's what I call a *devilish* dilly of a kiss!" called out Costner.

A round of applause caused the entangled ex-lovers to separate. Not knowing what else to do, Roger Hayes joined in the applause, announcing that Alicia Stone was in fact the one deserving of praise.

Alicia was amongst the first to leave the Miramax party and return to her hotel. Once in her room, she ordered champagne. When room service brought two glasses, she decided to drink for both herself and her imaginary companion. The bottle was almost empty when she butted out her cigar and dialled a number.

A nondescript and tired voice answered.

"It's for you, Mrs. Hayes," the nanny said, as she yawned. "She says it's very important."

Haley had just lowered her sleepy baby into his crib. As she walked to the telephone, she wondered how someone could have obtained this number. "Thank you. I'll take it from the bedroom."

At first, she didn't recognize the voice. In spite of numerous occasions where they met during the shooting of *Evil Deeds*, Alicia Stone and Haley Moor never warmed up to each other and never chatted on the phone.

"If you were in bed already, don't anticipate my apologies," a frosty voice rambled.

"Alicia Stone?"

"Don't dare hang up on me, *sweetie*."

Haley turned her head and eyed her husband. He was fully clothed, asleep in a drunken stupor. In that moment something clicked. It was as though a curtain was suddenly lifted from her eyes. She berated herself for being so dimwitted — for blindly trusting her husband. Strangely though, she felt calm.

"First of all, I want you to know that I've been screwing your hubby since the first week of filming." Alicia slurred. "Got that?"

"Alicia, you're drunk and delusional—"

"You stupid, spoiled bitch! I'm drunk, all right, but far from delusional. I've been *fucking* your husband for months."

"You're insane, Alicia. You're not his type even for a one-night stand," Haley said. "Take your story somewhere else."

"Don't you dare give me the fucking brush-off!" Alicia shouted. "I screwed your *holy* husband until I had enough of him. You don't believe me? Ask your mighty daddy. Go ahead. He will tell you how your hubby was *doing* me when he found us on the floor in my dressing room on his anniversary night."

Haley's lack of reply enraged Alicia even more.

"And in case you're going to kill yourself over this, I'll have mercy on you now. I was never going to let this out, if your pussy-loving daddy hadn't fucked up my chance at an Oscar. I deserved it. But *nooo!* Your daddy didn't think so. So he thrust his hand into that Oscar game he loves so much, and I got nothing. I suffered, so now he will. Indirectly, of course."

Alicia slammed the phone down, refilled her glass, and downed it with a short toast, "Burn in hell, Moor!"

Howard Stone didn't panic. In fact, he almost felt relief. It was the kind of feeling one had when they felt something was wrong. For some time, he had been suspicious.

He had lung cancer.

"So how much time do I have, Terry?" he asked his doctor and lifelong friend.

"Eight months to a year, if you don't undergo surgery," the doctor replied. "Three to five if you choose the knife/chemo package."

Howard Stone thought and debated.

"I'll take the long run, my friend. I'd be selfish if I didn't."

Alicia's father made a remarkable recovery.

Not that he was holding onto any false hopes and could be fooled by the temporary remission. Yet his newfound "lifeline" was a wish come true. It was painful enough to see his daughter's career and life in limbo, but he, at least, had a second chance to put things in order before it was too late.

As it turned out, George Carry's phone call on that cold day of January 1979 made a world of difference. He proposed a deal that allowed both of them to breathe a lot easier.

They merged their businesses.

After a three-day drinking binge, Adam finally showed up at the office. He was freshly shaven, looking more like his old self.

Miss Annette warned, "Alicia is away, but no one knows where. She has been calling your father daily, sometimes talking for hours at a time. I think she's cooking up something big and I'm really afraid for your father's health. From what I suspect, she's at it again."

Adam knew what *it* meant. *Selling her shares*. Alicia was pretty good at terrorizing the old man with that threat. He panicked and in the end gave her something in exchange for her renouncing the sell idea. Adam was too smart not to recognize that this time it was something different. There was something holier than the crude oil. A place in Hollywood. It was in the news: Barnes Moor was dead. Alicia would want to jump to the second chance to become a celebrity. That, to Alicia, was more valuable than anything else under the sun. This realization gave Adam chills, as he knew that if she sold her shares it would likely kill his father. Alicia wouldn't sell to the "family". She was too wicked to offer that satisfaction to Adam and his father.

The phone rang interrupting his gloomy thoughts.

"Adam Carry speaking. Ah, Garth, so soon...?" Adam said with little enthusiasm. With a sideways glance at Miss Annette, Adam massaged his pounding temples with his free hand.

Soon he was engrossed in conversation with Garth. They talked earlier that morning and Garth immediately took Adam's foul disposition as a cry for help. Garth wanted to improve his friend's spirits. "Just give me some time to think about it. She will come to you just like a mouse to a piece of cheese." Garth had said. However, Adam didn't really have much hope — not that he'd asked his friend to find a solution to his problem — that his friend would come up with a plan to get Eve back.

"Man, I could bang my head for not thinking up that one myself. You're a genius! To think of it, it's in fact what my sister suggested. Unintentionally, of course." Adam said and then hung up.

"Miss Annette, would you please find Sandy Radu's phone number?"

"Sandy Radu, the CFRN reporter? Why? Are you looking for more trouble than you can handle?"

"Please!"

"I assume, given the time of day, you want her work number," Miss Annette said still unconvinced of Adam's hasty decision of inviting his old flame into his mess. With the dexterity of a good secretary, she found the number, underlined it, and pushed the book before his eyes.

Adam punched in the number and a polite voice answered and requested his name.

There was a brief silence then a cheerful voice chimed in, "Adam Carry! I'll be darned. Don't tell me you're that very same Adam Carry I dated a hundred years ago."

Adam laughed. "The very same."

"How can I help you today?" Sandy asked.

"How do you feel about shooting an *exclusive?"*

"Exclusive?" she repeated. "Business or personal?"

"Both."

"Sounds *exclusively* crazy but okay. But let me remind you, as an old friend, that hanging dirty laundry in public can be quite damaging."

"I'm totally aware of that," he replied.

"I'll be darned!" Sandy said, laughing.

"Is that a yes or no?"

"When do you want it?"

"Is it too late for *Live at 6?"*

"Not at all."

When they met in front of the Carstone Corporation building, Adam produced a note with the questions he was "eager" to answer.

"Sixty seconds, Sandy, from now," one of the crew assistants called out.

She nodded. "You ready, Adam? We're on," she said.

"Five — four — three — two — one and *on!"*

"Good evening everyone. The oil industry plays a vital role in our lives. With less than seven years until the turn of the millennium, energy analysts are predicting a 'Golden Era' for the industry. Experts say the industry will be characterized by a scramble to generate a monumental boost in production to keep up with increased global demand.

"Major corporations are struggling to stay on top, and intermediate and junior companies struggling to maintain the float line. All of them are facing issues beyond their control such as access to crude resource, persistent aboriginal concerns, climate change, and endless provincial and municipal regulations.

"Not even the biggest competitor in this lucrative industry — Carstone Oil Corporation — is immune to these concerns.

"With its headquarters in this modern building behind me, the corporation was formed in 1979 via the unification of two average-size oil companies: Carry Oil Limited, which maintains control of fifty-one per cent of the shares, and W.S. Stone Limited, with forty-nine per cent. The merger produced this robust, profitable oil supplier whose reputation is renowned around the world. Canada generates 6.3% of the world's oil, and Carstone Oil Corporation supplies a good portion of it.

"However, parallel with this spectre of thriving business, the corporation is challenged with a critical internal issue, namely the divorce between Alicia Stone Carry and the heir of former Carry Oil Limited, Adam Carry. This divorce could literally break up the company. Although recently, the topic was picked up and discussed by a local news source, it was later dismissed as speculative, fictitious, and slanderous."

Sandy stepped to the left, bringing Adam into the spotlight. She introduced him properly with the professionalism of Diane Sawyer, and just like the legendary TV reporter, she got straight to the core of the subject at hand.

"Mr. Carry, is there any truth to the allegation that you and your wife Alicia Stone Carry are divorcing?"

"Yes, our divorce is in the final stage."

"As much as our viewers will appreciate your statement as being genuine, would you please explain why the statement issued a week ago wasn't accurate?"

"The fact that the information was expressed without my awareness or consultation makes it difficult to answer a good part of your question. However, what I am prepared to do is to correct that warped statement by simply invalidating it."

"I have no doubt about your word, Mr. Carry, but the information you're revealing now may have a decisive impact on the function of the whole corporation. I'm sure our viewers are wondering if the aftermath of a divorce would alter the image and integrity of Carstone Oil Corporation."

"Honestly, I fail to see how the divorce would represent a liability. Carstone will remain an industrial enterprise. I base my affirmation on the fact that the divorce won't change the state of the existing ownership. My father, George Carry, and my soon to be ex-wife, Alicia Stone, are the key shareholders and will continue to lead and serve the corporation to the best of their abilities."

"I believe your assurance is much appreciated, I truly do. But I was pointing more towards future years rather than months," Sandy said, pretending to scan her notebook. "Our source indicates that you are the heir of fifty-one per cent of the business; is that correct?"

"Yes."

"Last year, in accordance with your entitlement, you were acting as CEO and President of the company while your father was recovering from a heart attack. Is this accurate?"

"Yes."

"At that time, there were some concerns circulating — categorized as unfounded rumours by another Carstone spokesperson — but even now, those directly involved and affected are anxious to be provided with clarification, chiefly on the matter of employment retention and investment. Will the divorce bring about the disjointing of Carstone into two detached entities?"

"Our employees can rest assured. It's nobody's intention to transform someone's lifetime work into a garage sale. Maintaining the company's formation is the aspiration of everyone involved. My father's primary objective is to preserve an honourable place in the oil industry. His lifetime endeavour will stay in one piece, his wish respected with veneration when the day comes for me to be CEO. The best interest of Carstone Corporation will be my priority and I intend to see it succeed," Adam said.

"What is behind your desire to come forward tonight?" She made a gesture to offer him the microphone but then pulled it back to her mouth. "If, of course, the question is not too personal."

A look of astonishment crossed Adam's face.

"Consideration for others and veneration for the truth are two reasons. And yes, it is personal. Thanks for listening."

"Thank you, Mr. Carry," the reporter said and then, facing the camera, added, "This is Sandy Radu reporting for CFRN Edmonton. Back to you, Blair."

George had been in the shower when their housekeeper, Margaret, ran in to inform Janet about the interview, which she had caught on the kitchen TV. Janet was thankful that the interview was over by the time they settled down for a quiet supper later that evening. As a precaution, Janet had asked Margaret to keep the phone off the hook for the remainder of the evening.

She couldn't believe Adam would expose the corporation and *his* private life on television. However, she knew she would stand by him if there was any trouble. Even though she didn't agree with his unpredictable decision, Janet reflected on the implications. Would Alicia counterattack? And, of most importance, how would George handle the fallout? Underneath her façade of self-composure, she was terrified of losing him. And she loved him. Over all these years, he had been a good provider and a good husband. It was this reasoning that had led her to reinstating George into their bedroom only three days after kicking him out.

She reflected on how complex their relationship had been in the past few years and dreaded what complication this new TV stunt would bring to their family.

Adam slipped into the chair opposite Crista. She brought the boys to the hockey practice with one thought in mind. "You look better today."

For a moment, Adam looked puzzled. To the best of his knowledge, she hadn't seen him at his worst.

"Better than at 6:00 p.m. yesterday," Crista clarified.

"Ah! So you watched the news."

"*We* did. Mike, me, and a dear friend of ours. We can talk about that until sunset, but I don't have a complete report as of yet."

"If I understand correctly, you're trying to tell me that Eve didn't..." He searched for the right words.

"...buy it?" Crista offered.

"I wouldn't use that word."

"Man, you must be madly in love with her. I would give an arm and a leg to have Mike declare his love to me on the silver screen. I'll tell you something your ears are eager to hear. My dear friend Eve is lucky, all right, even if she won't admit it yet."

As he heard her words, Adam's face brightened, but his excitement was halted when their full implication sank in.

"Tell me that Eve believed me."

"I sincerely hope so," Crista said. "Not that Eve said yes, but I have a hunch in my heart that she was won over."

Adam sighed with relief.

"I think you should know that *I* was the one who told Eve about the scene from the mall. I should have minded my business and trusted Mike that you had a good reason for being there. But, no! I added it to the TV news from the previous night and...the rest you know," Crista said.

For her peace of mind she needed to come clean.

"For all the discomfort I caused, I'm very, very sorry. I didn't have the right to mess up Eve's mind with my precipitous, ill-conceived assumptions."

Adam's heart soared. He sensed that her apology was sincere.

"I have a great regard for Eve. We are closer than most sisters. I thought I could protect her best interests. But with my meddling, I've done her a disservice instead."

"You know, Crista, you may not believe me when I say this, but I have a feeling you're the kind of friend everyone should be blessed with. No, listen," he said, when he saw her interruption coming. "I really mean it. Eve is lucky to have you as a friend. It could have been just the way you imagined it. If anyone should carry the burden of guilt, it should be me. I kept details away from Eve for too long, especially a few essential things about myself. I only hope I didn't hurt Eve irreparably."

"Let's hope not. Don't ever entertain that idea."

"Where did you get the idea that I would hurt Eve?"

"I don't know. It's about time you realized how off-the-wall my mind can get."

"Really, Crista. Why are you saying that?"

"Well, I don't mean you would hurt Eve intentionally. How can I explain this...I really hope you see Eve for the great human being that she is, because if you think you can cool off your 'needs' with her while you're deciding who to be with next, you would represent an immense disappointment to Eve. You need to think about how Eve sees your intentions. Last night you made big waves, claiming *it was personal*, about *consideration for others and veneration for the truth*, remember? Eve would have felt that *she* was your personal matter. Do you understand what kind of hurt I'm talking about?" Crista answered for him. "The pointless, insubstantial relationship."

"Would you like me to start making promises?" Adam asked.

"No!"

He chuckled. "Good. Because I don't know how to convince you that I care way too much for Eve to ever cause her any harm."

"You don't need to convince me, Carry! *Her*. Go ahead. Call Eve. I bet she's sitting an inch away from the phone right now." Crista stood up. "You're going to need lots of patience while you're waiting for Eve to get to the same place as you. You'll probably end up hating Dr. Laura."

"Dr. Laura? Who is that?"

"You know, the famous radio talk-show host."

Adam still had no clue.

"Dr. Laura is one of those know-it-alls about love and life. Eve follows her rules. No shacking up with a man is rule number one. No sex before she has a ring on her finger and a date set is rule number two. And, as I know Eve too well, a clean medical check-up completes the 'must have' rules. Got that?" She paused. "Believe me, Adam, I'm doing you a favour by telling you this. While you will learn to hate Dr. Laura, you'll have your share of cold showers."

The hockey coach's voice startled them both.

"Who is with Anthony today?"

"The arm is fractured. Fortunately, there's no need for surgery," the doctor said, as he examined the X-rays. "All you need is a cast on your arm. How do you feel about that, bud?"

Tears welled up in Anthony's eyes. He was so scared, but he thought how much he liked it that Adam was there with him. He made a silent resolution to not tell his mommy that he still considered Adam his friend.

"I'm sure you're not afraid of a little needle," the doctor said, "but I think a Tylenol will do the trick. What do you think, can you chew one?"

Relief spread across the boy's face, and he grabbed the pink tablet from the doctor's hand.

While a technician put the cast around Anthony's arm, the doctor gave Adam basic information about the next steps. Adam asked Crista if she had called Eve. She shook her head and told him that *he* should do it.

Adam was half through dialling the number when the receptionist stopped him. "Sir, please refrain from using your cell phone," she said, pointing to a sign on the wall. "It interferes with the hospital electronic equipment." She gave him a piece of paper. "Please give this information to the boy's mother, in case she has any questions about Anthony's arm, and ensure that she provides us with his Alberta health-card number."

"I'm sorry. It was careless of me," Adam said.

The receptionist's instructions gave Adam an idea.

"...leave a message after the tone," Adam listened, his heart beating fast and hard. For a moment, he was thankful that the answering machine picked up. What was he going to say? Oh, yes, about Anthony...

"Hi. It's Adam. I'm at the Misericordia Community Hospital with Anthony—"

"Adam? What happened to Anthony?" Eve shouted.

"Nothing too serious. He fell when he tripped over somebody's hockey stick and broke his left arm, just above his wrist."

"He broke his arm? Oh, my God."

"He handled it like a real trooper. He was more frightened than in pain. They just finished applying the cast. I'm bringing him home soon. They need his health-card number, though."

Eve protested that she would come to the hospital at once.

"No need. We're just about to leave," Adam explained.

"Hold on, then. I'll give you Anthony's health-card number."

The clerk entered the number, glanced at the screen, and called Adam. "Excuse me. How old did you say the boy is?"

"He was seven in January, I think."

"Then this is the wrong number. It's valid but not the boy's. Same last name, but definitely not his personal information. It belongs to an adult female."

Adam called Eve again.

Eve donned a navy sweater and jeans. With the front door wide open, she waited anxiously while Adam's car moved up the driveway. She jumped when she saw Adam carrying her son's limp body.

"He's asleep," Adam said. "The Tylenol must have taken effect."

Adam followed Eve. "He can sleep in my bedroom, for now," she said, relieved that she didn't have to face him. It was only when she turned to grab a blanket that she realized that he was propping his body against the door frame and, yes, his eyes were on her. A surge of warmth washed over her. She continued taking care of her sleeping boy, caressing the tips of his exposed, chalky fingers.

"Thank you for driving Anthony to the hospital. And taking care of him. Crista may be sharp and flippant in everyday life, but she goes to pieces in a crisis."

"You're welcome. As for Crista, what can I say? She wasn't a pillar of support, but she gets full credit for being there," Adam said thinking of their earlier chat.

It was obvious that Adam expected an invitation to share a cup of coffee. Two hours later and with their skeletons out of the closet, their time together was well spent. When Adam left to fill Anthony's prescription, Eve marvelled at the revelation that — yes — she was in love with him.

# Four

"MY EARLIEST MEMORIES ARE OF NANA BELLA, MY BABYSITTER, and my sister, Cassidy. My parents were like guests in my life. I wasn't deprived of any material things, but as for love and affection…" A sigh followed. "I poured out my love and affection on my sister — she was like a little mother even then — and some on my babysitter.

"At the age of sixteen, I had the most coveted things in the world: money and a pair of absentee parents. One day in Grade 10, four of my friends and I decided to skip class and go to a park we liked to hang around. I was the only one with a car, so I drove." Adam shook his head. "It was a day I will remember until I draw my last breath. I would label it *The Doom Day* if I were writing an autobiography.

"Anyways, my friends and I were passing around our second joint — a ritual we indulged in when we got together — when a young man approached us with a tempting proposition. Coke for ten dollars a line. He said he'd already done two lines and felt 'super.' He seemed to us to be so cool.

"None of us had tried the stuff before, but we all had a 'what the heck' attitude. One of my friends, Dylan, had no money on him so I paid his share. I saw myself as the coolest guy in my own crowd, as I had money to give away.

"A bit later, Dylan collapsed." Adam fought back tears. "He never regained consciousness. The doctors said his brain was damaged by an allergic reaction to the cocaine. After three months, his mother decided to disconnect him from life support."

"And you blamed yourself," Eve concluded. "Adam, you shouldn't."

"But I bought his death, Eve."

The pleading tone in his voice melted Eve's heart. She never suspected a man could be so consumed by such a tragedy. Sitting beside him on her love-seat, Eve stretched her hand out and touched his face.

"So many years have passed. You need to put this tragedy behind you."

"After three months spent in an adolescent psychiatric ward, one has no alternative…" he replied taking her hand from his face, holding it between his own. "I was *there,* Eve. In a mental institution. Does that bother you? Knowing that I was once mentally unstable?"

Eve shook her head. "I think it would trouble me if you didn't react that way, as odd as that might sound."

"I was heavily sedated for most of it, with a cocktail of drugs," Adam started again. "I remember one instance so vividly. A psychiatrist asked me if I had ever considered suicide. At first I was too stunned to realize the implication of the question. I knew I had withdrawn from the rest of the world, but it was at that moment that it occurred to me that I didn't deserve to live, to belong in that world. I felt responsible for Dylan's death. It had never crossed my mind to kill myself, but maybe that was the price to pay for my mistake."

Adam paused, lost in his thoughts. The soft hand that stroked his face brought him back.

"I needed to get well, but needed to be absolved of my guilt. On May 12, 1973 – *The Absolution Day*, as I call it — I didn't know what day it was or how long I'd been out of it, but I felt well rested in both mind and body. It was as though a veil had been lifted off my eyes, and a peaceful feeling embraced my whole being. My guilt was gone, and I didn't know why, but I knew a miracle had happened.

"My mother was sleeping on a folding bed close to mine. I asked her what she was doing there. I learned later that the medication wreaked havoc on my body and mind to such a degree that, on those last days, even the doctors were frightened, so they allowed my mother to stay in my room. That day I *found* my mother all over again, or I should say we found each other. I asked her if I could go back to school the next day. I felt fit and sound, ready to go. She looked straight into my eyes as though she truly *believed* me, rather than just *wishing* to believe me...that what I was saying was true. Many doctors took turns examining me that day and unanimously decided to discharge me the next day.

"Later that evening, Mrs. Hewlett, Dylan's mother, came to see me in the hospital. She told me that Dylan had passed away that morning at 11:33. He was in a good place now, she said. She wanted me to go on with my life and to forgive myself. She told me that *it was not my fault*. She said that if anything should come out of this horrifying event, it should be a good lesson. She had a mission to prepare a video on drug awareness and needed my help.

"*Dylan's Story: the Hard Way to Learn a Lesson* came out the following year. I co-narrated it with Mrs. Hewlett. At the end, Mrs. Hewlett proclaimed that, 'If together we saved one life, someone's child's life, Dylan's would be redeemed. Every life is precious!'"

The irony dawned on him much later. It took three months for his friend's heart to stop beating, and just as long for his mental state to be restored.

Adam shared more of his past with Eve.

"I had a few 'puppy-love' flings but the first girl I was rally in love with was plucked from fairy-tales. That lasted a while. She was nice and well brought-up but in the end she took off with another guy. Just like that! Naturally, I was very upset, angry and hurt, you know. It seemed back then that her deceit was the biggest 'tragedy' of my life, but eventually I moved on.

"Then, there was Alicia. In retrospect, she was there to fill the void the 'nice' girl left behind. I didn't go looking for Alicia; she was already there. My father and Alicia's father were relatively new business partners. She started getting more involved with the company and we got to know each other well at work. Our parents encouraged the relationship, because the union of their successors was regarded as a blessing and relief to them and the company. I wish I knew then that this 'modern arranged marriage' would be a predestined failure."

Even with the lights dimmed in the room, the pain on Adam's face was evident.

"I stopped being bitter about my life when I met you. I decided that the past is best forgotten," Adam said. "If people hang on to their bitter memories, they waste the time they could be spending with other people. As you can see, I'm trying to make up for my long overdue silence. How am I doing so far? Does my autobiography interest you?"

"Just as much as you do."

Eve watched Adam settle down on the deep-cream carpet with a pillow. He stretched at the bottom of the panoramic view of Edmonton Downtown. She followed him.

"Do you believe in love at first sight?" Adam asked.

"Yes," she answered, thinking about the time she met William. "Do you?"

He nodded. "That Saturday morning when I came to pick up Anthony, it hit me. From the moment I saw you, I was simply in love! Not that the feeling was mutual, as I recall."

"You're right. I was not knocked off my feet by your charm then. I thought you were a bad man."

"*Bad* as in the big, bad wolf?"

"No! Bad as in all men are pigs."

"Ouch! So I was a pig in your eyes," he teased.

Eve shrugged. "Put yourself in my place. The children standing in front of us were the only thing that kept me from slapping you. How nervy of you to come in my house and undress me with your eyes and then kiss my hand. I thought you were Ryan's father…and that made you a first-class womanizer in my eyes. I made sure my wedding band stood out, but it just didn't work with you."

"Hmm," Adam grunted. "A pig, huh?"

"Yes, I thought the worst of you then, but don't sulk now," she said, and reached for his hand. "Soon enough I knew that my mind didn't stand a chance next to my heart."

"How soon?"

A mischievous smile played on her lips. "Five minutes ago."

"Eve!"

"Okay! Maybe after I'd seen you a few more times. I can't tell exactly."

He laughed. "Tease me without mercy, but be grateful that my impulsive nature didn't lift you up in my arms and kiss you senseless right then and there. Just for the record, when I saw you that morning, beautiful and tall, I was drunk with your Venus grace. I knew you were a widow, though I wasn't sure if you were available, and stubbornly I set my mind to conquer your heart anyway."

"Are you still that stubborn?"

He nodded. "More determined than stubborn," he said, before their mouths melted into one another.

For a long while, Adam pretended to be focused on the papers in front of him. He couldn't help but think about the challenges of maintaining a positive attitude towards the woman who thrived on destroying his nerves and sucking the life out of him.

He had asked Eve the night before how she felt about the fact that he was bound to be around Alicia during working hours. "Hope you're not jealous of her."

"Is there any reason?" Eve asked. "If you wanted her, you would be with her now and not here, right? I don't see why two civilized people cannot remain cordial to each other, especially at work."

He thought hard about her words now. If only it could be as simple as Eve made it sound.

Adam was slightly concerned about the possible side effects of his TV confession the previous Friday evening. It was not yet history, despite how he wished it to be so. When Alicia had summoned him into George's office, he was positive it was going to be addressed. Astonishingly, Alicia was the one who attracted George's wrath. George lashed out, criticizing her for airing their dirty laundry in public, a stunt that Adam only followed.

"At least he covered his butt — our butts — by making his speech genuine and credible," the old man snapped, surprising them both. "And in spite of what transpired, we came out clean and are still in a good position." His eyes bored into Alicia. "I declare that no permanent damage was done."

From there, they moved to the conference room for the weekly staff meeting. However, Adam was still musing over his father's words. Adam didn't believe for a moment that his father was letting him go unpunished.

George wanted something from him. It was a move he recognized too well.

He didn't care as long as he got Eve back.

"You've got to give her back that cell phone, if you don't want yours truly to be part of every one of your conversations," Crista said, before she handed Eve her cell phone.

Crista leaned back on the carpet of grass. There was no more relaxing place in the whole city than the little hills at the Muttart Conservatory. She was pleasantly surprised that Eve had stopped at the library and invited her for lunch. Her friend's renewed enthusiasm was palpable, yet there was something she wasn't saying.

"Okay, Adam. We'll talk about that later," Eve concluded and handed the cell phone back to Crista.

"What's that all about?" Crista asked, with her eyes closed and arms folded behind her head.

"Adam wants us to go out for dinner."

"And?"

"I'm not ready to be seen again in public together. You know what happened last time."

"Is this about *that* old issue?"

Eve pondered for a moment. "I don't know why, but I have this creepy feeling Alicia is watching me. I know she watches Adam or else she wouldn't pop up when least unexpected. Deep down, it bothers me that he's still attached. I wish time would jump ahead two months."

Crista pulled herself up on an elbow. "You're crazy, you know that? The man is smitten, ready to pluck the moon from the sky for you, and you hang on to those principles of yours."

"It's not that. There is something else. I don't know how to say this. It concerns Adam."

"Go on," Crista prodded.

Eve took a deep, ragged breath. "You know how dearly I always wanted to have another child…"

"Yes." Crista jumped to the conclusion that *the creep doesn't want a child to tie them to one another. That must be it.* His daddy's millions, which would one day slip into his bank account, were not for sharing.

Eve smiled as she read her friend's mind. She had exactly the same thought when Adam first told her the night before.

He had started off by saying that he had never felt so strongly for another woman. He also told her he'd felt so hopeless over the past week, when he thought he might have lost her forever. Suddenly, his eyes looked troubled.

"Before I say one more word, I think it would be only fair if I ask you a question — a very important one. To avoid it wouldn't be honest of me when there is so much at stake." He cleared his throat, "Do you plan on having more children?"

Eve thought about his broken marriage and that one of them did not want children. *So, it was he.* She cringed at the thought, but when she spoke, she kept an even tone.

"Do I wish to have another baby? Yes, I do. Do I plan to have more children? That's a totally different question. It's not entirely up to me," Eve said. "As far back as I remember, I always wanted at least three children. It seemed to me an ideal number, since I had only Jonathan to play with. I don't count Garry, because of the age gap. Garry and I grew closer much later when I was almost an adult myself."

If she thought for a moment that he had asked that question because he *wanted* them to have a child together, but was not sure if *she* wanted any more children, she now knew the truth. It was the sudden change in his eyes that gave her the insight. Out of politeness, Eve continued, "On the other hand, I should be thankful for having one healthy child. I had my share of difficult pregnancies and much disappointment. And yet, I have no regrets for trying."

This time she didn't make an effort to pretend she was not studying his reaction.

"Adam, you brought up the subject, and I certainly believe that I must be honest with you too. Undoubtedly, things need to be set straight between us, because it impacts our future," Eve said. "Am I deducing correctly that you don't want us to have children?"

Shaking his head, he said, "Your guess couldn't be more wrong, Eve. If there is anything in the world that I wish to have in my life, it's a child. *Our* child. But sadly, I can't give that to you. I *can't* help you conceive a child. I've known this for years…"

Recalling that conversation Eve became contemplative again. She needed a little more time to think. She knew that you can't get upset at something that is out of your control. As they say, what you cannot change, you learn to live with. Eve sighed.

"You know my friend, I don't like this silence."

Crista's words startled Eve.

"I'm sorry. I got caught in my thoughts."

"That's all right. Start from where you said that you dearly wish to have another baby and leave nothing out. You know that I'm a stickler for details."

"Crista, there is not going to be a baby with Adam. Not now, not ever. He is not able to have children."

"Really, Eve? This is the worst thing that can happen to a man. I can only imagine how Mike would react if he was not able to procreate. It bothers us — all right, me especially — whatever it is that is preventing us from conceiving now, after having done so before. But to be in Adam's situation? My God! It's the ultimate disappointment, I imagine."

*Exactly his words,* Eve thought.

"On the other hand, his inability to procreate is not the end of the world. You already have Anthony, and Adam seems to be getting along splendidly with him."

"I guess I have to make peace with the idea. Besides, as Adam suggested, we could always adopt. When I think how many unfortunate children are out there, I want to open my heart and arms to them."

"You truly love the man."

"Very much. Much more than I was willing to accept even days ago — much deeper than I thought I would ever love again. I love him even more now that I know about his impairment. He didn't have to tell me. He could have kept his secret to himself. Years would have passed before I'd have learned about this shortcoming and it would have been even too late to adopt."

"This must have played a part in the downfall of their marriage," Crista said. "Why didn't they adopt one, two, or as many children as their money could afford?"

Eve put aside her half-eaten sandwich.

"Adam told me that for years he tried to persuade her to start a family, and when he finally succeeded in convincing her, nothing came of it. They consulted fertility specialists. He was tested and the 'fault' was finally discovered. His wife — you're justified in calling her Cruella — never missed a chance to put him down, to reproach him about his inability to make their life complete by producing an heir. That hurt him immensely. He fell into a deep depression, like many other men and women who experience this particular problem. Can you believe what she did? She picked up a letter from the fertility doctor Adam had consulted and faxed it to Halifax, where Adam was on business. She called him first and asked him to stand by the fax machine, as she was sending him the proof of his 'virility'. Of course, the letter stated his chances to father a child were zero. What can be more vindictive than that? Of course, the adoption concept came into discussion. It was an option she never warmed up to. Once, she stormed out the night before they had to pick up a newborn baby boy."

For the first time ever life seemed to have a purpose, a direction. Everything seemed to be going well. A life that a year ago seemed so dull and bleak was now bright and blissful.

A sobering thought mingled through the seemingly flawless picture. Eve was reminded that on this day, two years ago, William had met his death. William died on Jessie's birthday. *Poor, sweet Jessie,* Eve thought. *Is it possible this is her last birthday?* Eve shuddered at the thought.

She called her brother in Sydney. Gloria answered.

"It's working, Eve. The treatment is *really* working. I wish you could see how good Jessie looks. Her hair has grown back. Oh, darling, I just knew she was going to make it."

Her heart full of sorrow, Eve was half listening to her sister-in-law. Suddenly, a dark thought came to mind. *Gloria can't be under the influence of alcohol, can she?*

Eve interrupted, "Where is Jessie? I want to say happy birthday to her."

"Oh, Garry has a couple of days off and took the girls to Bluehay. They love it out there, especially Jessie, who made Garry put up a tent so they could sleep outside."

"Why didn't you go with them?" Eve asked. The air was still for one moment and Eve wasn't sure if Gloria considered her rude for interrupting.

"I'll go next time. I've already taken so much leave from school in the past months."

Eve stared into space long after the conversation ended. She wished she were there to help. To lend her shoulder. To return the favour of two years ago.

The sun was high in the cloudless sky. He was blindfolded and enticed by a beguiling voice: Come, come! Her voice was sometimes so close and yet, when he swiftly stretched out his arm, he came up empty handed. Her laughter stopped. And it was not supposed to. She had promised not to run away. Chills brought goosebumps to his skin and panic made his heart pump cold blood into his veins. Hastily, he uncovered his eyes. She was there! She awaited him! No wonder she didn't answer when he called her name…

A dainty blanket of pink, red, purple, and white, heady, scented petals were kissing her naked, exquisite body. She smiled enchantingly and beckoned him with her right index finger. "I've been waiting for you," she said.

"Shh…Let's not use words," he said.

Oh, how the words titillated and awakened sensations. He groaned in sweet pain as her hand glided over his lower body. He guided it even lower…Tender, joyful, tantalizing shots surged through his body with the touch of her hand.

*The real touch,* which he knew was as real as him lying there on his own bed.

His eyes popped open.

In the next instant, he was on his feet, finally realizing that the dream transported itself into reality. A nightmare reality.

"Alicia! What the hell are you doing in here?" He demanded, fury surging through his body. He yanked the sheet and wrapped it around his waist, leaving the transgressing woman totally exposed.

"Don't be ridiculous, darling," she said with a defiant smirk. "There's nothing you can cover up with that stupid sheet that I haven't seen before. Too old and too late to be prudish, don't you think? Come back here." She patted the very spot he jumped from seconds before.

"Get out, or I'll drag you by force," he fired at her as he walked toward the adjacent bathroom. "You have the nerve to come in here and invade my privacy and break the rule on top of it."

"Darling, you make me laugh at your childish safeguard. We've been there before. Remember? A few times, if your memory doesn't serve you right at this hour."

"If you think that your old tricks are going to work again, you are about to be disappointed!" Adam shouted. He returned clad in pyjama pants. The thought that his body became excited under the touch of this manipulative, cunning creature made his stomach turn.

"Come on, darling, look at *it*. You got your thrills with every sweet bit of it before. Correction — you could never resist it, remember? You always came back to 'her majesty' for more," Alicia said, her fingers lazily touching that private part of her body. "Come here, sweetie. Didn't we always lose ourselves in sheer ecstasy after each separation?

Hey, maybe that's what we needed — another separation to rekindle our love for each other."

Alicia spread her legs even wider and fondled her wet softness.

"Don't insult my intelligence with your wanton show, you alley cat. You think I'm so dense to fuck you now and start the ordeal all over? After you shared your 'majesty' with all those cock-dipping men who eagerly raved about your 'formidable' sexual stunts the next day over their lunches? Do you really think I'm stupid enough to take you back? Get out of here!"

"You don't know what you're talking about," she counterattacked.

"Oh, you underestimate my abilities to locate and supply the proof. I'll have my lawyer hand it to yours. Plenty of it and at the right moment, *darling*. How about that?"

Alicia snorted and gave a faint shudder. "Oooh, I feel so terrorized by that blob-head lawyer of yours. Really mortified." She threw her head on the pillow laughing.

Adam seized the moment and grabbed her ankle, a move that brought her into a sitting position, her head yanking upward. He was fuming, but remembered Garth's admonition not to bring up "the evidence." And, most importantly, *not to touch her: not even with one finger.*

However, his rage overtook Garth's directions. He started dragging Alicia off the bed despite her vicious kicks and protests.

"Get your hands off me. You're hurting me."

"*You* asked for it," Adam said. He bent and grabbed Alicia's negligee off the floor and threw it in her direction.

"I take it you don't need me. You're fucking that long-legged Barbie doll now," she said.

"Isn't it too late to play the part of an injured party when you've taken every dick to bed, simply to get back at me? I thought you would at least be discreet. I was wrong."

A sneer spread across Alicia's face. She was far from being insulted.

"Dumbfounded to be proven wrong, aren't you darling?" The lines around her mouth changed into a smirk. "But you can't discount the fact that because of *that* our marriage worked. And if I were you I'd consider myself lucky that I stayed with you as long as I did."

"Some luck, indeed," Adam snorted. "Why didn't I see it that way, you bitch? Now get out of here before your Broadway performance makes me lose my temper and really hurt you." He skirted around her and with two long strides flung open the door. "I'm sure you know your way out."

Alicia swirled the flimsy piece of clothing and threw it over one shoulder before starting for the door. Passing him, she couldn't resist brushing her pointy silicon breasts against his chest. It was her way of claiming victory.

"Don't forget to put on some clothes when you go out to cool off your needs," Adam called out after her.

She stopped and turned, "How about you, darling, don't you need to cool off, too? Oh, what am I saying! *Barbie* must be taking care of that. You can't be too frustrated."

"Shut your fucking mouth and leave Eve out of it! She won't sleep with me, before I'm all finished with you! It's called scruples — a concept you have no notion of!" Adam said in one breath, instantly regretting every word.

"Oh, I'm impressed! I implore you to introduce me to your paragon of virtue one day."

The muscles in his jaw twitched, but he decided that Alicia's "supplication" was not worth a reply, so he slammed the door in her face.

Eve was ambivalent about Crista's plan to go out for her birthday celebration. First of all, they didn't have a babysitter. But the lack of a babysitter was not really the main reason for her reluctance. After all, Crista had said, if necessary she would bring down the "fat guy with the white beard from the North Pole" to watch the boys.

*The man with a beard*, Eve mused. The thought brought back the memory of her recurring dream. It had visited her again the night before. This time, a new sequence with a man sporting a beard was introduced.

Eve sighed as she sank into the armchair. Of course, Crista's plan was a nice gesture. She would have appreciated it if Adam were there too.

Last year for her birthday, when Crista and Mike insisted on an adult celebration, it turned out to be disastrous. Memories of happy, previous birthday celebrations that the two couples had spent together had haunted Eve the whole evening.

For a brief instant, Eve felt guilty that her friends' efforts weren't cheering her up, when she knew in fact that Adam's absence accounted for her foul disposition. Additionally, it was noon, and he hadn't even called to wish her happy birthday. He was in Toronto for a few days, and Eve suspected, didn't know it was her birthday. Knowing this didn't prevent her from jumping every time the phone rang. Like a foolish sixteen-year-old, she daydreamed about Adam wishing her happy birthday in person and wearing nothing but a smile.

It rang now.

She let it ring a few times before she decided that her voice wouldn't reveal her state of mind.

"Eve, there is a slight change in our plans for tonight," Crista said.

"Good! Then we'll leave it for another time—"

"Let me finish. I said there is a *change*, not a postponement. And don't interrupt me, I'm very busy here. We received another library's order by mistake and I noticed only halfway through unpacking—"

"So what's the change?" Eve interrupted.

"We won't leave from my place together as we planned earlier. Mike and I will meet you at the restaurant." Crista continued to ignore Eve's protests. "There is no room for 'No'. We've already arranged that you'll be picked up at your doorstep, like the birthday girl should be, at 7:00 p.m. Mike and I will take a taxi too, so we can celebrate like old times." Crista ended by assuring her that the babysitter matter was resolved, all Eve had to do was to bring Anthony to her house after school. "Look, gotta run. Happy Birthday!"

Eve was thoughtful. She wondered why her best friend wouldn't consider delaying the celebration until Adam was back in town. She was still miffed a few hours later, on her way to pick up Anthony, that Crista hadn't mentioned Adam at all when she called again. And not in a rush as before, considering that she took her time to advise Eve in great detail what she should wear to look "smashing," so that she wouldn't be able to tell her apart from her "co-national," Nicole Kidman. Why? Because the restaurant — its name remained a secret — was not "one's average drinking hole."

Eve decided to take Crista's advice regarding her wardrobe and hairdo. *After all, it would be nice to show them how grateful I am for their friendship.* From that moment forward, Eve was determined to face the day with more enthusiasm.

"May I help you, miss?" A polite voice startled her. She was still recovering from being brought to the restaurant in a white limousine. A *white* limousine!

"Yes, please," Eve said to the maître d'. "I'm supposed to meet my friends here."

"Under what name is the reservation made, miss?"

"Malone, I think. M-A-L-O-N-E."

The man relayed Eve's details to a young woman behind the reception desk.

"I have no reservation under that name."

"You can try mine, Eve Nelson, but I don't think—"

"That's it!" The receptionist's triumphant voice startled Eve. "Robert, would you please show Miss Nelson to table 2A?" She turned to Eve and said, "Have a pleasant evening with us, Miss Nelson!"

As Eve followed the maître d', she took in the ritzy surroundings. Crista and Mike must be deranged to go to these extremes. With a polite nod, she acknowledged where the man directed her: a private, cozy part of the restaurant. She thanked him and started to sit down, only to be interrupted by the ring of her cell phone. As she placed the phone to her ear, something caught her attention out of the corner of her eye.

"Happy birthday, gorgeous!"

*That* didn't come through the phone.

"Adam!" Eve exclaimed.

In that instant, everything became clear. The dress code imposed by Crista…the limousine service…the fancy restaurant. If she only was thinking harder, she would have known.

Adam met her with a tight embrace. They kissed and it felt exhilarating.

"Happy birthday, Eve!" he said again. "You look amazing."

"Thanks, but the word is *shocked*. I didn't know. I thought you were still in Toronto. I don't know what to say. If I say anything foolish, don't take it seriously. I'm afraid I won't be sound for some time. My first rational thought would be to throttle Crista, though."

Assisting Eve into her seat, Adam laughed. "I don't think throttling an innocent woman would be a good idea."

"Innocent woman? Are we talking about the same person?"

Adam nodded.

"But who else could it be, when she is the only blabbermouth friend I have?"

"I stand by Crista's innocence. Yes, she was involved, but it was at my insistence. Her cooperation was a valuable asset. As a matter of fact, *you* disclosed the details of interest to me," Adam said. He took his place in the opposite chair, and repositioned a vase of roses not to be a hindrance between them.

Eve's gaze followed the roses. One red amid over two dozen white ones.

Adam had no pangs about scheming to create this little "ambush"– as Crista called it — because he had such deep feelings for Eve. Yes, he could have called her more often in the past few days, but how else could he have created the intense surprise he wanted? He was smitten by her and if their relationship didn't take a step further soon...

"Remember the day Anthony broke his arm and I called for his Alberta health-card number?

"Yes."

"Well, the first number you gave me was *yours*," Adam said. "I was able to sneak a glance at the computer screen and saw your date of birth."

Throughout dinner, she felt euphoric. Although the restaurant was one of the city's most elegant ones, she only had eyes for Adam. When he invited her onto the dance floor, she was floating. She felt beautiful and loved and very special.

Before dessert was served, and between kisses, Adam asked, "Did…I…tell you how beautiful...you are?

"Twenty-four times in the past hour alone."

"But did I tell you how the dress clings to your beautiful body? Oh, yes, I think I said that too. But I remember I didn't tell you there is something amiss with it, did I?"

"Is there anything wrong with my dress?"

Standing behind her, as he had just seated her again, he bent over the table and picked up the red rose that, to Eve's surprise, had the stem cut short and was encased in a little vial of water. He dislodged the rose from the vial. She didn't move an inch as Adam tenderly adorned her hair with the red velvet rose.

"I've had many dreams of you, but none of them did you justice."

His lovely words had the most heady effect on Eve.

"I also dreamed of *this* complementing your dress," Adam said, producing a yellow satin, square box from under a napkin.

Eve opened the box gingerly. When she saw the necklace, she was overwhelmed with emotion. Mesmerized, she traced the diamonds with her fingertips, one after another. There were seven in number, three on each side of a larger one in the middle.

"It's exquisite, Adam. I truly love it, but I think it's too much, too expensive, I can't—"

"Too much? Too expensive? I won't hear of it. My only regret is that I wish it were a ring instead."

She was thoughtful for a moment. "I'll love it as if it were that. But really, Adam, you shouldn't have. It's too much," Eve reasoned, as she let Adam fasten the necklace.

When Adam sealed her wavering acceptance with a lingering kiss, she responded willingly.

She felt drunk with happiness. In the embrace of her Prince Charming, she could dance the night away. She couldn't remember ever being this happy.

Crista was in a triumphant mood. She knew that at this hour Adam's surprise was in action. She was ecstatic that she could help Adam put together the little details to create a memorable evening for Eve. If she had to keep the secret for one more hour, she would have exploded. She had been so afraid that she would accidentally reveal the surprise to Eve.

With the boys playing Nintendo in Brandon's room, Crista contemplated her upcoming fairy-tale vacation, which she had planned in its entirety. She had read about the luxurious lifestyle on a cruise ship in romantic novels and had seen it in movies. She wanted the same. She had bought herself a couple of evening gowns she found on sale at J. Michaels, and envisioned her dashing husband inviting her to the dance floor. She concealed her new dresses carefully together with some "light garments" that were bought on the sly. She scanned her husband's side of the closet. Surely, he would need some dress shirts, so she pulled out three that she liked and deposited them on the bed to send for dry cleaning.

"Holy, shit!" she said under her breath, slapping her forehead. "Better not forget Mike's tuxedo." She gasped at the possibility of forgetting about that particular garment; Mike would have been the only one unable to attend the Captain's party.

Now Crista took the tuxedo out of the closet and added it to the dry cleaning pile, but not before she went through its pockets. She discovered a loose button in one pocket. In the next pocket, she found a wad of Kleenex. From the last pocket, Crista fished out a little booklet that, at first glance, she was inclined to throw away, but as soon as she placed it on the night table, a suspicion crept into her mind. She picked up the booklet with shaky hands. Her suspicion proved right when she realized it was a receipt from the Bernadine Jewellery store. It was for a ring purchased on April 3rd. The receipt was stapled to a page inside the brochure that also included a colour picture of a diamond ring. The price: $7, 215.00!

She brought the picture closer to her eyes. She was certain that the ring was the most exquisite thing she had ever laid eyes upon.

But she was not the recipient…

Crista did what she always did in such situations: She panicked. She called her husband a gamut of unkind names. She called his number but hung up. He was working late again, a routine she hadn't been suspicious about until now. His phone would be on call forward after hours. She was realistic enough to know that every relationship has issues, and no one's life was perfect, but this was deplorable. The fact was that, the man she trusted more than anyone in the world was cheating on her. There was no doubt in her mind, because the proof was before her eyes. At that very moment, another woman was probably gloating and showing off that beautiful ring.

This was her worst nightmare.

Crista's fear sunk in. Their marriage was a sham.

*My God*, she thought, *what should I do first? Call a lawyer? Call Eve? Call his parents?*

Passion.

No inhibitions.

No regrets.

Only longing and willingness.

The unspoken desires of two people, who have love and admiration for one another, were finally unleashed. When Adam had whispered his fervent intentions in Eve's ear at the restaurant, she only asked for one alteration in his plan — her place as opposed to the hotel room upstairs. The limousine that delivered Eve to the restaurant had been waiting outside when they finished their dinner.

Their eagerness was evident by the trail of discarded clothing scattered all the way to Eve's bedroom. There was no rush however, as Adam discovered places on Eve's body that he'd only imagined before. Both were only inches and seconds away from total fulfilment. And when they thought that the ultimate passion would be finally achieved…

"*Eve!*"

When her name was repeated a second or third time in a distraught tone, they knew it was not their imaginations.

"It's Crista."

"Crista?"

"Oh, God! Anthony got hurt, or else she wouldn't intrude." She jumped off the bed, grabbed a housecoat and disappeared without looking back. As she made her way down the hallway, she quickly collected their cast off clothing. She returned to the bedroom and gave the mound of clothing to Adam who was waiting naked behind the partly open door. The furious knocks on the front door continued.

"Crista? What's the matter?" Eve said, her heart in her throat. "Where is Anthony? Did something happen to him?" As soon as she stopped long enough for an answer, she saw the sombre faces of the two boys standing behind Crista. The children walked past her and headed up to the second floor upon Crista's request. "Where's the fire?" Eve asked. "Mike? Did something happen to Mike?"

All of a sudden, Crista looked devastated. "Yes, indeed *something* happened to Mike. It appears that my 'loyal' husband may be more loyal to someone else."

"That can't be true, Crista. Mike is not that kind of man."

"His actions suggest that he *is* that kind of man," Crista said.

Eve tried her best to calm her friend down. She knew from past experience that if she didn't do something Crista's reaction would escalate.

"Hush! You don't want the children to hear this. Tell me what happened," Eve said. "But first make sure you've thought this through and that you haven't overreacted."

"Overreacting? Look at this. It speaks for itself," Crista said, and threw the jewellery brochure in Eve's direction. Crista was silent for just a moment before she started sobbing.

Just then, Adam entered the room barefoot, with his shirt buttoned up to the last two buttons and only half tucked into his pants. He had rolled up one sleeve and now was fumbling with the other.

Crista lifted her eyes. She examined Adam from his bare feet to his dishevelled hair. "Oh, my God! I must have lost my mind. I totally forgot about your plans for the evening and all."

"Maybe Mike bought the ring for you," Eve said, and passed the brochure to Adam.

Adam gave it a perfunctory glance but refrained from giving an opinion.

"Do you see me walking around with the fucking ring? Look at the date it was bought on. One month *after* our anniversary. *One month!* Don't you think he would have bought it in time and it would be on my finger now? Okay, I would have gladly overlooked that he gave it to me late," Crista said, then added, "Oh, my, God! He bought it with the bonus money. He told me that there was no bonus this year and here is *this*."

Eve handed her the box of Kleenex and Crista blew her nose noisily.

For a while, everyone was silent. Eve and Adam exchanged a glance, their thoughts connecting at the same time. Adam escorted Crista into the kitchen for a soothing drink while Eve made a hasty escape.

The coolness of the evening had a calming effect on Eve's nerves, though not as much as she needed. With every passing moment, she was more convinced that Crista was not overreacting. The proof was there on the passenger seat: the brochure from the jewellery store with the purchase receipt inside it. Her thoughts flew back to another time when Mike had gotten rid of Crista ungraciously…

Ten years ago, when Eve and William came to Canada, they truly appreciated Mike and Crista's friendship. Mike was a wealth of information, particularly regarding William's new workplace.

Crista offered Eve the heartfelt assistance that any foreigner needed when settling in a new place. Eve fell in love with Crista's boisterous ways and was grateful for her encouragement and support after the loss of her first pregnancy just months after their arrival in Canada.

It was Crista's candid manner that attracted Eve. But the special bond between them came from the fact that both of them experienced starting all over in a new country. Originally from New York, Crista came to Canada when she was about six years old. Her parents were never married. Her mother, a young, white woman, killed herself when Crista was five. Her father, a black man, abuser, and drug addict, in a rare moment of clear thought decided to "make things right" for his daughter by sending her off to live with his sister in Ontario. When Crista was sixteen, her auntie died and Crista ran away to escape possible abuse from her uncle.

She once confided to Eve that she was dating Mike, but that she harboured no false hopes of building a life together. His family was in the way. "It's not me they are adamantly against. It's my skin, if you know what I mean," Crista had explained. Eve knew that only too well. Some people had a problem with the colour of Crista's skin, one of them being her husband, William, which disturbed Eve a lot. He carefully masked his prejudice but continued to make remarks about "statistics of interracial relationships" and "cultural differences".

About a little bit more than a year after they met, Mike had paid them a visit alone. When Eve had inquired about Crista's whereabouts, he casually said that they had broken up. After a while, William told her that Mike was dating a *white* woman whose partner was dying of cancer.

Eve missed Crista's company and her infectious laughter. She wondered what had become of her and why she never tried to contact her.

At the beginning of that May, Eve stopped at a Safeway store in Collingwood to buy a bouquet of flowers. While her cashier wrapped the flowers, she saw Crista. She was running a cash register towards the end of the lane.

Eve took notice of her smooth brown face, a bit rounder than before, which gave her a beautiful aura. But on further observation, something else about Crista caught her eye: the hopeless expression that hung around her. This apathetic Crista took Eve by surprise.

Gone was her old smile. Gone was her cheerfulness and joviality. This Crista looked bitter, beaten, and resentful.

Taking her purchase, Eve moved one step sideways and saw something unforeseen: Crista was expecting...

Eve turned her attention to the road now. She didn't know what to expect when she faced Mike. Something did not add up. Moments ago she was certain that Crista was right, but now that she had more time to cool down, she had some doubts.

Once at the bank, Eve knocked on the glass door to get someone's attention. There was light on in a few offices, and she could see Jeff Robinson approaching from the other side.

"Mrs. Nelson! What a surprise!"

*Indeed,* Eve thought, as she stepped inside.

"We aren't usually this late, but the boss is back tomorrow and there are certain things he likes to have in order," Jeff said.

"I was wondering if Mike is still here. I tried to call him but only the machine picks up," Eve lied. "I was in the neighbourhood and thought I'd stop by."

"Let me check. I saw him earlier," he said and retreated a few steps to have a better look. "Yes. He's at his desk."

"Eve, what are you doing here?" Mike asked.

"May I speak to you in private?"

"Yes, sure," Mike said, and with a quick, almost imperceptible nod, dismissed the young assistant in his office.

"What happened? Why are you here?"

Eve was silent for a few seconds.

"Is everything all right? I didn't pick up any calls. We are so busy here, with Victor returning tomorrow."

"Very considerate of you to do your best at work, although it seems to me, you would rather be here than at home."

"I don't like your tone of voice and the insinuation, Eve. What the hell has happened since I last spoke with you?" Mike asked. "Weren't you supposed to be with Adam, celebrating your birthday?"

"Oh, so he does remember other people's plans!"

"Most positively *he* does," Mike countered. "Now, would you please tell me what the hell is going on and what brought you here?" He studied her face. "Let me ask you a question—"

"No! Let me ask you one. Are you cheating on Crista again?"

*"What?"* Mike spat the word. "Where did you come up with that idea? And what do you mean, *again?* Did Crista fill your head with some kind of garbage?" He jumped out of his chair. "My God, you seem determined to incriminate me. I can see it on your face."

"You're damn right. Who is it now, another widow-to-be? Or maybe your taste has changed," Eve snapped, tilting her head towards the door. "It's that young…fellow you were tête-à-tête with when I came in?"

"Stop it. You're not the type to jump to such dimwitted conclusions. That's Crista's territory. We both know she overreacts ninety-nine per cent of the time."

"Trust me, this is that one per cent when she is not overreacting, my friend. I brought the proof with me."

Mike shook his head. "If I recall correctly, your saint of a husband was counselling me against marrying Crista. I didn't marry Crista to please you or to displease William. Don't get me wrong, I truly appreciated your intervention back then, but it was my decision to marry her, and I did it because I realized how much I loved her. *Still* do," Mike said. "Take note of *that*, for your 'investigative records'. I don't know what you brought as proof of my so-called 'infidelity'. All I know is that whatever it is it must be a piece of crap. *Crap.* Do you hear me?"

Eve grew alarmed. Could it be that, in spite of the seemingly solid evidence, there was an innocent gesture behind buying that ring? Mike was glowering. She felt the confrontation had taken a wrong turn.

"You know what's odd?" Mike continued. "Of all people, *you* want to find fault in someone else's husband's conduct. You never seemed to question your own husband's acts of infidelity."

"Leave William out of this!"

"If you were meant to know about your husband's escapades, I don't think there is a better time than now. His visits to Europe were not strictly business related. Nor were those long-distance calls to Belgium. You want to play fireball? I'm game."

Eve was appalled. She had never questioned William's faithfulness. She had thought that he was too success-driven to make time for an affair. Could she have been wrong?

Eve realized that Mike's hand was extended.

"The least you could do is to show me your *evidence*," he requested.

"This will speak for itself."

Mike glanced at the brochure Eve put in his hand. "Ah, this. How in the hell did she find it? I considered the tuxedo the ideal place to hide it." He laughed. "Isn't it like Crista to make a mountain out of a molehill? I bought the ring for her. Is it such an impossible thing to conceive? I can't believe that you went along with her ridiculous accusations."

Eve's face showed that she was not convinced.

"It's impossible to think otherwise, especially, when you see the date of the purchase. Why didn't you buy it one month earlier for your anniversary, if it was for her?"

"For the simple reason that I wouldn't be able to spend seven thousand dollars on a fucking ring without her noticing, that's why," Mike retorted. "I bought the ring when I got the bonus. It was already late for our anniversary, so I decided to make a nice romantic event of it when we were on the cruise."

Eve still looked doubtful.

"You think my explanation is hogwash, don't you?"

Mike darted out of the office. He returned holding a manila envelope from which he produced a ring box.

"I had our initials and anniversary date engraved on it." He passed the ring to Eve. "See for yourself."

A luminous, proud moon lit the path to her car. She desperately needed to release long-restrained tears of irritation and confusion, but they refused to tumble out, simply because she couldn't quite believe that William had soiled their marriage. Did he know some woman in Belgium? Was he so good at fooling her that she never questioned any of his trips out of the country? She would never know. Besides, once Mike calmed down, he admitted he was making an assumption without evidential support. He tried to convince her that he had been enraged by her accusation and had fired back without much thought.

*Was he telling the truth then, or the first time?* Eve asked herself, as a wave of depression attempted to engulf her.

As promised, she delayed her return to give Mike time to get home before his wife arrived. Eve went along with his plan to "surprise his darling, preposterous wife" with the ring right away. Eve also offered to keep their son overnight to let his parents celebrate.

Eve parked her car in the garage. As she entered the house, she fashioned her face to give away nothing. How can one question the fidelity of the dead? She pushed the matter to the back of her mind, undecided if it should ever be revisited. As she entered the family room, the dim light from Anthony's fish tank revealed the feminine form crunched up on the sofa. She assumed Adam was supervising the bedtime process for the two boys. She had called to say that Brandon would stay overnight.

Crista felt her presence and sprung up.

"You did it again, girl," Eve started laughing softly. "And I most certainly must have gone mad to forget that you are always expecting the worst to happen. You are—"

"A Calamity Jane?" Crista supplied.

"Exactly. That should be your middle name," Eve said. "You can put your mind to rest, and put the guns away. Mike bought the ring for you. The ring bears your initials and the anniversary date on it. It was bought with the bonus money and was supposed to be a surprise on the cruise."

The two women shared a steady gaze for a long moment, a moment broken by Adam's appearance.

He was dressed, socks and all. The sleeves that were rolled up previously were now tamely disciplined by gold French cuff-links. Eve made an effort to shunt a surge of disappointment.

"I couldn't help but overhear that things were not as bad as previously thought," Adam said.

"I'm the world's most irrational fool," Crista said. "The biggest, I should say, because there is no bigger fool than a suspicious, jealous wife. I jumped to conclusions too quickly. I've been a jackass tonight and ruined your perfect evening with my assumptions. Please forgive me. Next time don't pay any attention to me at all. Don't even open the door for me."

"Consider it a deal," Eve chimed in.

"I second that," Adam said.

Eve picked up the cue.

"Help me show this 'trespasser' her way out."

Adam hardly resisted the impulse to invite himself for lunch. He already envisioned a scantily-clad Eve opening the door, whispering in his ear that she loved his pretext for lunch, which could wait, of course. First, they would finish what they started the past evening…and the further his imagination went, the more he added to his daydream.

*What if I just showed up there?* Adam thought for a moment but reconsidered. It would look too cheeky to just show up unannounced.

So, flowers it would be instead! The night before, when he left her place, the bouquet of roses from the restaurant looked pitifully lifeless as they had been abandoned in the foyer when Adam and Eve rushed in.

"Cash or charge, sir?"

"Pardon me?"

The young florist repeated her question.

"Oh! Cash," Adam said.

"Is there a message, sir?"

"I'll write it myself," Adam replied.

He licked the tip of the tiny envelope after he inserted the card with the short message on it.

"Thirty-one white roses. One red, in the middle," he said. One-hour delivery. Correct?"

"One thing I know for sure, Mike Malone. You get crazier as you get older!"

Mike burst out laughing.

The night before, when she had stepped inside the house, the flickering candles were casting long, dancing shadows on the walls. She steered clear of the two tall, cinnamon-scented candles and followed the guiding, illuminated path. Soon her sense of curiosity was overpowered by her arousal, which engulfed her with every step.

This surpassed anything Mike had ever surprised her with. As she followed the path, she knew it would lead to Mike. She visualized him holding up a candle at the "destination," which would be a room where he wished to make love to her. She opened the bedroom door but didn't see him. *Now, get logical,* Crista told herself. She reviewed all the rooms, dismissing closets and other alcoves as she slowly turned to retrace her steps. It dawned on her that the only room she had not checked was the kitchen.

As she approached the dining room, he appeared from behind a wall, surprising her.

And, he was holding a candle.

Reflecting the soft light, the ring was the only object he was wearing.

Crista brought her mind back to the present, and the restaurant with its busy lunch sounds.

"I could guess what you were thinking about," Mike whispered.

"Say it then!" Crista challenged.

"Of us getting pregnant? I promise you a gorgeous baby girl, just like her mommy."

Crista liked his guess. Indirectly, her thoughts were leading down that way. She liked the "baby talk" and the sweet stuff he showered her with. How could she ever think that Mike would want another woman but her?

"A baby girl, hmmm? What if we get another boy? No one we know has girls. Look at Eve, three pregnancies — all boys."

As soon as she said that, Crista's face changed. The mask of guilt was way too noticeable for Mike not to ask.

"What is it?"

"Well, I was just thinking about my ill-timed intrusion on Eve and Adam. They didn't have enough time for a quickie, let alone making love."

Mike laughed. By now, he knew the whole story about his wife's reaction to his "cheating."

For a moment, Crista debated whether to bring up the subject she knew was disquieting. She didn't want to ruin the mood.

"I forgot to tell you that Adam is dry in the sperm department. Eve told me about it the other day. I guess he wanted to bring all his skeletons out of the closet before they went any further."

Mike was baffled. "What about Eve? Is she all right about not having more babies? I mean, ever since we met her, she was either pregnant or wanted to get pregnant. How is this new piece of information settling with her?"

"Eve has adopted the attitude that you can't have your cake and eat it too. And considering the complications she had with her pregnancies…I hope she finds peace with having just one child. At least she's about to get a perfect substitute father for Anthony."

"You may be right about that," Mike said. "Baby, you must promise me something: Let these two experience their own ups and downs. We need to stay out of their personal business."

"I promise — and I intend to keep this promise — not to barge into their lives again like I did last night," Crista said and solemnly placed her right hand on her chest. "I feel awful about that. She deserves to be happy. I know she was a 'good girl'. Not that making love to Adam would have turned her into a monster. If anything, *it* would have made her…better. I mean, she would have felt like a normal, gratified woman, just the way I felt last night."

"Did you, now? Why don't we go back home for a bit of afternoon delight?"

"Peter Ghana from Falcon Ford called," Miss Annette called out as she saw Adam coming in. "I left his message on your planner. He stressed that it is urgent."

Moments later, a little light was flickering on the intercom panel. "Yes, dear?"

"What's Ghana's story? He's not in his office right now."

Twenty minutes later, Adam was fuming. "He told me they had the exact model I'm looking for in Calgary, but it has apparently been sold." He started pacing the room. "He told me there would be no problem delivering it in less than forty-eight hours," Adam said. "Check with another dealership for me, please."

One hour later, Miss Annette brought in unsatisfactory news. "No one has the SE in stock for another month or so. A different colour maybe, but not in white," Miss Annette said.

Adam stopped at the window, hands crossed at his back.

"Adam, dear, going back to Peter Ghana, he said he'll have the car in three weeks. The vehicle he talked to you about was taken out of the lot as you two spoke. The man actually pulled some strings and learned there is an auto-cargo scheduled to depart for Canada tomorrow. When I spoke to him, he said they would have enough time to pull another car out and have yours loaded in."

Adam was still quiet, lost in thought.

"I didn't know you have a penchant for bigger cars now."

"Now, that was a low blow, Miss Annette," Adam laughed and turned around. "We both know who the car is for. Nice try, hiding your question under the pretence of that statement. I thought you liked Eve."

"My liking her is irrelevant. It's just how you are showing her that seems overboard. But what do I know about expressing feelings?"

She may as well have been speaking to a deaf person.

"You really must stop sending flowers, Adam," Eve said, pointing to the vases filled with enormous bouquets of flowers in her living room. "One rose per evening is more than I need." She complained softly, but still thanked him with a kiss for the yellow rose.

Like clockwork, every evening at 6:00 p.m., Adam crossed her threshold with a rose in his teeth. For him, that moment was what he looked forward to all day. It was like being a teenager all over again.

"Why did I have the impression that you needed more?"

Tonight he couldn't misread her longing by the way she clung to him in a tight embrace.

"Adam, guess who signed my cast today at school?"

Eve and Adam jerked their heads to the sound of Anthony's voice. He approached the boy and bent down to be on eye level with him. "Let me see it." He recalled Eve saying that three *Oilers* hockey players had visited Anthony's school that day.

Beaming, the boy extended his plastered arm.

"Is it Dave Manson's?

"No."

"Then maybe Gordon Mark's?"

"Noo!"

Adam contemplated aloud. "It can't be Gretzky's, because I have his signature on a glove at home and this doesn't look like that."

"Whoa!" Anthony exclaimed. "You have Wayne Gretzky's autograph? Can I trade with you for it? Maybe Todd Marchant's?" The boy pleaded, pushing his cast in Adam's direction to reveal the identity of the autograph. Anthony stopped speaking when he saw the reproving frown on his mother's face.

Adam glanced back and forth between the boy and his mother.

"Let me talk to your mom in private for a minute," he said and winked.

Anthony scurried upstairs.

"What was that for?" Eve asked a minute later when Adam stopped kissing her.

"Hmm?" he asked, planting another passionate kiss on her parted lips.

"Why did you ask Anthony to leave us alone?"

"I was making a point. A very good one, with delicious help from you. If the mom gets what she wants, the boy gets likewise."

"Since when did you become an expert in child psychology?"

"I'm not. I haven't raised children, but I sure remember being one. If I can give Anthony the attention he needs and deserves, that helps not only him but me also."

Eve was quiet. Then tilting her head, she teased, "I have no choice but to get used to having to contend with two boys instead of one from now on, right?"

"Afraid of being outnumbered?" Adam asked, and capturing her hands at her back, kissed her tenderly.

She let him kiss her without protest.

"May I have the glove, Mommy?"

For the second time, Adam and Eve jumped apart in surprise. And again, Adam took the lead.

"Your mom said you can have it. She's very hard to convince though," Adam said, glancing at Eve. "I have a few things signed by hockey players. I think you can have them. If I correctly remember, I have…"

Eve watched as they departed, completely absorbed in manly stuff. She was not aware that she was smiling. Even so, she felt a bit uneasy. Wasn't it premature for Adam to get so serious, so soon after his failed marriage?

Eve wondered if Adam would be as eager to think of a future together if she was not so dead set on adhering to her principles. They had come so close to breaking her rule on her birthday. Now she used that example as a point of reference in her mind. If they had made love then, she would have guessed now the order of his priorities.

To compound her indecisiveness and her concerns, something else happened that prompted profound contemplation.

On Saturday, Adam's nephew celebrated his birthday. Amongst those invited were Anthony and Brandon. Eve encouraged Adam to spend the afternoon with his parents where the party was taking place. He hadn't visited with them often since he spent all his spare time with Eve and Anthony. He agreed with her suggestion, but to Eve's surprise, showed up at her place claiming he was an "outcast" among the young group.

Eve offered him a consolation prize: freshly baked cookies, served with plenty of kisses.

Unexpectedly, Crista brought Anthony home an hour later. She couldn't stay, explaining that Brandon was in the car and had just been punished with "no phone calls, no visits with friends for one week."

"Brandon is not the only one being punished. Your beloved nephew is under the whip as we speak," Crista said to Adam.

"What happened?"

"I'll let Anthony tell you. He was there and witnessed the mischief. To be fair, I must tell you that he didn't cause the trouble," Crista said.

Eve and Adam looked at the boy. He stood there in complete silence, chin trembling.

"I didn't do it, Mommy. I didn't do it. It was not my bubble gum," Anthony started crying.

"Ryan 'borrowed' Brandon's bubble gum, who in his turn planted it on Mrs. Adam Carry's seat when she got up to fill up her wine glass. I think from there on, you can use your imagination," Crista explained and left in a hurry.

"Anthony, did you know what Ryan was going to do with Brandon's bubble gum?" Eve asked him as soon as she had him seated on the couch next to her.

The boy nodded.

"Do you remember when I told you that if you see others doing something wrong and say nothing, you are as guilty as them?"

"Yes, Mommy."

"It was naughty of you not to advise your friends against doing it, darling. Not doing anything about it meant that you agreed with them, and took part."

The boy's head lowered another notch.

"Anthony?" Eve asked. "Remember I told you once what happens to people who take joy in watching bad things being done to other people?"

"Yes, Mommy. Those bad things may happen to me, too."

"Right!" *He only needs a reminder from time to time,* Eve thought. She doubted that the two older boys would have listened to him. She was ready to "pronounce" the sentence and send him to his room when he surprised them.

"But Mrs. Carry enjoyed kicking Max, Ryan's little dog. Will she get punished for doing that?"

With the bravery of someone already in trouble, Anthony plainly explained how Alicia saw Max sleeping on one of her shoes and kicked it hard in the ribs. That made the little dog yelp, which, of course attracted everyone's indignation.

The last piece of the puzzle fell in place. The children counterattacked in response to a vicious act of animal abuse.

Adam sensed that Eve was preoccupied.

"I didn't know *she* had planned to attend the family celebration," Adam said after Anthony went upstairs to his room.

Eve gave him a weak smile, "I don't expect everyone in your family to sever their ties with Alicia just because you two are divorcing. I'm not so self-absorbed and stubborn to think or demand that."

It would be a serious talk, Adam decided. When she smiled, he realized it was a different kind of smile, a polite smile. Regardless of his reticence to discuss the subject, it could not be avoided. By all means, he needed to straighten out some things.

"Besides, my position is hardly endangered by Alicia's presence," Eve said, managing to sound normal. "You are inevitably bound to run into each other throughout your lives—"

"No! Let's not even go there. It's not going to be like that."

"Tell me how it's going to be then."

Adam sighed in exasperation, massaging his temples as he always did when he was hit over the head with the subject of Alicia.

"Look. As unpleasant as this discussion is, we have to have it to ensure we're on the same page. I know this situation is upsetting you. I don't like it either and I agree that something has to change so it won't interfere with our lives," Adam said. "At this point, I don't know what to do about her and her foolish conduct. I expect, in time, she will stop showing up where she is not welcome. I'm sick and tired of her acts."

*Me too,* Eve thought, watching her hands on her lap, doing her best to avoid his eyes. Certainly, Alicia was at the celebration only to wreak havoc on Adam's nerves. He wanted *her,* and under the circumstances, there was no clearer proof of his sentiments than his presence here, with her, and not at his parents' house.

Adam took Eve's hands between his, "It's time for a major move on my part. And I'm ready for it. Ask me anything that is in my power to change. Anything. I would relinquish my position at the corporation and leave town—"

"Adam, stop it! You really scare me. I'm not such an unreasonable and selfish person to ask you to uproot yourself and traipse from town to town in search of peace of mind. Besides, you can't just walk out on your parents and your duties here."

"And why not? I think it's the only solution. Eve, you are the most important thing in my life. All I have there has brought me tremendous unhappiness," he said, pointing towards downtown. "It's probably for the best that I leave it behind. I'm serious. What good is this position and power without the love, support, and understanding that I need? I now realize that these two type of elements clash and I must choose one over the other. And by God, I certainly know what I would choose. You."

Eve thought for a moment. This kind of seriousness didn't take her by surprise, but it threw her off balance.

"You can't just walk out and abandon your father. You are his only *son,* and every man's son is his pride and joy. I have never met your father, but he must have done at least one right thing to warrant your respect. Every father wants to pass on his legacy and success to his son."

Adam interrupted her, "Do you think you can find a sitter on short notice?"

"Why?"

"I want to show you something, but I have to take you to the right place."

Eve became intrigued. "Let me check with my neighbour's daughter."

Half an hour later, Adam assisted Eve out of the car, now parked on the premises of Carstone Oil Corporation.

As they made their way to the building, Eve believed he was making a mistake. He was exposing the huge gap of wealth and privilege that lay between them.

Eve recalled when she found out who he really was. Now, just like then, she felt a wave of anxiety. She shook her head to clear her muddled thoughts. If Adam was set to scare her off with this outing, he succeeded. Yet, part of her knew that Adam would do his best to assuage her fears.

Once they were in the building, an official came out from behind the welcome desk and greeted them. He smiled and shook Adam's hand.

"Good evening, Mr. Carry. Where to?"

"Seventeenth, please. Roy, please meet Ms. Nelson, a very good friend."

"Ms. Nelson," the old man said, with a smile and a small bow.

Eve returned his smile.

Adam placed his right palm on a glass hand-print scanner built into the desk and waited a couple of seconds for his clearance.

An elevator door opened soundlessly to Eve's right, startling her. Adam ushered her in and the door slid shut.

A moment later, they stepped into an open area. She looked around at the upper-management office area, and realized the elevator serviced only that floor.

It took Adam fifteen minutes to brief her on the layout of the headquarters executive suite. They walked hand in hand through the deserted offices, their footsteps echoing along the corridors. As they walked, Adam stepped ahead to open office doors as each was equipped with hand-print electronic devices. Those particular offices contained highly guarded documents and only three people had the "power" to open them, Adam explained. Eve could easily guess who the other two "gods" with similar power and privilege were.

When Adam and Eve reached a wide corridor, he told her to keep close and mimic his movements. His warning made her heart beat faster, as she realized that they must be crossing into an ultra-sensitive area.

"Don't be afraid," Adam encouraged. "If we do slip up nothing precarious happens."

Eve stepped so close behind that a few times the tips of her shoes bumped into Adam's heels. He squeezed her hand to assure her. Abruptly he stopped. Eve froze.

"Just pretend you have to pass over an obstacle about a foot high, just like that." He made a large step into the air and she followed. Finally, they arrived in the 'free zone' and she was able to breathe easier.

"It'll be easier on the way back. I've got some special eyeglasses in my office that distinguish the rays," Adam said. Seeing Eve's reluctance to move, he advised on a cheerful note. "Darling, loosen up. You can move now."

"Are we on a candid camera?" Eve asked.

"No!" He lied. "And this is Miss Annette's territory."

Eve assessed her surroundings. She liked what she saw. Marble and stainless steel dominated the reception area. Leather furniture in slick shapes was placed throughout the spacious waiting area. A few live plants, whose top branches were almost touching the pyramid glass ceiling, looked sturdy enough to climb on. On the wall across from the reception desk, there was a huge oil painting to which Eve was instantly attracted. A hint of recognition piqued her curiosity. She got closer to the right corner of the painting and then stepped backwards.

"Wow! I've seen this before. I didn't expect to see it in Edmonton," Eve said. The painting bore Thomson Pares' signature. She knew that this one, titled *The Waves*, was auctioned in Toronto several years ago. "It's stunning! One of Pares' masterpieces, for sure."

"To be honest with you, I never liked it. I was not the one who picked it out," Adam said.

"Why Adam? Doesn't *The Waves* sway you?" she asked.

"For the money we paid, it sways me all right. Come, I'll show you my office."

Adam's office was nothing like she had imagined it. Many times she envisioned him seated behind a massive desk. As she slowly pivoted on one foot to view the whole room, she saw it was a far cry from the ultra-modern picture she had in mind. She moved about the spacious room. Her natural, artistic curiosity led her to a heavy framed portrait. Her training told her that the artist's hand was experienced with portraits. The light fell in just the right place. She was fascinated with the colours; an inexperienced eye would think that the man in the portrait posed for the artist, but Eve guessed that it had been taken from an old photograph. She was surprised to discover she could identify the subject. Adam's father. No wonder that when she had met Adam's mother she couldn't find a whole lot of resemblance between the two. Adam, she realized now, strongly resembled his father. Less aloofness in the eyes and a lot less of the sense of entitlement she heard the old man possessed.

"That's my grandfather, the founder of this oil company," Adam supplied.

"Oh! I thought it was your father."

Adam laughed. "I have not met anyone yet to mistake us. My father and I, I mean. But your instincts are right. Fifteen years from now, you won't distinguish my portrait from this. Funny, how the genetics work."

Adam wrapped his arms around her. She turned towards him. She had resolved to be patient, as she guessed he had a unique way of revealing his intention for bringing her here.

"You really surprise me. Most of the time you speak your mind, regardless of the issue, which is just fine with me. Yet, there are times when you keep your thoughts exclusively to yourself. Like right now, you're probably thinking, 'What the heck has he brought me here for?' Am I mistaken?"

"I'm desperately curious. But I'm trying to be content waiting. You know the overused saying, good things come to those who wait."

"How good?"

Eve shrugged. "I don't know. It all depends on how long one waits."

Adam laughed. "No further questions. I owe you an explanation. And I'm happy to oblige, but let's have a seat." He indicated a beige leather love-seat.

Eve proposed, "Take your regular chair and I'll have this comfy one across from your desk. I'd like to watch you speak. I have a hunch you give great speeches."

He agreed, and after they settled in, he began his speech. "For a very long time, it has occurred to me that I resent where I stand professionally, as well as in other areas of my life. If I didn't do anything to fix that, it was probably because I didn't know how to fix it, or worse because I was afraid everyone would think I'm being selfish. I was born with a silver spoon in my mouth, and as insensitive and unappreciative as I may sound — I want it all to go away.

"My grandfather, I was told, was a very wise man. He created this enterprise from scratch. My father, on the other hand — also a smart man — continued my grandfather's legacy to a degree that would have made my grandfather proud. Certainly, I'm expected to lead the corporation to even greater heights. But honestly, Eve, I don't believe I belong here for the simple reason that I *don't* have the drive for oil and money like my predecessors. Never had, never will." The creases on his forehead were more prominent now.

"I dread thinking about the promises I made in that interview with CFRN. To be honest, I was stretching the truth about one important thing. No way will I do what I don't like just for the sake of keeping the business together. I know, you might say I'm a spoiled brat. Or worse, with all the hardworking ancestors I've been blessed with, I turned into a prodigal son—"

"Adam, I prefer to voice my own opinion. Like you said, I speak my mind sometimes and this is one of those times. I appreciate your straightforward and genuine point of view."

"Good, because I wasn't sure I was making sense," Adam said. He seemed to weigh his next words with considerable thought. "The truth is that I finally feel that I've gathered the strength and wits to change my life..."

If this was what he couldn't say anywhere but *here,* Eve was confused. Yet she decided to be patient.

"With each passing day since I met you, it dawned on me that it's in my power to change it. I firmly believe now that people should share their life with the person they love, cherish, and embrace." Adam held Eve's stare. Eye to eye, heart to heart. "I can do what I always wanted, Eve. And, if I have you by my side, I will have achieved the most important accomplishment of my life. Everything that you see here I want to leave behind in exchange for a normal life. A life with you."

Eve felt her life was about to change. The experience was so intense that she had to pinch herself to prove she was not dreaming. All she had to do was look in the mirror and catch the flicker of the diamonds at the base of her throat and her heart soared. Adam made her promise she would wear them all the time, and so far, she hadn't gotten tired of them. There were some moments, spontaneous moments, when Eve surprised herself by thinking how wrong she had been before to think that life was bleak and wasted without William. How different she knew now! She was like a child counting down the days until Christmas, as she waited for Adam to be a "free man".

She had come a long way.

# *Five*

WEDNESDAY MORNING, ADAM FOUND OUT THAT HE HAD TO GO to China the following day for at least six weeks. He shared his plans with Eve. They agreed that it was a long time apart, but by the time he returned, they would both be free to plan a life together, because by then his divorce would be final.

Eve didn't waste time sulking in a corner. She developed some plans of her own. She would go visit her brother's family and be back before Adam returned. Her decision was prompted by a recent conversation with Garry, who shared the horrifying news that Jessica had only a couple of months to live.

Content that her personal life was stable, Eve made space and arrangements to be with her brother and his family in their time of need. She would have to relinquish her responsibilities for the upcoming exhibition. Luckily, Nora's youngest daughter, a university student, offered to help. Nora understood that Eve needed to support her brother and his family.

Eve buried herself in a myriad of tasks in preparation for the exhibition. There were some necessary changes in positioning for a few pieces of artwork, because the initial plan overlooked the influence or lack of proper lighting — an extremely important requirement for certain pieces. Eve also needed to arrange the appropriate legal authorization for Nora to sell Eve's works.

Eve banned Adam from her mind during her busy days. At night, though, he was there exclusively. As he had predicted, he was too busy in China to contact her. "It's going to be truly a probation time, darling, I'm warning you," Adam had said. "When I'm there, I mean business. It's the nuisance cycle: work, eat, sleep, work, eat, sleep."

Week after week, as many times as she left the house in one day, the first thing she did upon her return was checking her answering machine. Every time she hoped he had called. After discovering he hadn't, she brooded.

More than once, she almost gave in to her restless heart to call him. If she wanted to get in touch with him, she just had to call Miss Annette to get his number. But she thought it was important to stick to their agreement to use this as "probation time."

And yet, how she wished he would call.

This time the nightmare did not consume her. Yet she wondered if this had any significance. With the sole exception of one instance, all the sequences of her nightmare were portentous of events that affected her life. It woke her up, but she was not in the mood to analyze it any further.

Outside her window, the moon was almost full, shining and defiant. A daring, opaque cloud briefly shrouded the moon's surface. The hint of its pale aura stood on guard.

A car passed on the street and the lamp by her door lit up automatically, making the night's atmosphere seem alive. Eve returned to bed, the promise of a good night's sleep slipping away.

Seeming to shake off the smothering restraints, the moon materialized like an auspicious companion. Eve could see it from her bed.

When the phone rang, she was awake, although her mind was sluggish as she had been on the verge of falling asleep.

"Adam!"

"Aren't you asleep like a good girl?" he teased, amid a muffled buzz.

"I was awake, but that doesn't make me a bad girl. What are those noises? Is there a party going on?" Eve inquired.

He laughed. "None to which I was invited."

A broadcast of some sort in the background was competing with his voice.

"Are you in some airport?" Eve asked, not being sure if her voice carried to the other end. "Are you coming home?" The static filled the line intensely. And then again the buzzing sound came on the line, as if Adam was operating some powerful tool while he talked. Suddenly, it grew fainter and fainter as if someone had closed a door, cutting off the source of the nuisance. "You're in a plane. Don't deny it, Adam!"

"No, no. Why are you saying that? I'm half way through a conference." He paused as if trying to attend to something. "Actually, we just took a break and I thought I'd give you a ring."

"A what?" Eve said annoyed at being unable to decipher his voice through the noise.

"Eve, darling, I can't hear you well, but if you hear me better, I want you to know that I'll call you later. Hopefully, we'll get a better connection. Okay? Bye."

Eve turned the pillow over and punched it a few times, hoping to get some relief. She picked up a book to distract her from her frustrating mood but soon tossed it aside. Two hours deeper into the night, Adam had not called her back. He had said "later." She was furious, because he didn't choose a better place to call from.

Morning came and with it her poor disposition. She had stayed up too late, and inevitably slept in. Anthony was late for school. He panicked, cried, and cringed at the thought of reporting to the principal's office. She assured him that she would go with him and explain.

And there were no messages from Adam.

She met Crista for lunch at a new place that had just opened and was supposed to be excellent and priced decently.

"You still haven't heard from Adam, have you?"

"What? What's that supposed to do with anything?" Eve asked. "As a matter of fact, he did call me."

"Oh?"

"What do you mean by 'oh'? Tell me, please."

"'Oh' because he is alone and so far away. 'Oh' for you being *so* lonely. And 'oh' because he is *officially* an eligible bachelor now. Don't tell me you forgot that *that* time had come."

Eve laughed. No use to restrain the excitement she felt. Crista always said exactly what was on her mind. Of course, the big day had come painfully and slowly, but it had come...and he was far away.

"I'm sure he's thirty thousand feet in the air on his way to see you," Crista predicted.

The seed of suspicion grew until it was a reality. If she got the number in China, and he didn't answer it, it could mean only one thing: Adam was coming home. To her. He must've called from some airport given the cacophony of voices and the announcement system in the background. Eve flung open her little phone book. Feeling jittery, she strode to the phone with Miss Annette's phone number in hand, but just as she was about to pick it up, it rang.

"Adam! Where are you? I can hear you very well now. Wait a second. You're not fooling me. You are coming home."

"Yes, I am," he laughed.

"When are you arriving? You said you wouldn't finish business there for another couple of weeks. Can I pick you up from the airport?"

Adam laughed again. "In about two hours, I'll be there. Regretfully, I'm on a very short visit — sort of run away from my post, for a maximum of twenty-four hours. And don't come to the airport. I'd love that, but I've arranged to have a car waiting for me."

"I could come by taxi—"

"No. No need for that. You want to do something constructive? Find a sitter for Anthony for tonight, sleepover package. I want us to celebrate my freedom tonight. Freedom. How does that sound? By the way, do you want to go somewhere? Should I stop home for some formal clothing?"

"Are you kidding? How many times can you change clothing in twenty-four hours?"

"I love when you scold me."

With two hours to go, Eve hoped she could stay calm and sane. Too excited for a relaxing bath, she was washed and dressed in ten minutes. Next, she called Crista, spilled the news of Adam's homecoming, and asked her to pick Anthony up from school and host him for the night.

Crista happily agreed.

There is a misconception that lawyers have reptile blood running through their veins. That they are self-centred, cunning creatures and liars to the core. They can make the innocent bow and let criminals loose. Some will do anything to *not* lose a case.

Brad Johnson knew these things. He had been a lawyer for many years and those qualities described him and many people he worked with. Part of the job. However, when a case was personal, the reptile fled its casing, leaving behind a warm-blooded human being.

And this case was personal.

Almost nine years ago, Brad and Cassidy Johnson had adopted a three-month-old boy who had just been released from the Neonatal Intensive Care Unit at the Royal Alexandra Hospital. They had named him "Ryan" long before anyone called him anything but "Twin B." It took months for the baby to overcome some health problems so that he could be discharged to the adoptive parents. He was considered theirs since they knew that his biological mother failed to contact the hospital authorities upon her "free-will" discharge.

Ryan's biological mother had been brought in by air ambulance from the Northwest Territories to give birth to twin boys and then ultimately vanished with the healthy one. Attempts to locate her were unsuccessful. Eventually, "Twin B" was placed in permanent government guardianship until he would be adopted.

Cassidy Johnson was not only the baby's paediatrician, and an interested prospective parent, but also acted as a surrogate mother. She spent every spare moment sitting by the tiny incubator, and as he grew bigger, stronger, and healthier, by his little crib. She was the first to feel the grasp of his tiny hand and the first to be rewarded with his innocent, mesmeric smile. Cassidy introduced her husband to the baby, and he too fell in love with him.

By his first birthday, Ryan was no different from any other infant his age. He continued to become a very handsome boy indeed. His face reflected the worry-free life of an upper-class child. One might think he was spoiled, if they didn't know that every material thing he had came as a reward for good work in school and extracurricular activities.

In mid-June, Brad opened an Express Delivery envelope with the address of a Yellowknife law firm. After a quick glance at the contents, he decided to take refuge in the only place he didn't need to explain — the bathroom. The contents were very disquieting. Ryan's biological mother wanted to reclaim her rights over Ryan. She didn't want just contact, she wanted to "reinstate custody."

Brad didn't waste any time. He contacted people with good knowledge of the matter, close friends who were willing to help. He exhausted the subject with Leon Hill, his long-time friend, who volunteered for the case and equipped Brad with arguments and counter-arguments. Yet Brad was reluctant to share the disturbing news with his wife. It took him two weeks to find the "proper" moment.

As expected, Cassidy took the news hard but didn't fall to pieces. Sharing the discomforting news was one thing but telling his wife about the possibility of losing their son was another. Unfortunately, the subject arose when they met with a judge who Leon Hill contacted for private advice.

Judge Parson assumed that all present in his chamber were briefed ahead of time. When he said that Brad and Cassidy would need to familiarize their son with the fact that they weren't his biological parents, Cassidy transformed.

"No. Definitely not. I will not do that. Can you imagine what that would do to my son?" she sprang to her feet.

Three pair of eyes stared at her.

"Honey, sit down," Brad said. He had briefed her but hadn't enlightened her about *this* particular possibility. Yes, she was tough as a doctor, but she was also a sensitive human being and mother. Leon was the first to tell Brad that it could come to the point that the boy must be informed of the situation. Furthermore, when Ryan reached the age of eleven, he would have his own voice in the matter. It was this issue that enraged Cassidy.

Brad managed another glance in his wife's direction.

"Do you people hear yourselves? It is preposterous to even suggest we tell our son we are not his real parents."

For a moment, everyone looked powerless.

Parson tried to reason with her. "This is only a supposition—"

"A bad one, I'd say. How can you men be so clinical? Why don't you just tell me to pack my son's belongings and send him to the NWT on a one-way ticket?" Cassidy was exasperated. She stared down at her husband.

"Calm down honey and please sit down," he advised, as he gently placed his hand on her arm. "No one suggested we give up our son. We agreed though—"

"We agreed on what?"

"Darling, no one here wants to see Ryan in this situation, but we have to examine all possibilities. We'll do everything we can to avoid exposing our son to this. Time is on our side. We're not talking about next week or even next month."

"Next year is just as soon," Cassidy retorted.

Judge Parson interjected, "Cassidy, I want what's best for Ryan and I believe he is best taken care of by staying where he is — with you. Even if he were only two years old, I'd argue that he should stay with the couple he knows best and lived the longest with. But I also know that no one can stop the biological mother from initiating a legal battle. Statistically, very few succeed in getting a child back after freely giving it up. She would have to prove that she can offer more for the child. She would also need to prove — and this is important — that the adopted parents present an environment that is detrimental and injurious for their adopted child. I firmly believe no one ever would doubt your best interest for your son. As for the former factor, it is safe to assume that her limitations preclude matching your ability to provide for Ryan."

Judge Parson had everyone's attention, Cassidy's in particular, who was won over by the judge's use of her son's name. In her eyes, this little detail made this judge a caring human being.

Parson cleared his throat. "I assume her lawyer wants to wrap things up before the boy's eleventh birthday. It seems quite calculated that they waited to make this sort of move. However, we must consider if some other factor prompted this." He paused for a few seconds. "From what Leon told me, you suspect the mother is interested in money. Be very careful investigating this," Judge Parson said. "You can leave the boy out of this for now and proceed with the offer."

"Yes," Brad said. "We'll be careful."

Leon nodded in agreement. "We both decided it's worth the try. That woman may be more interested in cash than her son."

Judge Parson chose his words with caution. "I trust you know what to do, and most importantly, how to do it properly. It must preclude her from having a case next time, if she decides to make this move a routine," he said and started to rise. He shook hands with both lawyers and Cassidy. "It's going to be okay, Cassidy. You'll see. Try not to worry." To the lawyers he said, "Do it soon and cautiously. And keep me informed. Any hindrance of any kind, contact me — day or night."

At the door he stopped. "I wish you good luck."

Eve decided to surprise Adam by waiting for him at the airport.

Once there, she checked which flights coming in around 5:00 p.m. were possible connections from China. Then she bought a newspaper to hide behind and screened each group of arriving passengers.

AC621 arrived from St. Paul, which of course didn't bring Adam. Its passengers came through Arrivals, collected their luggage and visitors and departed. Next, there was a flight from Vancouver at 5:10 p.m.

Eve's heart leapt as she saw Adam.

She put one foot forth to break into a run towards him, but in the next instant, she saw Alicia reach Adam and envelope him in a warm, animated embrace.

Frozen behind the newspaper, Eve turned around and found refuge on a bench. Her mind refused to come up with a rational explanation for what was happening. All she could think of was that Alicia was there, in Adam's arms, to claim him. *Is that the reason Adam didn't want me to come to the airport?* Eve wondered.

It took her two hours before she found enough strength and willpower to get up and leave.

It was a depressing drive home. Eve didn't know what to think. Part of her wanted to believe there was an explanation for what happened. She wished she'd been brave enough to watch them for a few more moments.

When she got home, she saw a strange car in her driveway and hurried into the house to find Adam sleeping in her bed. It was then that she understood that Alicia was at the airport for the sole purpose of creating chaos.

Eve stood rooted to the floor, mesmerized. He was there before her eyes. What better proof that he wanted *her*. His suit was hanging on her closet door. In the corner, on a chair, lay a grey carry-on garment bag. A wave of shame washed over her as she could almost hear him saying, "When are you going to learn?"

How many times could she be wrong about him? How could she be so brainless, and tumble head first to such a hasty conclusion?

Eve almost giggled as she scanned the white cotton robe he had on. She bought the garment the other day from Hudson Bay. She also brought home a sheer nightgown with the thought of driving Adam crazy. She left both items on the armchair before she rushed to the airport. Now she was pleased with herself. Adam had not only made good use of his, but it seemed he had fallen asleep cuddling hers. Her mind had created a thousand scenarios for the moment that would bring their first lovemaking, but none of them came close to the intense reality of this moment. She quickly removed her clothes.

Adam's eyes popped open. "Eve! Where have you been?" He tried to prop his body on his right elbow but was gently pushed back.

"Shhh! I'm here now. And so are you," Eve's soft voice was reassuring and sensual.

She straddled him naked. She bent and kissed him slowly. She fumbled with the tie of his robe, and when she finally slipped her hand inside it, he closed his eyes and groaned in utter ecstasy.

"No, no. Wait a second," Adam said when he had a chance. "There is something I want to say...and ask you...and do..."

"Then let me help you *do it*, darling," Eve said, easing open the robe.

Their bodies touching produced swift intakes of breath.

"Isn't this what you wanted to *do*?"

"Oh, yes! More than anything..."

Still breathing hard, Adam said, "Oh, God, how I've missed you. And wanted to make love to you." He kissed her. "You must have made a bet with someone to see if you could have me spent in the first five minutes. You are the sweetest, most lovable, and most sex-starved woman who ever existed," Adam said. Their bodies, shining with perspiration were still entwined.

"Feeling victim of my Midas touch already?" Eve teased. "You haven't seen all my abilities yet. I may not turn everything I touch to gold, but I can turn you flat on your back. That I can promise. Don't say you weren't warned. It's not too late to change your mind about getting involved with this crazy woman."

Adam laughed, "I don't doubt that, but I'm afraid that since you brilliantly shanghaied me, it's too late for my initial plan—"

"I didn't shanghai you. You let yourself in and made yourself at home in my bed."

"But you pinned me down."

"And you liked it."

"Liked it, loved it, and could die for it, but I imagined we'd start it a little bit differently," Adam said and stretched over Eve. His chest brushed Eve's rosy breasts, erect and welcoming. Thousands of volts lit up his nerve endings from his head to his toes, but he was determined to ignore their incitation this time around.

"I imagine — no, I planned — to ask you something *before* we made love," Adam said, and pulling something from under her pillow, he came to a kneeling position.

"Darling, will you marry me?"

Eve was silent for a moment. She pulled herself into a seating position.

"You have no idea how much I have come to love you in this relatively short time. Yes, I will marry you."

When Adam adjusted the ring on her slim finger, she was beside herself.

"This is far and beyond the most beautiful ring I've ever seen." She looked at it with her hand stretched out.

A minute later, her thoughts sobered. "Adam, I know you didn't have to steal to buy this gorgeous thing, but I think it's too expensive."

"Honey, nothing is too expensive for you, don't you know by now? Besides, I got a good deal on it. Fifteen per cent off the regular price."

"When did you buy it?" Eve inquired.

"Last week in Singapore. All Hollywood celebrities are adorned with their jewellery. They're known for their top quality."

"Nice to know! But I'm not the Hollywood type."

"Perhaps Hollywood is not on par with you, but they will have to endure our presence there. Perhaps, for our honeymoon. That, of course, after your exhibition."

"Oh, Adam! Let me adjust to one piece of news at a time. I'm still in shock about this," Eve said, admiring the ring again. "I don't know if I'm—"

Adam covered her mouth with his.

"Don't you know that I believe you are worth it? Whatever I can offer you is only a small fraction of what I'm getting in return. Please get that through your beautiful head."

A soft smile played about the corners of her mouth. "I'm working on that. I promise." She shook her head, half-amused and half-amazed. Never in her wildest dreams had she ever thought of being proposed to while naked.

"Oh, Adam. I want to tell the whole world how happy you make me feel. Since you came into my life, I stopped waking up in the morning with that dreadful feeling that life is passing me by. I have even stopped feeling guilty about leaving the past where it belongs. I thought it was only natural that when you live with enormous sadness for so long, it's just a part of who you are. I used to think no one would ever replace William in my heart. But I was wrong. You changed all that."

A pregnant silence followed.

"Darling, I almost forgot. Crista gave me specific 'directives' to carry out. One of them obliges me to assume the responsibility of using a condom. If you had waited half a second, I would have grabbed one."

"You are kidding, right?" Eve said and then kissed him. "You mentioned Crista again. What has she to do with anything that relates to our lovemaking?"

"Much more than you know. You have a true, caring friend in Crista," Adam said laughing. "She once told me that I need a freshly acquired medical, a ring, and a date before I'd succeed in making love to you. Those supposedly being Dr. Laura's rules, which you live by. The divorce decree was another condition and it needed to be black on white. More or less those were your friend's assigned conditions. Mind you, she may want to see those to ensure their authenticity."

They laughed together, each for their own reason: Adam because he was finally on the other side of the "conditional" obstacle, and Eve, knowing how protective her impetuous friend could be.

"I have a two-month-old check-up, but not with me...hence the condom," Adam further clarified.

"Adam, stop the nonsense talk. I'll have a serious talk with Crista about her 'friendly' interference and tactics," Eve said, and getting closer to him, started nibbling on his earlobe. "Tell the truth, how many condoms do you have? You already saved one."

"You got me. I have only one. I bought it from a dispenser in the Vancouver airport. Sorry, I only had a toonie in my pocket. As for the divorce papers, they must be in some post office somewhere. Garth told me on Tuesday that the divorce pronouncement should have made its way to my mailbox by now. That's the *real* reason I stopped at home first. I left him a message, but he didn't return my call." Adam explained. "Anyways, I'm famished. How about you?"

For a split second, Eve thought he was changing the subject. The distant look in his eyes said that it was something he kept guarded. *Perhaps, it's some work issue that bothers him*, Eve thought.

Later, at the dinner table, he said, "You know my darling, it took all my mental resolve to stay away from you in those last days before I left for China. I sensed that I had made my way into your heart, but I wasn't so sure there wouldn't be any misgivings on your part if I pushed the envelope."

"Why didn't you at least try?" Eve surprised both of them with her question.

"Would you have let me make love to you, if I did?"

"Maybe."

"Too late now. I promised I wouldn't push you into intimacy before you were ready. I realized you weren't prepared for it until I was finished with the divorce. That's why I said, before I left, that my going away would signify 'probation time' for us. I'm delighted to say that we passed that with flying colours." He laughed. It seemed to him that, since he returned to Eve, he was either laughing or smiling. It felt wonderful.

"So, while fighting the demons called testosterone and respecting your ethics, I had my share of cold showers."

"And I thought you no longer found me desirable," Eve joked.

"I found you extremely desirable from the first day all right, but I found you also worthy of respect. I wanted us to remember dating in its finest and purest form."

"Not the bumpy times though. Those I don't want to remember."

Adam nodded in agreement.

Eve had seen a vague yet troubling expression in his eyes a few times this evening, but it disappeared so fast that she wondered if it was only her imagination. If anything else was floating around, Eve didn't want to fret about it now.

"Where were you tonight when I came in?" Adam asked.

"Oh, Adam. I wish you hadn't asked that."

"You were at the airport, weren't you?"

Her eyelids dropped.

"Aha! Gotcha! Why didn't I realize it before? You went to the airport, saw my ex, and got frightened and confused. Eve, when are you going to learn? We've been there before." Across the table, he squeezed her hands. "Oh, my poor darling, what went through your mind?"

"Never mind that," Eve said. "I wish I'd remembered your previous scolding before I freaked out. But in that moment, my mind didn't work. I saw her there hugging you…What would go through anyone's mind? It was only when I came home and saw you sleeping in my bed..."

"It's obvious you didn't watch the whole episode. I was taken aback to see Alicia there. My mother was supposed to bring the car for me. Had you watched for three seconds longer you would have been amused by her foot stomping when I refused to give her a lift into town in the car she brought for me."

"*No!*" Eve pictured the scene he described.

"Oh, yes. Anyways, tomorrow — today, that is, I'll meet my father and *her* for a full report," Adam said looking at the clock. "Come here. I want to show you something," Adam took her by the hand and led her into the living room. The full moon cast a soft light over the driveway.

"See that white SUV?" Adam asked, once they were in front of the living room window. "I would like you to have it. It would really make me feel better knowing you drive a reliable vehicle."

Eve gasped. "Oh, Adam!"

Adam laughed and kissed her forehead. "It took a few weeks to get it in white. I know from Mike how unwavering you are about this particular colour. It is my engagement present to you."

The moon witnessed their lovemaking on the lush carpet in the living room. No limitations, no restraints. Eve felt as if she could burst with happiness and enveloped Adam with those feelings. Finally, the gift of giving was there for sharing until Adam would leave again to finish his business in China.

Time, for the moment, lost its meaning and pace under wonders and spells of love.

Eve's agitation awakened him shortly after he fell asleep. She had given a shrill cry and flailed her arms in her sleep. She was comforted by the fact that she was not alone. Unlike other times, now she could share her dream's ghastly details and her own fears.

"You must've had a nightmare."

"Oh, Adam, it was awful. It was the same old, frightening one." She cried. "Awful, awful…I've had it two nights in a row, now."

"Shh, it's a dream," Adam said, and held her close.

"The recurrence of the dream doesn't puzzle me," Eve said, when she finished narrating the dream to him. "What really puzzles me is that, every time the dream comes back, there's a new element to it. It's almost like a movie sequence, things start where they left off. What is so queer about it is that, in my dream, I realize that it's a dream, but I can't wake up. Or maybe I simply don't want to until the new part kicks in. I never believed that dreams had a meaning or a connection with real life, but after I have it, something significant always takes place — usually something unpleasant or disturbing." She yawned. "Did I ever tell you that I had the dream the night before we met?"

"Yes, but didn't it bode well then?"

Tired, Eve nodded. "That was the only time it had a positive interpretation."

Long after Eve fell asleep again, Adam remained awake. He tried to interpret the dream through his own mind.

In her dream, Eve had given birth to a baby boy, which to her knowledge, was her first one. As soon as the baby was born, the obstetrician started laughing behind his mask. A nurse cut and tied the umbilical cord and hastily wiped the baby's wet body. Wrapped in a bundle, she handed it back to the doctor, who was still laughing manically. He removed his mask and Eve was surprised that he had a beard. But what surprised her more was that the doctor was her late husband, William. Hope rose in her heart, but it was short lived as she saw him leaving the room with the baby in his arms. She shouted after him, demanding her baby back, but no one seemed to care. She would have jumped off the bed to rescue her baby, but her arms were tied to the bed.

Exhausted from the effort of deciphering Eve's dream, Adam felt his body slipping into a deep sleep. He placed one hand under Eve's neck and curved his body against hers.

When Eve's eyes adjusted to the bright light pervading the room, she realized that she was alone in bed. From her bathroom came the muffled sound of running water. Satisfied, she smiled and stretched. A mild muscle ache reminded her of the unrestrained lovemaking of the night before. A warm, tingling wave of excitement rushed through her body, causing her an unruly, swift arousal. She yawned, letting a satisfied moan out in the process.

"You're awake," Adam said, poking his head out.

"And you are dressed," she complained. "So soon?"

"My darling fiancée, it's nine forty-five." He knelt by the bed and kissed her. "I wish I could stay forever, but I have to meet my father," Adam said, taking her hands in his damp ones, and kissing them on both sides.

Eve understood, but she liked to tease him. *I will have him for a few more minutes,* she thought, *minutes that I want to feel loved.*

"What's wrong with that? Staying forever, I mean."

Adam laughed.

"Please, don't go yet!" Her whisper felt like an incantation in his brain.

Before he had time to answer, she started to undo his tie. Adam hesitated for a very short moment. His voice grew raspy. Any protests would be unconvincing and futile.

"Would love to stay forever more..."

Eve didn't miss the cue. She kissed him and he kissed her back. And that's all it took. With trembling, anxious fingers, Eve worked her way down to his fly. With his breathing increasing, Adam swiftly removed his clothing.

"I must warn you. I may not have time to come back before I catch the plane," he said.

Eve's heart soared with the sight of Adam's smooth nakedness on top of hers. She gave him a feline smile.

"I'd rather have the bird in hand than the one in the bush."

Adam groaned and plunged his mind and body into the ocean of love.

It was the perfect summer day that the city's inhabitants look forward to. The flowers looked as if they were dressed for a royal visit, even putting to shame species from much warmer climates. To complement the picture, the birds were in full concert. Their chatter was the first thing Eve's mind registered that late morning. Then the sound of the doorbell pealed through the house. That, she thought — changing her mind — must have been the sound that woke her. A jolt of profound expectancy and a new longing embraced her. Eve jumped out of bed. *Adam's back!*

The thought of putting on her sexy nightgown briefly crossed her mind. Instead, with a swift move, she grabbed the white cotton housecoat that Adam scarcely wore the night before. She had gone to sleep after Adam left, depleted and fulfilled at the same time.

Before she opened the door, she contemplated a seductive line. She didn't know why but a strange wicked attitude had gotten the best of her. She didn't recall having such thoughts before. But then again, she didn't remember being as happy as she was now.

All erotic thoughts fled Eve's mind when she opened the door and stood nose to nose with a woman in a tailored two-piece business suit. The woman gave Eve a quick once over. Eve knew she looked dishevelled enough to warrant the look. For one short moment, she directed her gaze downwards to the woman's shoes, which appeared to have left some snake rotting skinless somewhere. Overall, the woman's looks were impeccable. If her mind had been rested, Eve would have made the connection to her identity much quicker. The confidence this woman had led Eve to recognize her.

*Alicia. The ex.*

She had seen her that night at the restaurant, mostly from behind. That was enough to be certain this was the same person now standing within arm's reach. To properly introduce herself would have been redundant. It never crossed Eve's mind that things would come to this moment, but it was obvious some kind of confrontation was on this woman's agenda.

Eve took a step forward to deter Alicia from stepping into the house.

Rather than stepping back, Alicia lifted her chin a notch higher.

"May I help you?" Eve asked.

"I have a feeling I don't need to introduce myself, but for the records — I'm Adam's wife."

"Then I might be of assistance to you. Mostly, to update your records. You are Adam's *ex*-wife. I take it your marital status didn't catch up with you. Or perhaps it hasn't sunk in yet," Eve replied.

"Actually, you've got it wrong. It's this misunderstanding that brings us — you and I — face to face. I have a very legitimate reason to believe that I'm not the one who is not updated. Nor the one who lives in a fantasy world, dear Ms.—"

Eve wouldn't help her complete the sentence.

"Or else I wouldn't be here in this delicate posture."

"I don't recall inviting you here. Now you must excuse me," Eve said, and gestured to the intruder that the conversation was over.

But Alicia was not finished. "Perhaps you have my intentions wrong. While I benefit indirectly, I'm here to do you a priceless favour."

"Oh, please. Take it with you. Don't you think that's a little tacky, given the circumstances?" Eve was fuming by now.

"Not at all. When family matters are at stake, I would endure even more pain or awkwardness. I don't mean to be cruel, but as you don't give me a choice, I will state this simply and briefly."

Eve was astounded by the woman's impertinence. She had said in plain words that she was not buying what she was selling and she still persisted in bothering her.

"Adam and I reconciled."

"Really? When? During the night?"

"I'll pass on your insensitive comment because you don't know any better at this point."

"Oh, thank you. You don't know how much your benevolence means to me. Now that you delivered your punch line, would you mind leaving my house and tending to your own business?"

"This *is* my business," Alicia said. "And part of it is to make *you* mind *your* business and leave my husband alone. Yes, Adam and I reconciled, and I'm afraid he didn't have the guts to tell you. I realize, and safely assume, that you'll be disappointed about losing such a *precious liaison*, but since he doesn't have the backbone to end his 'escapades', I'm the one who has to sort out the confusion he creates."

Eve hardly could suppress a vulgar expletive. What she really wanted to do was push this woman out of her house and close the door. She heard that in some divorces, one of the parties passes through the denial stage. Adam was justified in trying to escape the traps laid by this woman. Adam not having strength of character? This woman must be talking about a different person. This was too much for an angry woman — an ex at that — to understand. If Eve had one shred of concern about his gallantry and honesty, she would have gotten married in the middle of the night as Adam suggested.

"You're right about one thing," Eve said. "There is a misunderstanding. However, it's on your part. You need to accept the fact that Adam is through with you and has moved on. As for your calling my relationship with Adam a 'precious liaison' you have no right to make such comments. But, for your peace of mind, you should know that I'm not after Adam's money. Now take your 'good intentions' and leave my house," Eve said and took a step backward to close the door.

As Eve removed her left hand from her pocket, Alicia blinked in surprise as a bright sparkle hit her like a lightning bolt. She masked her reaction as best as she could. She inched forward.

"What if I tell you that *I know* that your intimate adventure last night with my husband was your first and only episode? Would that make you reasonable enough to listen to what I came here to say?"

No one else could know that Adam and she had made love for the first time the night before. Eve hadn't had the chance to tell anyone. Did Adam let it out? She stood her ground. She reminded herself there is nothing this woman could say that would impact her. She had Adam's love on her side. She didn't see the need to defend herself.

"Yes, you heard that right. Adam told me everything this morning. Some details of which I had no interest in knowing," Alicia said, her voice softening a degree. "Look, I'm trying to tell you that Adam and I patched things up. Something came up last week, and he agreed on ending our separation. It happened when it was almost over — in the eleventh hour, so to speak. As you may know, this wasn't our first separation — who knows if it's the last. But we were able to meet halfway and put things back on track. Adam made some promises, and I was able to forgive him."

Alicia's smirk had disappeared. Her smile was sincere and the moist gleam in her eyes was quickly wiped away before it could roll down her cheeks.

"He wanted to call you with the news from China. I insisted that you deserve better and he agreed to meet you in person and tell you." She shrugged. "I suppose that he wanted *something else* to happen instead. What needed to be said was left to the wind."

Alicia, Eve knew, was not a saint. Or anything close to that, from what she had witnessed that night at the restaurant or learned from Adam. She almost heard Adam saying, "Don't be a fool. Don't listen to her." She held onto that thought as though it was a lifeline. Alicia's strategy was not going to work. Eve knew that Adam wouldn't discuss the intimate details of the night they spent together with anyone, let alone Alicia. She made an effort to ignore the doubts in her mind. The faraway look in Adam's eyes the night before, his musing, pensive gazes into empty space at times, as though he couldn't help it. Eve deliberated. If she chose to believe Alicia, she must distrust Adam. If she chose to believe Adam, she could get hurt. Why couldn't things have just stayed the way they were last night?

*Smile and don't show what's in your heart*, Eve heard Grandma Evelyn advising. If Eve was disturbed by Alicia's information, she tried to not display it. She had no idea how Alicia found out the details of the night before.

"Suppose any of this is true, I'd accept Adam's apology. He can call me and set things straight." Sensing that Alicia was not finished with her story, Eve continued, "He struck me as a responsible adult not a snotty, unruly child who someone else has to make amends and compromises for. If he doesn't call me, I'll contact him for clarification."

"No. Don't do that. Please, don't contact Adam." Alicia's voice began to tremble. "There is more about Adam that you don't know. I feel like I'm betraying his confidence by unveiling his secrets, but at this stage, my personal pride is not as crucial as the situation my family is in," Alicia said. "I didn't come with the intention of unsettling you, but I felt that you must know. Adam suffers from a mental disorder. He was diagnosed with this many years ago, when he was young. His parents believe it was triggered by a love affair gone sour. The girl he was dating took off with another guy leaving Adam heartbroken. He was shattered and his mind snapped. He spent three harrowing months in a psychiatric hospital. I guess, he didn't tell you about that."

Eve's heart sunk. "Actually he did, but..."

"Oh? I never knew he ever talked to anyone about *that*." Alicia fumbled in her purse, extracted a tissue and dabbed at her eyes. "For my part, I was in the dark about his mental affliction for about two years after we got married. With proper medication, it's hard to notice if anything is amiss. When I fell in love with him, he looked perfectly sane — the perfect Mr. Right. Of course, his family kept his secret safe. Who could blame them?" Alicia explained.

"One can only imagine what a shock I had on our second anniversary, when out of the blue I not only discovered his little secret but he also told me that he wanted a divorce."

With Eve's attention captivated, Alicia gained terrain.

"My in-laws, extraordinary people who are like parents to me, were devastated by his outrageous decision on one hand, but relieved on the other. The event gave them the opportunity to share his condition with me. It was up to me at that point to leave the marriage with my dignity intact, or I could wait, as they suggested, until his 'airs' — as his father calls Adam's antics — were over and done with, and Adam would be back to normal."

More dabbing.

"Well," she continued, "I loved him before I knew all this, so I chose the second option and went through it three more times. I couldn't give up on my husband just because he had a condition he couldn't control. I knew he didn't want to hurt me. It was his sick mind that upset things, not him. From what his parents have said, since he was rejected by a woman he loved deeply, insecurity engulfs him periodically so he rebounds to that state, even if his present relationship is stable." She shook her head. "Each time this occurs, he finds himself a good-looking woman — always a strawberry-blonde one, the complete opposite of his old flame — and imagines himself falling in love with that woman. He showers her with ridiculous pricey gifts and money and a couple of months later, when the romance fizzles out, he comes back to me full of regrets and promises."

"And you took him back each time," Eve concluded, her mind still stuck on Alicia's mention of the "ridiculous pricey gifts." Like the ones Adam showered her with the night before. And before that, Eve thought of the diamonds around her neck.

Alicia looked confused. "Why not? Why does anyone take his or her cheating spouse back? I suppose there isn't one simple answer. I still believe in honouring my marriage vows. It has its moments of trial and hardship. No marriage comes with full satisfaction guaranteed.

"Perhaps I feel responsible for the thousands of employees under our joint leadership. You see, the collapse of our marriage would surely lead to Carstone's disintegration. Inevitably, those people would be jobless. But mostly, I believe that love has its own magic power. The least I can do is to find understanding in my heart to accept, forgive, and forget Adam's transgressions. With the help of medication and tender support, Adam has long stretches of time between episodes," Alicia continued.

"This time is going to be different, though. We are adopting a child — a baby boy, from Russia. Last week I learned we have the approval at last! Adam promised he would not change his mind this time around — like a few years ago, when he got cold feet just the night before we were all set to go and pick up a baby from Romania. If things work out well, one day we'll adopt a second child. Adam was thrilled when I called him with the news in China, which, by the way, increased his longing for the reconciliation. We could've adopted years ago when we learned that we couldn't conceive." Alicia's face brightened as Eve's flattened. "We're leaving today for Europe, where we'll spend as much time as necessary for our baby to be ready to travel with us. Adam is so happy with the prospect of starting a family. He is so good with children. It gives me the confidence that it will help Adam's mind stay on the right track for a long, long time."

"I can see that," Eve said.

She could see it. She didn't like how the conversation had turned around, but the clarity it gave her was overwhelming. Adam had used her in the most appalling way. Was the vague, faraway look in his eyes she observed the night before a glimmer of him losing control? She didn't want to believe Adam was as unstable as Alicia said he was. Perhaps it was more of a controlling manoeuvre on his part. She could understand how a love deception could cause a mental breakdown but not the off and on behaviour Alicia described.

"I ask that you not contact him," Alicia continued. "At this moment, his mind is the most fragile. While he made up his mind to start a family, I believe he is also torn about 'breaking up' with you," Alicia said. "We had lengthy conversations on the phone this week about his feelings for you. He praised you as being an intelligent, honest person who was not interested in his bank account and who deserves compensation for involving you in a doomed relationship." A mixture of painful humiliation crossed Alicia's face. "Yes, he was confiding in me and consulting with me. His wife! Can you imagine? He was fretting on the phone asking me if providing you with a new SUV was enough of a gift for the suffering he caused you."

At that moment, it was impossible to tell that Alicia was the very same haughty woman who had set foot in Eve's house moments earlier. She looked pitiful. With half her makeup washed away, she had aged ten years in ten minutes. The smeared mascara underneath her eyes gave her the air of a housewife, caught at her most untidy hour. The mighty woman who came to her door huffing and puffing indignation from her nostrils seemed to have diminished in stature by the minute.

*She's just a woman,* Eve thought. She's a victim caught in the web of love and sickness, pride and money. Certainly not someone to envy. She felt sick to her stomach. Hours ago, she considered herself fortunate with the last piece of happiness in place. All of that was gone, vanished. It was obvious she had to put the past four months behind her. She had lived through worse times than this and survived. She would obliterate this from her mind, she decided. One night of foolish sex wouldn't damage her permanently. But first and foremost, she would do the right thing.

"Here. Give Adam his presents for me," Eve said, with as much determination as she could muster. With automatic steps, she turned around and grabbed the cell phone from the kitchen. Coming back she also fetched the keys of the SUV. Finally, she took the ring off her finger and thrust it into Alicia's hand.

"No offence, but I'm sure I could live just fine without your husband's sick generosity..." Eve said, her voice trailing off just as the other woman interrupted.

"Oh, my Lord. This is *my* engagement ring."

"What?"

"I can't believe he did *this* again," Alicia said, checking the ring from all angles, her face crumbling with visible anguish. "He told me he keeps it in a safe deposit box at the bank." She clasped her mouth with her free hand. "In 1982, Adam took me on a surprise trip to Singapore. He proposed to me there." She managed a frail smile. "Even then he was the type of person who made decisions on the spur of the moment. I was so infatuated with him and his exciting life that it didn't cross my mind to question his impulsiveness. When I saw this ring, I fell for it. He said that Singapore adorns all Hollywood celebrities with their jewelleries. He bought the ring on the spot. The salesman was so pleased with the rapid sale that he gave Adam fifteen per cent off on the spot." She almost snorted. "Its enormous value apparently didn't stop Adam from offering it to another woman when we separated for the second time. She felt *very* offended when I took it back from her," Alicia explained. "How can I forget this and forgive him for another humiliation?"

Robot-like, Eve shoved the rest of the things into Alicia's scooped hands.

"Perhaps like other times," Eve suggested curtly.

"Yes, perhaps like other times." Tears bathed Alicia's cheeks anew.

"Now, please leave," Eve said. "I have nothing else that belongs to Ad—your husband. And don't worry, I have no desire to contact him."

"You don't know how much I appreciate your help," Alicia said, biting her lip. She turned to leave. "But…I'm not sure if we proceeded in the right fashion though. I don't think *I* should be giving these to Adam."

"And why not?"

"It just occurred to me that by taking these back, he would know that I got involved and cleared things up for him. Adam probably intends to send you a letter acknowledging these gifts as the proper compensation."

Eve thought about this as she massaged her temples. *Why should I care? I'm not a marriage counsellor.* Though Alicia did have grounds for concern, it would be simpler to just close the door behind her and avoid his phone calls.

*Who cares about my wounded heart?* Eve thought.

"I think *you* should send Adam all of these along with a short note stating that *you* had second thoughts about your relationship. This way, it would give his fragile mind a most welcome break. Yes, unquestionably, this is the best thing to do."

"So, I would be 'breaking up' with him."

Alicia's smile flattened. "Do you mind?"

Eve was silent for a moment. The gaze in her narrowing eyes passed the other woman's shoulder, and focused on a distant, imaginary point. She shook her head.

She thought she heard Alicia saying something about taking the car to return to the company…something about gratitude… and thankfulness.

Eve wished all this were only a bad dream. A sequence of her niggling nightmare.

Yet she was sure that what just happened was real.

And that she had lost...

Up in the air, things seemed to settle. Dinner had long been served; extra drinks were delivered at the discretion of flight attendants. The thriller, *Lethal Weapon 3,* flickered on the silver screen and was entertaining those who were still awake. The fussy infant's cry from the adjacent seat rose when his mother's appeasing pleas couldn't soothe his anxiety. Alicia struggled to catch some sleep. Not all the money in the world helped when business class was full. She had received a phone call and had to leave her seat to find a quieter place to tend to that conversation. While there, she made two more calls. The news was good with promises of progressing into great. She forced a smile back at the apologetic mother and her little tormentor and mentally scowled at Adam, who was sleeping soundly, in business class section, with a smile etched on his face, seatbelt buckled across his lap.

Nearly two weeks had passed since Eve's life fell into disarray. She did not make a federal case out of it, complain, blame, or burden anyone else with the turmoil her error in judgement caused. The emotional chaos she created was her cross to bear. With each passing day, her conviction grew stronger and stronger that her situation was a result of her reckless judgement. Adam? Adam was someone she didn't know. She only thought she knew him, but the facts contradicted her. He was what he was, the mentally ill man exempt from responsibility.

She had to concentrate on getting her life back on track now. It took a great amount of willpower and stamina not to mentally collapse. She had to stop analyzing the breakup. It was of no help. What was done belonged to the past.

It was not the tactic Mike and Crista suggested for closing the "tale of Adam". When they promised to keep out of it, Eve was more than content. Crista had expressed her desire to get her hands around that "crook's neck." It seemed to Eve that her friend's reaction was subdued compared to the day Crista found her in an awful state — totally crushed in spirit.

That day, Crista had called Eve several times, each time getting a busy ring. She was excited to see how Adam's visit had gone, but more pressing was the question of whether or not she would need to pick up Anthony from school again. She had no idea of the real reason Eve was not answering her phone.

Shortly after one o'clock, she had the feeling something was not right. She let herself into the house to witness an odd sight. Eve was in a trance, the bleak, straight stare in her eyes brought back memories of another dark time. It was as though she had crawled back into her widowhood shell. She had looked like that after Williams's urn went into the ground.

Crista couldn't convince Eve to lie down on the couch, to take a shower, or eat. It was only when she mentioned that it was almost time to pick up Anthony from school that Eve started moving about restlessly, randomly tending to small chores. She offered a few succinct details of the whole deplorable situation at Crista's insistence.

"What's done is done. No use in losing tears over a charlatan," Crista said. She then suggested contacting Adam on his cell phone and was surprised to see that her friend wasn't opposed to the idea. Only doubtful.

"You think so?" she asked.

"Definitely. Who knows how honest and truthful or ill-intentioned that woman was? Every story has two sides," Crista said.

Eve showed the expensive ring to Crista. Eve never mentioned the car. She thought it was ridiculous to admit that she was gullible enough to accept a car. "The gift" was no longer parked in her driveway by the time Crista showed up. Alicia must have come by taxi and left with the SUV. Of all the things Eve handed to Alicia to give back to Adam, she picked up only the car keys.

Alicia made her promise not to contact Adam, but Crista said that she didn't need to keep that promise. Eve felt a gnawing feeling that tugged at her insides, but she knew Crista was right. But who was going to protect *her* interests? Surely not Adam, with his mental sickness.

In the middle of dialling, she backed off. "No, I can't do it. I need to wait for his call. I made a promise, and I don't want to break it, because I can't handle the stress."

"Don't be silly," Crista said. "There are promises that only fools keep. This is one of those."

Eve was lost in thoughts. It occurred to her that Adam's story about the ring was exactly the same as how Alicia described the purchase of her engagement ring. Alicia could only have known those details if Adam had bought the ring in her presence.

"Let's forget about it," Eve said.

Crista lost her patience. "Give me his office number then. We may find out something from his secretary," she suggested. She grabbed the phone from Eve's hand and dialled. "May I speak to Mr. Adam Carry, please?" Crista asked in a sugary voice.

"Mr. Carry is not in the office. May I ask who is calling and what it is in regards to?"

Covering the mouthpiece with the other hand, Crista whispered, "How old did you say this Miss Annette is? This broad sounds insanely young."

"Sixties," Eve guessed.

"Can you put Miss Annette on the phone? Is she there?"

"No ma'am. Miss Annette is no longer working here. Who is inquiring please?"

"A close friend of Adam's," Crista said. "I would like to contact him as soon as possible, if *you* don't mind," she said.

"I don't mind, but I can't contact Mr. Carry yet. Mr. and Mrs. Carry left this afternoon for a vacation in Europe. Would you like me to take a message for him?"

Crista slammed down the phone. "Yes. Good riddance."

On the long road to recovery, Eve determined not to wallow in self-pity. She made a decision to go to Sydney as soon as things were settled for the exhibition.

With Crista and Mike gone for their "getaway for two," Eve found her days empty. She missed Crista's spontaneous calls and visits. When

Eve took Brandon for the weekend, she mentioned to his grandparents that she would soon be leaving for Australia. The Malone seniors promised they would let Crista and Mike know.

Crista called just days before Eve left town. "Have you heard from Adam at all?" she asked.

"Adam who?"

"I take it that you didn't. Hey, don't lose sleep over the jerk. The sun comes up each morning. It will just take a while for you to see it shining through these clouds. Think of it this way: No permanent damage was done."

*Yes,* Eve thought, *at least no permanent damage was done.* At least on the outside. Not even her best friend could guess how bruised she felt inside.

Anthony came to the table jumping with excitement. He plopped onto the chair and started eating ravenously. He knew that today his cast would come off.

Eve forced herself to swallow some scrambled eggs, which seemed to taste as greasy as the bacon. She had a busy day planned and was almost certain that supper would be her next meal. Suddenly, she felt sick. At first, it was just a hint of disgust in her mouth, but then with more vengeance, the food heaved up in her throat. She didn't rush to the bathroom until she was out of Anthony's sight.

When she lifted her head and looked in the mirror, she was shocked by what she saw. The skin on her face had faded into a pale-fleshy tone. Her reflection blurred as tears filled her eyes. A second episode came on as unexpected as the first.

Pounding on the door brought Eve back to her senses.

"Mommy, Mommy what happened?"

"Nothing, darling. I'll be right out," she said, trying to sound natural. On the other side of the door, she could hear Anthony's frantic whimpers.

She quickly cleaned the sink and washed her face with cold water. She put on a smile and opened the door.

"See, I'm okay, honey."

"Mommy, please don't die," Anthony cried and embraced her. "I don't want you to die."

Eve's smile, as phony as it was, disappeared.

She knelt and hugged her son. She had no idea that her son feared losing her, too.

"Darling, I'm not dying. I bought a different kind of toothpaste with a yucky taste that made me throw up. That's all. See? I'm just fine."

For the third time, she read the warning: *If you think you may be pregnant, please advise the X-ray technologist.* They were waiting in the little change room for Anthony's name to be called when she took notice of the warning on the wall. *Oh, my God. Oh, my God,* her mind kept repeating. *I may be pregnant...I feel pregnant.* And finally, *I am pregnant.* She felt just like the other times. She had been sleepy and tired recently, but she had blamed the feeling on her strained nerves. And now she was plagued by the unmistakable pregnancy queasiness.

With the cast finally removed, she drove Anthony to school. Then she bought a home pregnancy kit. She was not sick. She was giving life.

*Great,* Eve thought. She was having Adam's baby. The realization hit her hard. He had fooled her into believing he was not able to conceive when *that* was the very thing he really wanted: to impregnate her and then to take away her baby. Eve had this vision of him planting her baby in Alicia's arms nine months from now. She was certain that Adam knew what he was doing. Eve wouldn't be fooled now of his intentions.

*What am I going to do?*

Dr. Summer posed the same question, the next day. "There is evidence of pregnancy," he said.

Eve's reaction was unreadable.

"Considering the date of your last period, you may be as far as—"

"Sixteen days. I'm exactly sixteen days pregnant. That part I'm not confused about."

"Oh?"

"Please don't get the wrong idea. I spent on night with this man, but it was not a one-night stand. He courted me for a few months. I thought we were in love with each other and suddenly he vanished from my life. Actually, he went back to his wife," Eve said. "He was separated when I met him. He had me convinced that reconciliation was not in the cards for him. And here I am, pregnant."

"What are you going to do?"

Eve blinked, breaking her dazed expression. "I'm having the baby, I guess. You know how I feel about abortion."

"Do you plan to discuss the pregnancy with the father?"

"Of course not."

Her terse answer made the doctor more tactful. He was too seasoned not to recognize that Eve was unusually defensive. But if she wanted this baby to replace the one she lost after her husband's death, she would be misleading herself.

"Believe me, it's not selfishness that's sworn me to secrecy. It's fear. The fear of losing the baby. My chances to keep the baby are practically zero. The father is very rich and has a wife who can't conceive. Wouldn't that make you a bit fearful?" Eve gave a shallow laugh. "You see, he lied to me that his marriage was over because he was infertile. I can see that he would take my baby away from me and they would raise it as their own. Do you understand my fear?"

The day Eve and Anthony left Edmonton, she gave directions to the taxi driver to an address she only vaguely recalled. It was for George and Janet Carry's house. One evening, before Adam went to China, he took her for a drive to show her the "outback of Alberta," as he put it. He hinted that he had in mind a place to build a dream home. On their way back, Adam cut through a secluded area where his parents lived, an area where the homes resembled palaces.

Turning onto Preston Cove, Eve glimpsed the impressive, English-style house on the left. She felt her stomach churning. She wondered how much Janet knew, if anything, about her son's ultimate deceit. Before the door opened, she made up her mind that she would be polite and keep the visit short.

She need not have worried.

Margaret, the housekeeper, opened the door and Eve introduced herself. After her inquiry about Mrs. Carry, the woman said that Mrs. Carry was resting for the moment. "Janet broke her right leg last week and is hardly able to move now."

Eve felt relieved that she didn't need to face Janet Carry. When she spoke, she was surprised she sounded so natural.

"There is no need to disturb Mrs. Carry at all. I'm here to deliver this parcel for her son. I'm leaving the country today. I assume that leaving it here is as good as with him. Have a good day and please give Mrs. Carry my best wishes."

The flight from Edmonton to Vancouver was smooth with no significant events other than Anthony getting sick in the airbag shortly after departure. On the second plane, towards Honolulu, Anthony bumped his head in the washroom when the plane hit an air pocket. A flight attendant brought him some ice to apply to his head and a colouring book.

After they boarded the connecting flight, Anthony seemed to relax and made friends with a little boy three rows behind. He forgot about the bump on his head. Later, exhausted, he finally fell asleep.

A nun was sleeping next to Eve. Eve closed her eyes, agonizing over her thoughts until she too finally fell asleep.

She woke up with a jolt only to see that everyone around her was being violently jerked from one side to the other. Panic rose as each second passed and sleeping passengers started to wake up and fully comprehend the situation. The lights went on and a voice streamed through the speakers.

"Attention everyone! This is your captain, Scott Hills, speaking. We are experiencing some turbulence. Please return to your seats and fasten your seat belts. If we lose altitude, and the oxygen masks drop, ensure that you put one on yourself before proceeding to help children or others who might depend on you. Please remain calm and pay attention to the flight attendant's instructions."

"Oh, God," Eve said closing her eyes. "Please, God don't punish Anthony for my transgressions."

"Ma'am, are you all right?" A flight attendant was patting Eve's shoulder, trying to get a response. She pressed the service button. Another flight attendant arrived with a cold compress and applied it to Eve's forehead.

"Ma'am, do you hear me?"

"I thought she was sleeping," the nun said. She then turned her attention to Anthony, who had woken up and unbuckled his seat belt to go to the washroom. "Wait a few more minutes," she instructed in a soft tone and refastened his seatbelt.

Just then, Eve opened her eyes. She slowly took in her surroundings. Her first instinct was to check on Anthony, but the friendly nun assured her she had already done that.

As she waited for her brother at Arrivals, Eve checked her face in a small mirror. She was satisfied that her cheeks had a close-to-natural tone. *You pulled yourself together all right*, the mirror reflection said. Yes, she had a big scare on the plane. She smiled down at Anthony and noticed a concerned look on his face. "What's the matter, darling?"

"Mommy, were you scared that the plane was going to crash?"

Eve imitated Mike's voice as she replied, "Me? *Noo!*"

She knew he was questioning her about the second time the plane went through turbulence, when they both were awake. Eve was surprised by how confident she sounded. Indeed, she was not as scared as the first time, when she had fainted. It was in that moment that she decided she wouldn't be dragging her children across the ocean for a vacation any time soon. Then a new thought crossed her mind. Her children! Up until now, she hadn't thought of the life inside her body as a child. *Her* child.

"There you are!"

Eve hadn't noticed someone moving directly towards her. She took a second look, her mouth falling open. He looked like a much older version of Garry.

But it was Garry. Apparently the younger version of him no longer existed.

"Jessie?" Eve asked, but she knew the answer.

"Last night. In her sleep. We didn't expect it so soon…"

In a flash, Eve was in her brother's arms.

"No. No. *No!* Please don't tell me I'll never speak with my sweet Jessie again," Eve cried.

And in the next moment, Eve turned pale. Garry caught her before she hit the ground.

They stood there in each other's arms, in grief too deep for words to describe, too raw for the mind to accept, as tears poured down their cheeks. Anthony was clinging to his mother.

"Mommy, why are you crying? Mommy, are you okay?"

Anthony's plea pulled her back from her despair. At the same time, Dr. Summer's gentle advice came through: "You must stay away from stress of any kind to avoid pregnancy complications or miscarriage."

The days that followed in her brother's household felt numb and hopeless. The family focused on giving solace, comfort, and counsel to Gloria, whose grief was beyond words.

The day of the funeral was, ironically, sunny. A considerable crowd gathered to pay respects to young Jessica Natalie Davis. Jesse's classmates came, each bearing a farewell rose. Their teacher organized them into a compact, obedient group. She was holding a box of Kleenex in one hand and a rose in the other. She was handing the Kleenex out, one after another and using many herself. Others who came were neighbours, colleagues, acquaintances, whose lives Jessie had touched to various degrees.

"…may the Lord rest her body in peace and raise her soul to heaven…"

Eve closed her eyes as her mind transported her back in time, when her husband's urn and the baby's coffin were lowered into the ground. The same words were spoken at that time but held less consolation.

In the last few days, she had made a Herculean effort to detach herself from time and space. Yet the moment she feared the most was here. She couldn't avoid it.

"...ashes to ashes..."

Eve felt an acrid smell in the air, a sour taste filling her mouth. And all of a sudden a hot sensation moved through her body.

And then the darkness took over.

"She's regaining consciousness!" Eve heard someone saying, not fully realizing what was happening. Her brother, she learned later, had been keeping a vigilant eye on her. He was standing between his wife and sister, supporting them both with his arms. As the coffin was lowered into the ground, he heard Eve mumbling something only to realize that she was fainting. In a flash, he summoned Gloria's sister, Corrine, and her husband who were standing not far behind.

"Thank you, Corrine," Eve was seated now in the back of the car. "I still can't believe this is real."

"None of us can, darling. Fortunately, these kind of tragedies sink in slowly or else they would consume people," Corrine said.

Eve eyed her. Corrine was in her last trimester, and it appeared to her as if she was uncomfortable with the thought of sharing her joy in the midst of these sombre circumstances.

Eve couldn't be more wrong.

"Good of you to come, Eve. My sister is very fond of you and...I believe with all of your experiences she will be looking to you for help in her healing process. I hope you don't mind. Helping, I mean. I would do it myself, but as you know, Gloria and I don't always see eye to eye on things. Besides, I suspect my sister will find it very difficult to embrace my little one when she just lost Jesse."

Gloria always had a big heart where family was concerned. Eve knew the two sisters were not the best of friends, due to the unfair distribution of their parents' wealth and support to each sibling. Couldn't they just put aside differences and overcome the hostility?

About two weeks after Jessica's funeral, something reminded Eve of that conversation. She was helping Gloria organize a photo album that chronicled Jessica's short life. A few of the last pictures were taken at Maggie's birthday party. Maggie was Corrine's ten-year-old daughter from her first marriage.

"Maggie must be at the end of her patience waiting for a little sister or brother," Eve observed.

Gloria shrugged and busied herself with the pictures.

"Does Corrine know what she's having?"

Again, Gloria didn't reply.

It was then Eve recalled the conversation with Corrine.

"This is the last picture of Jessie. I took it three days before she was gone," Gloria said, as if her daughter was off to summer camp. She placed the picture where it belonged — at the end of the journey. Without another word, she went to the serving table, poured half a glass of brandy and retired upstairs.

For a long while, Eve watched after her sister-in-law. Gloria was drowning her pain in liquor. Today was not the first time she had noticed that. She had suspected this from their past telephone conversations. She hadn't expressed her concern to anyone yet. She was hoping that, in a moment of sobriety, Gloria would recognize that alcohol was not the best catalyst in dealing with her loss. Also, Eve couldn't help but notice that, since Garry had returned to work, he was working very long hours. Perhaps he buried his pain in a room at the back of his mind where he could deal with it in small increments. While Gloria's drinking was not a viable solution, Garry's running away from dealing with the enormous grief only added to the problem.

Eve found herself in the middle of a very taxing situation. A seed of realization formed in her mind: Moving away from Edmonton was not really "coming home."

Anthony's welfare had to be considered, also. She brought him into a situation of intense sorrow. Schooling arrangements were another matter. Anthony finished grade two when they left Edmonton — where it was now summer vacation — but in Australia, the school year was not over until December. She needed to make a decision.

Her financial situation caused constant anxiety as well. Nora Murray's reports were not encouraging. Sales were not satisfactory, and if that didn't change, she'd have to sell her property in Edmonton in a hurry to secure financial stability for a couple of years. She also found herself wondering about the new life she was secretly carrying within. How was *it* going to change her life? How was Anthony going to feel about *it*?

Despite the way this tiny life began, Eve found peace and calmness in its existence. Maybe it was meant to happen that way, she tried to convince herself, touching her lower abdomen and transferring warmth to it through her palms. If it's a girl, I'll name her Victoria, after the triumph of overcoming the difficulties before she came into this world.

"Oh, how much I'm going to love you, baby!

# Six

Waking up late one morning, Eve found her son playing a game with Mrs. Olsen in the family room. Garry's family had employed Mrs. Olsen since Jessica was six months old. Initially, she had been hired as a nanny, but over time, she had become like a member of the family. Eve liked and appreciated the older woman and knew that now, more than ever, she was indispensable to this household. Mrs. Olson knew exactly what had to be done to make the house run smoothly.

"Good morning," Eve said, glancing around the room as she descended the last few steps. She saw only the housekeeper and Anthony. "Sorry, I slept in." She bent to kiss her son's forehead. "Have you had breakfast?"

"Actually, darling Anthony didn't have breakfast yet. He *insisted*," Mrs. Olsen said on a cheerful note, "on having it with you."

Eve took a deep breath to push down the nausea. "That's very gentlemanly of you, darling. I'll set the table while you wash up and make your bed."

"You know, I've been thinking that you might want to arrange to have Anthony in some kind of activity with children his age," Mrs. Olsen said, following Eve into the kitchen after the boy went upstairs. "Maybe it's not my place to say this, but it breaks my heart to see him doing nothing until his cousin Dianne comes home from school. I feel bad when she is busy doing her things and can't pay attention or include him. He seems really bored."

"You're right Mrs. Olsen. I'm afraid my thinking is hazy these days. I thought it would be beneficial for him to have his vacation time, but I realize now that Anthony needs to interact with children his age. There must be some day programs for school-age children that are not strictly academic. I'll talk to Gloria about it."

"I'm sure there are," Mrs. Olsen said, as an upstairs door was closed with more effort than necessary.

Gloria was, as Eve had come to expect at this time of the day, wearing pyjamas underneath her housecoat. Her blonde locks were roughly tied at the back of her head, giving her pale face a shallow appearance. She descended the stairs slowly.

Eve's smile quickly left her face as she exchanged a knowing look with Mrs. Olsen.

*For Pete's sake,* Eve's heart cried out. *She's already had something to drink and it's only 9:40 a.m.*

Taronga Zoo was busy. A school group on a field trip was gathered at the monkey house, daring the animals to mimic them. Coming to the zoo was not her ideal pastime, but Anthony was happy. Now that she had loosened up a bit, Eve realized how imperative it was that her sister-in-law receive help with her grief. Eve decided to talk to Garry as soon as possible, to urge him to assist in his wife's recovery. Eve would help, but she could only do so much.

With that thought in mind, Eve breathed a little easier. But she was hit with another discomforting thought as they sat down for lunch, reminding her that, in her efforts to help others, she had forgotten about Anthony's needs.

"Mommy, why don't those kids talk like me?" Anthony asked between bites of French fries. "They sound funny."

"What do you mean?"

"They talk different than us. I don't think they understand what I say. Twice a boy asked me, 'Padon, padon,'" Anthony said, trying to imitate an Australian accent.

"Ah, don't worry, darling. In time, you'll get used to it. I used to speak that way too; did you know that?"

"But you don't anymore. I always understand what you say."

That evening, while Eve anxiously awaited her brother's return from work, she recalled Anthony's concerns. He had grown so observant lately, Eve realized. It was different than in the past summers when he was communicating in a small child's language, more through gestures than words. She told him not to worry, but even as she said that, she knew with certainty that to say "don't worry" didn't necessarily make things right. How many times was she going to lie to herself that this innocent child hadn't been impacted by her decision to move here permanently?

She was still debating over a solution to help Anthony integrate with the Aussie children when Garry arrived.

"I asked Mrs. Olsen to take the children out for ice cream. They had supper," Eve explained and signalled him to follow her. "Gloria is upstairs sleeping. I need to talk to you. It's actually kind of overdue."

They walked into the library where Eve sat next to him on a leather couch. The library served mostly as his home office and the room bore his signature — plain and simple.

"Let me be very blunt with you," Eve started. "Gloria drinks. A lot. I'm sure you know this. We all know how tough this is for the two of you, but for you two to grieve separately is an aberration. Gloria needs help. Your help. Grieving together is not easy, and it doesn't make the pain go away overnight. But it is more..." she grasped for the right word, "beneficial. Right now, it looks like you two are avoiding each other, almost as if you're blaming each other for Jessie's death. I think she needs an intervention of some sort, which only you can carry out, because your pain is as great as hers."

Garry held his face in his hands and sighed deeply.

"I tried. I talked to her several times. I understand how death can mess up a person's mind, and although I don't condone this vice, I can't totally blame Gloria for losing control. Her drinking problem started innocently enough after we got Jessie's diagnosis. I hate myself for having suggested that a drink would calm her down. We both had a couple of drinks after we put the girls to bed, and talked and talked for hours, turning the facts and the situation on all angles.

"After a while, I noticed that she had already been drinking before I came home and I insisted she stop drinking altogether. But it continued. We had awful brawls in the mornings, when the girls were out of earshot, and she was sober. Yet, nothing helped. For a while, I put all the hard liquor in there," Garry said, pointing to their father's huge walnut cabinet, "under lock and key. She bought her own and hid it. As selfish as I may sound, I am so glad your visit coincided with this awful time. You two always got along and I was hoping you could have a positive effect on her. At this point, I really don't know how her drinking problem can be fixed."

"Her drinking habit is not the problem," Eve interrupted. "Stop seeing it in that light. The *grieving* is the element that's destroying her. Help her through that, and she won't have the urge to drink anymore. For Pete's sake, she is not an alcoholic. Alcoholics don't need a reason to drink. She has an overwhelming reason to do so."

Eve watched her brother. It was terrible not to be able to help more. There were no words to be said, no deeds that could be done that had the power to erase the unbearable experience that had knocked down her brother's family.

Garry took a ragged breath. "You know, I never saw it that way. I have been so engulfed in my sorrow, I forgot that Gloria and I have our grief in common. This night won't end until I find a solution to salvage my family. It's my duty."

Garry embraced his sister. "Thank you for the reminder."

"I'm merely returning the favour. Remember?"

The next morning, when Gloria came downstairs, a half-empty bottle of liquor was on the table. Around the table were Garry, Eve, and Mrs. Olsen.

Gloria glared at Garry, "How *dare* you check my closet? Is this your idea of respecting someone's privacy? Or maybe someone put some weird ideas into your head," she said, giving a black look in Eve's direction.

Her harsh words almost made Eve flinch, but she maintained her position. She would take any accusation to stand firmly behind her brother. He had told her he would drive Dianne to school and Anthony to Corrine's. He was determined to take as much time off as necessary to help his family recover.

"If you're looking for this, come and get it." Garry said, holding up the bottle. "That is, if you don't want or need your family."

"Is that a threat?"

"It is if you want to take it that way. You need to choose. But by God, you will live with that choice."

"I didn't realize I had welcomed the enemy under my roof and at my table!" Gloria shouted, looking at Eve as she turned to leave. But Garry was quicker. He grabbed her arm and pulled her back.

Eve cringed at her brother's force. "Gloria, I did express my concerns about your drinking to Garry. I wanted to speak to you, but I just couldn't find an appropriate moment—"

"A sober moment is what you meant to say," Gloria filled in.

Garry sighed in exasperation. "Darling, I know how devastated you are right now. We feel—I feel the same—"

"No, you don't. Someone who feels my pain can't go back to work the week after they buried their child. And can someone who pays social calls to her friends or goes to the zoo possibly comprehend my pain? I'm not judging anyone's feelings so give me a break and don't judge mine. I'm grieving my way and if that includes drinking, that's my business," Gloria said, as tears of frustration rolled down her cheeks.

Gloria turned to leave, but Garry obstructed the doorway.

"Get out of my way. And tell your sister that if she feels offended by my actions, she is free to leave. No one is keeping her here. I would have peace knowing that no one is spying on me. And don't tell me she was doing it to help, because she can't help. And you know why? Because she doesn't know how deep my wound is. She never lost a child this age. Her situation wasn't the same. Her memories of her tiny baby are gone by now. How can it be compared with my grief of losing Jessie? Even losing a husband — could that be compared to the agony of losing the flesh and blood you gave life to? It's absurd to even try to compare our situations. You and your sister must recognize that." Gloria was pushing her husband now with both hands. "Now move out of my way!"

Garry's response came instinctively. He embraced his wife, and stroked her head, which she rested on his shoulder.

"Darling, I can't let you go. We must help each other through this. I know you don't mean what you say about Eve. She wants to help you — us. She can't be indifferent to what is happening here. I know I am to be blamed for letting the suffering take its toll on you. Please forgive me for that. Eve reminded me that I needed to look after you."

Gloria started sobbing, which prompted Garry to start crying, too. And, as if on cue, so did Eve and Mrs. Olsen. They were tears of loss, but they brought relief.

"I thought no one could help, because I thought I was the only one feeling such agony."

"I feel the same, darling. Jessie was part of me, too. That's why it's so important to talk about it with each other," Garry said.

"I want you two to share your pain with me," Eve said, embracing them both. "I'll do my best to understand. You both helped me once, remember? Please let me do the same now."

"Oh God, I'm so ashamed about what I said earlier," Gloria said, after she took a sip of her coffee. They were all sitting at the breakfast table for the first time since Eve came to Sydney.

"We know you didn't mean it, darling," Garry said, gently squeezing his wife's hand.

"Of course I didn't, but I despise myself for speaking so irrationally. If I think about the time when Eve was in pain, she didn't order me out of her house or say ugly words like that."

"I didn't do that because in my bereavement I refused to see anyone around me trying to help. I was so self-absorbed, which made the healing process even harder, believe me. But in the end, you reached me and I'm thankful for that. Once you understand the pain and share it with loved ones, it will feel less and less overwhelming. In time you'll heal; I know this."

It seemed to Eve that the confrontation had really helped. Gloria hadn't had a drink since then and slowly opened up to her husband and the others around her, which seemed to bring her great relief. With that and her sober mind she started picking up the pieces of her life.

Eve was amazed at how things changed and for the better. The pain was still there, but the atmosphere was not of pessimism and dejection any longer. What most surprised Eve was her own strength; she had not become a nervous wreck, despite the emotional torment she was exposed to.

Eve pulled out a lounge chair from the garden storage and lay down in the afternoon sun awaiting Gloria and Garry's return. They had taken Dianne on a week-long vacation in Melbourne. When they returned home, they looked closer, more contented. Garry worked normal hours, whereas Gloria worked for three hours every afternoon. The principal of the high school where she taught suggested she start with a reduced schedule, increasing her hours as she felt more confident.

It was a balmy, breezy day. Eve inhaled the rose-scented air. The garden looked majestic and heavenly. A professional gardener cared for it. Eve had never before noticed the garden's beauty.

Eve placed her sketching pad aside and closed her eyes for a few minutes. She had started to occupy her time with things that didn't require too much concentration or stress, as per Dr. Summer's advice.

The sound of broken glass woke her. "What's the matter?" Eve asked sitting up quickly. A few feet away, she saw Gloria standing by, a frozen expression on her face, a carafe filled with juice in her right hand, and a glass in the other. The second glass was now in pieces at her feet.

"Are you all right?"

"Mrs. Olsen said you were in the garden. I thought you might want some fresh juice. Sorry to wake you, but a glass slipped out of my grasp." She placed the carafe and unbroken glass on the table.

Mrs. Olsen came out quickly and then returned to the kitchen to fetch another glass.

"What it is?" Eve asked. "You look a bit upset. Come and sit down here with me."

"Well, some things still shake me up. About Jessie, I mean. When I came out and saw you on this lounge chair, I thought for a moment that you were Jessie. She looked like you, Eve. She did, you know...just like you looked when Garry and I started dating, except that you were older. The day Jessie died, she was lying on this seat right here. It was her favourite spot."

"Oh…"

"That's all right. I can talk about it now."

Mrs. Olsen came back, removed the broken glass and poured the juice for them.

Holding her glass tight, Gloria started, "In her last week, Jessie lay down most of the time. She was such a sweet girl, Eve. The day she died, she told me, 'Mummy, why don't you change the garden statuettes around? I get bored seeing them in the same place.' I told her that I'd call John, our gardener, and ask him to do that. She said, 'I know how it should be done', and showed me with her finger where each piece was best displayed. Garry wasn't home or we probably would have moved the statues by ourselves right then.

"Then Jessie asked me to help her get closer to the fountain. I knelt by her chair and took her hand and to my surprise, she got up. I followed her, holding the IV bag up high. She stopped in front of the fountain and said, 'Can you hear them Mummy? They have beautiful voices.' I asked, 'Who has beautiful voices, darling?' But she didn't answer, she just said, 'What a marvellous light!' I asked 'What light, darling?' This time she just pointed towards the fountain and the sky. 'This,' she confirmed. I assumed she meant the fountain and its water. She said she was tired and wanted to go inside to rest. I started to help her into her wheelchair, but she said she could walk by herself, so I just followed her with the IV pole. A few weeks earlier, we moved her bedroom downstairs into Mrs. Olsen's quarters so we didn't need to carry her up the stairs, but she told me she wanted to sleep in her old room this time. She walked up all those steps steady and with conviction. Mrs. Olsen and I walked behind, one with the IV bag and the other with the pole. We both thought we were witnessing a miracle.

"After she died, the doctor told us that Jessie's sight and hearing could have been heightened in the last hours of her life. Eve, she knew she was dying and didn't want to tell me so I wouldn't be saddened. How can a child be so considerate, so good, gentle, loving, and not a bit scared of dying?

"It was six fifteen when she went to her room and I realized she was supposed to take her medication. I asked Mrs. Olsen to bring it from downstairs. But Jess said, 'Mummy, please don't make me take it this time.' And I said, 'You must take it darling or else you won't get better. She said, 'I'm better, Mummy, don't you see? I'll be just fine.' And at that moment, I was convinced it was true.

"She asked about people she loved and missed. She asked about her dad, if he would be home soon. She asked about her grandparents — my mum and dad. About my sister and you and Anthony. She looked tired, so I said, 'We'll talk later, darling. You need to rest. She said, 'No. Not yet, not yet.' I said, 'I'll be sitting here until you fall asleep,' and took a seat by her bed. When I thought she was asleep, I left. Jessie's voice stopped me just as I reached the door. She said she wanted to see the dress you sent her, with her portrait, for her birthday. She loved it very much!

"Then she asked, 'Mummy, am I going to be an angel? You know, like Auntie Eve's baby after he died? When you came from Canada, you told me that baby Jacob died and became an angel...that when children die, they all become angels in heaven.' I went back to her bed and took her hands in mine, and said, 'Darling, you are not going to die. Your father and I won't let that happen. Don't forget that. If you are to be an angel, you are, here on earth, right now.'

"Her mouth stretched into a wide smile. 'I love you, Mummy, for saying that. And everything else. I want to rest now, but I can't fall asleep if you stay here,' she said, and those were her last words. I'll never forget her words and that smile…"

Eve knew what happened after that from her conversation with her brother. When he came home, Gloria was euphoric about what seemed to be signs of Jessie's recovery. But Garry knew better. He charged up the stairs to his daughter's room two steps at a time.

"I never heard a shout so deafening," Gloria continued. "How I got up the stairs, I don't know, but I remember opening Jessie's door to see Garry on the bed holding her body in his arms. I never saw your brother cry before. I felt at a complete loss watching him. The last thing I remember was Mrs. Olsen's voice, before I fainted. From then until after the funeral, I don't remember much."

Gloria didn't realize she was crying until she noticed Eve was crying.

"What do you think of arranging the statuettes just the way Jessie wanted?" Eve said, after their tears dried. "We can ask Mrs. Olsen to help."

"I'd love that. It's about time. I can't believe we haven't done it yet."

"Perhaps there is a time for everything."

"Darlings, this looks heavenly!"

"Garry!" Two startled voices greeted him.

He took turns kissing and hugging the two women. Then he said to his wife, "Our little angel would be pleased. She is watching from above, you know."

Though happy to see her brother and his wife healing, Eve knew another evening would pass without her being able to find the courage or appropriate moment to share her news.

The following evening Garry took everyone out for dinner, Mrs. Olsen included. Upon returning home, they sat down in the family room. Anthony and Dianne were playing a card game, their laughter rising above the adults' conversation. Mrs. Olson retired to her room.

The opportune moment for Eve to open up arrived when she least expected it.

She had actually been thinking she could hold back for another day when Gloria suddenly asked her, "What am I going to do when you return to Canada? Who will have tea with me after supper?"

"Well, actually, there is something I wanted to share with you. I'm staying in Australia," Eve said, glancing at Anthony who was engrossed in his game with Dianne. "I mean permanently," Eve whispered.

"When did you decide this? This is great news!" Garry said.

"I don't know exactly," Eve lied. "Maybe in the back of my mind the idea started growing after William's death. I don't know. Maybe I've come to the realization that family is more important than anybody else I left behind."

Eve knew the whole truth would come out eventually, but was not yet prepared for complete disclosure.

"I'm thrilled!" Gloria declared trying to keep her voice hushed.

"I'm so happy for you. Well, for all of us. Welcome home! This house is more than big enough for both our families," Garry said.

"Actually, I've been thinking about moving to *Bluehay*. For my work, I need a quiet place. I feel like the inspiration always found me when I was there."

"As long as you stay in Australia, where you live is totally up to you, darling," Gloria said. "I think your announcement warrants celebration."

If Eve was worried, it was justified. She was reminded once again that dealing with children required skilful tactics. How was she going to tell Anthony? She had enrolled him in a private school in Sydney at the beginning of August, and although the academic level was not demanding, he was constantly complaining. Every time Eve asked how school was, she braced herself for a disheartening answer.

The teacher, a competent, young woman, listened to Eve's concerns about Anthony's anxiety around the fact that he "talked differently" than the other children, and devoted extra attention to him. She praised him for little things he did or said. Later, on the playground, Anthony was harassed ruthlessly.

When the teacher told her about the bullying, Eve wanted to pull Anthony from the private school and enrol him in the public school. Garry said that, if this happened in a private school, it would be even worse in a public school.

"But he *was* in a public school back in Edmonton," Eve pleaded. "We should at least try."

"Children are all the same," Garry remarked. "If one starts teasing, the others always follow suit."

"I have to go now. I've decided to take Anthony away from school during lunch breaks. Maybe that will help—Wait a second," Eve's face brightened. "Alexia has two of her girls in home schooling. One of her neighbours teaches her children and Alexia's. Why didn't I think of that before? That would be perfect. A small group of children could be much better for him. Besides, Anthony already knows Bonnie and Dakota."

"Sis, try not to fret too much about this. There may be more solutions we just can't see right now. We have to look at it from all angles. Children adjust more easily than adults do. And don't forget that it's not as if Anthony has to learn a new language. It's just a petty accent; he'll pick it up in no time."

Eve laughed and hugged her brother. "Isn't that the truth?"

"You better work on your 'bloody' accent too, or else you'll be laughed at. And take better care of yourself. You look kind of pale and frail these days. I'm afraid I'll break a bone when I hug you."

For a moment, Eve debated whether to let out her secret then and there. Yet, for some reason, she just couldn't bring herself to do it.

"If you tell me that *this* was a coincidence, I'll leave," Eve said under her breath, as soon as Brian excused himself to make a phone call. Twice when spending time with Alexia, Brian had shown up. Although Alexia was nothing like Crista, this behaviour was reminiscent of something Crista would do.

"It's not a coincidence, but it's not what you're thinking either. I met Brian at the supermarket last week. He asked if I had any news from you. I couldn't lie; I said you were in town and—"

"We're having lunch here, today," Eve concluded, her voice low. "We will talk about this later." She saw Brian hang up the phone and head back.

Eve was curious as to why he wanted to talk to her. To apologize? To ease his conscience? It was hard to disguise her shaking hands and make decent conversation with the guy. And all of this after what… eleven years?

"Hmm?" Eve said, shaking off her thoughts.

"I said it's a nice day, don't you think?" Brian repeated his prosaic line when he was seated across from Eve.

"Yes, it is." *At least it started that way,* she thought. The past Tuesday at The Lagoon, their short encounter had permitted only a limited conversation, because Brian had his own table reservation with other people.

"I talked to Suzanne yesterday. She is delighted with Anthony," Alexia said, starting her dessert. "She said he's very polite, easygoing, and smart. All the girls have a crush on him."

Eve laughed for the first time since their meal began.

"I'm happy to hear that."

"What's going on with your son?" Brian asked.

"My son goes to Alexia's neighbour for home schooling. She teaches her daughter, disabled son, and two of Alexia's girls," Eve explained. "I'm so happy we finally found a solution to his schooling situation in Australia. He was teased mercilessly in private school."

"Why does he have to be in school? Isn't the school year over in Canada now?" Brian asked.

"I've decided to stay longer in Sydney. All things considered." She felt terrible about lying. "He can't just lose instructional time in the interim," Eve continued and right away regretted it. She didn't intend to let Brian know about any of her plans.

"Such a loss...about Jessie, I mean. I'm sure your decision to spend more time here is a blessing to Gloria and Garry."

The three of them were quiet for a few moments.

"Well, I need to run," Alexia said, and stood up. "I'm sure they have me on the missing person list by now."

Eve didn't want to be left alone with Brian, so she got up, ready to leave as well.

"Eve, you don't need to rush, I don't know about you, Brian, but Eve has time," Alexia added, before she departed.

"Actually, I'm going somewhere and don't want to be late," Eve said.

"They don't expect me at my office for a bit," Brian said, "I could drive you wherever you're heading. That is, if you didn't drive here."

She shook her head. "I'm walking to the Adelle Vo Clothing Gallery. It's not far from here."

"I'll walk you there."

They passed through the old Musshi Verdi market with its cluttered little stores and food stands, which Eve had loved to visit when she lived in Sydney. However, now the smell of overused, burned oil made her sick to her stomach.

"Want some ice cream? I presume you still like vanilla."

Eve smiled. "Sure, but a small cone for me." Once they were seated at a small round table under an old umbrella, Eve said, "You remembered that I like this flavour."

"I remember a lot of things, Eve," Brian said. "About our past, I mean. I don't know if you ever think about it, but I do." He laughed. "Not that it does me any good. If anything, it reminds me of something precious I lost and was never able to replace."

Eve was silent. Indifferent.

"When I heard about your husband's death, I felt terrible for you. I kept in touch with Alexia over the years. I understand you had a wonderful marriage. You were entitled to happiness."

*So were you.* Eve silently scorned him. She was only half listening to him. After all these years, Eve knew there was nothing left in her heart for this man. Yes, he was her "first true love" and she had thought, at one point, that he would be the "one." Yes, she was nervous when she saw him again. But no, there was no magic anymore. Surprisingly, she harboured no bitterness or regrets, either.

"Eve, did you ever think how our lives would have been if I hadn't strayed?"

Eve was aware of the meaning behind his question. He didn't say, "we parted" or "broke up". He said, "I strayed", which was the absolute truth. She appreciated the accuracy of his statement.

"Brian, I'll be honest with you. I don't know what you expect out of these 'accidental' meetings, but please don't get any false hopes. We share some memories, but as far as I'm concerned, that's all. In answer to your question, yes, there was a time, long ago, when I hoped we would be reunited, but that didn't happen and the time has passed." Eve continued, "I met William and started afresh. Moved on to a new phase of my life. It's possible, you know. Even after the loss of first love."

"Not for everyone, Eve. Not for me. Letting you go was the most dimwitted thing I ever did. Many times I ask myself how I could have sacrificed our chance of sharing something so special."

"I'm sorry to hear that."

"Don't be sorry for something you are not responsible for. I chose my path in life. I'm only sorry for the pain and anguish I caused you," Brian said. "I guess you wonder why I insisted on seeing you. I felt I owed you an apology."

"Apology accepted," Eve said. "People make mistakes, Brian. What we think is best at one moment sometimes ends up turning our lives upside down. But the positive side of it is that we learn from our mistakes."

*Are you talking from your own experiences?* Eve's conscience demanded.

Eve looked out the window, her H2 pencil in hand. Two black-faced monarch birds had broken her concentration. She watched as they wrestled over a morsel of food. How serene life was here! It hadn't changed since she lived here close to twenty years ago.

She knew she'd made the right decision to move back to Bluehay. Later on, after the baby arrived, she would move back into the city. It would be impossible to take care of the baby without help. For now, she was happy that Garry and Gloria didn't question her schedule of three nights and four days here and four nights and three days in

Sydney. She needed to work and they respected her independence. Anthony was also being cooperative, which was helpful.

The thought of her son made her pensive. It was not just how she had recently changed his life, but it was the fact that she did it without consideration for his feelings. Guilt engulfed her more often than not. Though he was content with the school arrangement, and tried to be brave, she suspected it was only for show. If Eve found any comfort in this new arrangement, it was that now Anthony and Garry could bond.

Anthony had stopped asking when they were returning to Canada. It impressed Eve how maturely he behaved when told about the "prolonged" visit. Eve had explained to him that they needed to stay longer and help his uncle's family, especially Auntie Gloria. It seemed the most natural explanation and he seemed satisfied with it.

The telephone rang through the quiet house, startling Eve. *Who would be calling her?* She always called in the evening and talked with everyone, as was their agreement, so no one disturbed her during her working time.

It was Gloria.

"Did I disturb you, darling? I just wanted to let you know that you have mail from Canada."

"No, I was taking a break. Where's it from?" Eve asked. She couldn't explain it, but she feared that one day a letter from Adam would arrive. Just the thought of him finding her mailing address made her heart beat faster. *Stop it!* she ordered herself.

"There is a letter from Crista and one with an artistic logo, from Nora Murray," Gloria reported. "I know you're uneasy about the progress of the exhibition, so when I saw her letter, I thought I better give you a call."

*Uneasy*? Eve thought, *No, I'm tormented.* The pieces she had displayed were the result of a year of hard work, which would bring in much-needed income. She was hoping to earn enough money that she wouldn't need to work for at least a few months after the baby came. Feeding her baby between brush strokes wouldn't be ideal.

"Great! Thanks so much for calling. I can't wait to see what news Nora has for me. I'll come back tonight."

She went to Sydney a day sooner than scheduled, and by the end of her visit, wished she hadn't come at all. Lying awake that night, Eve came close to hating herself for the decision to return to Australia.

The visit had started nice and calm with a delicious dinner of crab roulade with broccoli and cheese on the side. As usual, after dinner they all retreated to the family room where the adults joined the children with their games.

A game of cards was nearing its end when Garry mentioned, "A guy named Brian called here last evening. Is he the *same* person we know?"

Eve nodded. "The one and the same. What did he want?"

"I didn't ask, but he'll call again tomorrow evening. I didn't know you were coming tonight," Garry said. "I heard that the Malones wrote."

"Yes, just a few words, mostly reproaches. Crista wrote that my 'stubbornness' to stay away longer will reflect badly on her, because she doesn't like to write letters. She would rather call but the time zone difference irritates her." Eve took a long sip of tepid tea.

"Any good news from Nina Murray?"

Eve's face brightened. "Yes, actually impressive news! Almost unbelievable. She will go to Calgary alone...taking her work only, because almost all of my pieces have deposits on them. Imagine that!" Eve said. "She said that she'll sell the rest on the condition that the purchases are displayed in Calgary for the next two months, for the benefit of advertisement. She suggested that next time I should stipulate this on the contract. But of course, there won't be a next time. Nina doesn't know that..." Eve said, as her voice trailed off.

"What do we play next?" Gloria asked, trying to divert the children from the adult conversation.

"Monopoly!" Anthony and Dianne shouted simultaneously. They ran out of the room to fetch the game.

"Do Crista and Mike know about your moving here permanently?" Garry asked.

Eve assumed a casual air. Inside she felt miserable as the reality of a permanent separation from her friends hit her for the first time. She missed them terribly and felt guilty for keeping them in the dark. "No. Mike and Crista don't know we're not returning to Canada."

"Mom!"

All adults turned their heads in Anthony's direction.

He was a few feet away, his cousin holding the Monopoly game under her arm. From his expression, it was obvious he had heard part of the conversation.

Eve got up and handed her teacup and saucer to Gloria.

"Anthony, I wanted to talk to you about that but—"

"I don't want to stay here. I want to go back to Edmonton," his little voice trembled. "You said we were staying longer because Jessie died and Auntie Gloria needs our help, but you lied to me."

Eve inched closer, but he ran up the stairs, shouting, "Liar! Liar! I hate you! I hate you!"

Good to his word, Brian called Friday evening.

"Hello, Brian."

"Hello, Eve. Were you surprised that I remembered your brother's phone number?"

"A little," she said. *More that you had the nerve to use it.*

"I was wondering if you and your son would like to go out for supper this evening."

"I already had supper," Eve said. "Besides, my son is not home right now."

"Maybe ice cream then. Or a walk. Just you and me?"

Gloria lifted her head from her book, alerted, and implored her sister-in-law with a series of hand gestures that said, "Go ahead."

"All right."

Brian picked her up fifteen minutes later, during which time Eve tried, to no avail, to relax. She wasn't sure how to conduct herself around Brian after so many years. Certainly, she didn't wish to encourage him to pursue her by accepting his invitation.

He suggested a drive to Luna Park, but Eve refused because it was too reminiscent of old times. He settled for ice cream, which he bought from the old kiosk on the corner of Sierra Street and Gale Point. Cones in hand, they strolled into Crescendo Park and sat down on a bench close to the bronze statue of an anonymous athlete.

"I had a good time, Brian," Eve said later, as his car pulled in front of her brother's house.

"There seemed to be a few moments when you were not there with me," he said. "Is it so hard to share your thoughts with an old friend?"

The fact that Brian was able to read her mind took her by surprise. Until that moment, she thought her feelings were not obvious to anyone. The revelation made her realize what a caring person he was.

"Oh, Brian, I'm so sorry for not being an appreciative audience. You're right, but I assure you, it has nothing to do with you," she replied. She turned her gaze towards the house. There was a light on in Anthony's room. She let out a sigh.

Brian looked at her puzzled.

"I had a squabble with my son last evening. We're not on speaking terms. I'm afraid my motherly charm is fading."

"It can't be that serious."

"Anthony didn't know until last evening that *I* had decided to stay here longer. He wants to go back to Canada to his friends and the routine he knew there. He refused to talk to me or go to school today. At lunch time, Garry came and took him to work with him in an attempt to break his mood, but I don't know if it worked."

"I hope your son doesn't hold a grudge for too long," Brian said, as Eve got out of the car.

"I hope so, too."

# Seven

Crista was more fractious than curious. "She did what?"

"She got married. How many times do I have to tell you?" Mike responded.

"I heard you the first time. But…but how, when, and why? I mean…" Crista sounded downright incensed at him for being short of answers.

"You can listen to her message when you get home," Mike directed, but realized that Crista had hung up.

When Crista got home she played the message on the machine until she knew it by heart.

"I thought you would be pleased to hear that I got married. However, we will be staying here for a little longer. We miss you all. I'll keep in touch." She gave a new phone number and said a rushed goodbye.

"Mike, I know her too well. It's not like her to fall head over heels for someone in such a short time. And to tie the knot, on top of it. Something is not right with this picture."

"Maybe it's not someone she just met," Mike said. "She knows people down there, because she lived there before, remember? Didn't she tell you once that there was a guy before William? What's his name?"

"Brian," Crista supplied. "No, Eve wouldn't give the time of day to that shit-head."

"Maybe the guy has changed for the better and Eve had a change of heart."

Crista ignored her husband's remark. "Where's the number she left?"

Across two oceans, in a picturesque country house, Eve rolled in her sleep. When the phone rang, she wasn't worried. Anthony was sleeping in the next room.

She answered after the second ring.

"Crista? Do you know what time it's here?" Although Eve's voice was croaky from sleep, it didn't sound annoyed. She could never be upset with Crista, especially now when she owed her an explanation.

"What do you mean you got married? Is this a joke?" Crista asked without preamble.

Eve laughed. "I know it's quite a surprise, but it's true. I got married," she said, and paused to give Crista time to register her words. "Brian and I were married last month."

"Last month? Brian? The same guy who cheated on you years ago?" Crista's voice was downright disparaging.

Eve laughed. "Same one, yet not the same."

"Sure."

"He's really changed, Crista. He turned into a really good person. He still cares about me after all these years."

"And how about your feelings for him, girlfriend? Were they rekindled overnight?"

"Yes. Does that surprise you?" Eve asked.

"Frankly, yes. Adam broke your heart, your wound healed, and you fell in love in record time. An old boyfriend, I grant you that, but still..." As usual, Mike was signalling her to watch what she was saying. He imagined Eve's new husband might be awake by now and listening.

"I'm sorry. It's so rude of me to not congratulate you. I know you'll bring out the best in Brian. By the way, what's your last name now?"

"Kid. K-I-D."

Crista couldn't suppress a chuckle. "No kidding, Mrs. Kid."

"Congratulations, Eve. Forgive my wife's ungracious approach," Mike said, speaking into another phone.

"Hi, Mike. You were there the whole time and didn't bother to come to my defence!" Eve said, with feigned indignation.

"I didn't see the need. You're quite capable of defending yourself. I wanted to wish you two well. I'm looking forward to meeting the lucky guy in person. When are you coming home?"

Eve hesitated. "I don't know for sure. We haven't decided on a date yet. I'll let you know as soon as we know."

Later that day, reminiscing about the conversation with Crista and Mike, a wry smile graced Eve's face. *My dear friends, you are surprised now? Wait until I deliver the news about the baby.*

Eve had married Brian all right, but not when she told her friends. She needed to lie to cover the baby's due date. It needed to appear as though she married Brian and conceived soon after she arrived in Australia. Then her baby could be born "prematurely" without suspicion.

To get back into Anthony's good books, Eve enlisted Gloria and Garry's help. Garry remembered that his nephew wanted to learn horseback riding. There was an equestrian centre — *From the Horse's Mouth* — not far from Bluehay, so Eve called and booked a class for Sunday morning.

She was in the bathroom applying sunscreen when the doorbell rang. No one had paid her a visit there, and the realization that Anthony was downstairs alone made her nervous. She didn't have to worry, though. Through the closed door, her son took charge.

"Who is it?"

"This is Brian.

"I'll get my mommy."

"Good boy!" Eve said, as she walked towards the door.

To the unexpected visitor, she was a bit icy. "What are you doing here?"

Brian had called her Saturday morning inquiring about her son's disposition. When she mentioned the plan to go horseback riding, he asked if he could tag along. She protested and the subject was dropped.

But here he was.

"I decided I need to improve my riding skills too. Aren't you going to introduce me to this young man?"

This made Eve smile. "Where are my manners? Brian, this is my son, Anthony. Darling, Brian is an old friend of mine from...school."

Brian extended his hand and Anthony gave a manly imitation of a handshake.

"Did you know my daddy?" the boy asked. "He was the best. He liked my mommy's paintings."

Eve and Brian laughed at the boy's naive boastfulness.

"I never met your daddy, but I heard a lot of good things about him," Brian said. "He was a brave man. You should be proud of your father."

"He died in a fire, but he saved lots of people he worked with," the boy announced. "On TV, they said he was a hero. I was five years old so I remember some things about my father," the boy said; then a pout crossed his face and he added, "But not many."

Eve interjected, "We're going to be late if we don't leave soon."

"Do you like horses?" Anthony asked Brian, as they ventured out.

Brian had insisted on driving. He and Anthony engaged in manly conversation on the way, which made Eve aware how much her son craved male attention. However, the resemblance to Adam's involvement in their life made her more uncomfortable.

The first part of the lesson took place in the stable. The instructors familiarized the young riders with their riding partners.

Eve was basking in the sun, which was not yet at its peak. She sat down and propped her back against a hay bale. She removed her sunglasses and closed her eyes. The queasiness was subsiding. She had dreamed about Adam the night before. It was the first time she remembered having a dream about him and she felt depressed just thinking about it.

Her mind switched to the tiny baby in her womb. She wondered if every time she looked at the baby it would remind her of Adam. If it were a boy, would he have his father's face? Or if it were a girl, would she have his dark hair? She knew that if the baby took after him, she would love it all the same. She wondered if she still loved Adam, but was afraid that she knew the answer to that question all too well. She couldn't bring herself to hate him.

A moment passed before she realized that a shadow had fallen over her face. When she opened her eyes, she saw Brian studying her.

"You're going to fry in no time, even with sunscreen."

"Oh! I think I fell asleep," Eve lied. She put the sunglasses back on.

Not far away, the galloping and neighing of horses filled the air, momentarily announcing the end and beginning of a new loop.

"Anthony seems to be having a good time," Brian said to fill the silence. "He didn't protest like some of his fellow riders did when the instructor said that, for the next step of the lesson, parents should stay behind." He gathered some hay and settled himself on the ground by Eve.

"Can I ask you something?"

Eve turned her head towards him. "Sure."

"Is my being here upsetting you this much?"

She didn't reply at once, so he decided to rephrase his inquiry. "I mean that I showed up at Bluehay totally unexpected."

"No, not really. I mean, not any more. It has actually been nice to have someone else accompany Anthony, especially when the smell of dung hit me hard."

Brian didn't dare laugh until he saw Eve smiling. "I bet that's the real reason why there aren't many ladies in attendance today."

"Or many who aren't holding their noses tight and breathing only when necessary," Eve said and laughed.

"True!"

"Brian, can I ask why you create these opportunities to see me? What do you expect to achieve? What part was not clear to you when I said that I'm not looking for a companion, a date…a man?"

"Eve, I won't lie to you. I tried to get you off my mind a long time ago. At some point, I even thought I had succeeded. But with you coming here and staying longer this summer, everything changed. I feel like I would regret it if I don't pursue you. So I'm working up a plan to win you back. I want you in my life, Eve." He paused. "Don't shake your head. We're both free. I told you the other day about my life and how I messed it up, but I've turned it around and left my bad habits behind. I want to know your son, to treat him as my own. I have a lot of love to offer him and you. I'm sure Alexia told you that I want to leave Australia. Why not move to Canada? At least think about it and give me a chance—"

"A chance?" Eve interrupted him. "A chance of what? Of creating more unhappiness? To me, love is something sacred, not something I fool around with. It culminates in marriage, where mutual love is the most important element. We *loved* each other a long time ago, but those feelings have long since disappeared, and we can't bring them back."

"Eve, except for a brief period of time when I was making a fool of myself, I never stopped loving and caring for you. You cared for me once, and I hope, in time, you'll care for me again."

"I don't love you, Brian. I can't. I simply just can't imagine you in my life," Eve stated.

"You love someone else."

"Yes," Eve said quickly, answering with her heart, and not her mind. "No. I mean, that's not relevant." By now tears appeared at the brim of her eyes. "My God, why don't I tell you the truth?"

He looked at her in confusion.

"All right, I lied to you. I'm not staying here for a while as I told you before. I returned to Australia for good. Forever. Definitively. I made the decision even though my son is longing to return to Canada. I'm actually running away from a situation I got myself into. I'm two months pregnant. The baby's father is another woman's husband. I'm hiding here in Australia, Brian. Do you understand? I am just trying to keep my family intact by staying here. There are so many days when I feel completely overwhelmed. Love and marriage have no place in my life right now. Your insistence to be in a relationship with me is almost pushing me over the edge. I don't know what tomorrow brings for me. You need to understand why I am so determined to keep you at a distance and not get involved."

"How did you get involved with a married man?" Brian asked. "I'm sorry. I didn't mean to ask that in such a disparaging way. I have no right. What I meant—"

"It's all right. Really. The way I see it, this is the kind of reaction I expect out of everyone who cares about me. I've disgraced myself by falling that low."

"You said you're hiding. Does that mean the father doesn't know you're carrying his child?"

"Correct. This man and his wife are very, very wealthy. The wife can't produce an heir, which caused friction and several separations between them. I came in the picture during their last separation," Eve explained. "The wife wants to adopt. Obviously, he had a better idea. Why not have a child of his own. It was an idea that I didn't suspect until it was too late."

"I presume he's back with his wife, and you're afraid he'll try to snatch your baby once it's born."

Eve nodded. "Exactly. And it scares me to death."

Brian drew in a sharp breath. "Marry me, Eve."

"What? Are you—?"

"Crazy?"

"—sure you haven't lost your mind?" she continued.

"No, no. Don't get the wrong idea. Just listen. I'll marry you and give your baby my name and protection. It will be a union of convenience, if you like. What do I lose? What do *you* lose? If anything, it helps you out and I can prove I'm still worthwhile. This way you and Anthony have a chance to go back to Canada. And so do I."

"Now I know you're crazy. Be realistic, Brian. How could I impose on you? That would be *using* someone in the crassest manner. Besides, I'm safe where I am and the father doesn't even know I'm pregnant."

"I think you're ignoring how you were taken advantage of by this guy and his wife. What if he shows up looking for you? How do you convince him that his math is flawed and that this baby isn't his?"

"That won't happen," she responded softly. She was worn out, and it was only midmorning.

"You may want to consider moving to Northern Siberia, changing your name, or even becoming a brunette—"

"Are you trying to scare me?"

"No. Quite the contrary. I'm trying to open your mind to my offer, which would significantly simplify your position. Trust me. If I were that man, I'd have already suspected that you might be carrying my child. Your disappearance without a forwarding address might highlight that. Don't you think?"

Did she think? What else had she done over the past two months? Every day she thought about every possibility related to Adam finding her. Maybe once she found the guts to tell Garry, he would confirm that she didn't need to let Brian take the burden off her shoulders. No, she could not accept that. It was one thing to let him take charge of Anthony in the barn, but it was another thing to make him an instant father.

"I'll tell you what I think," Eve said with conviction. "I think we shouldn't see each other. My plight doesn't concern you, so let's just call it quits."

She still couldn't believe that, despite her resolve not to take Brian's proposition seriously, she actually married him. It happened two days after their conversation at the Equestrian Centre.

Eve was outside filling the bird-feeder when she heard the phone ringing.

"Hello?"

"Sorry to bother you," Mrs. Olsen said, in a hushed but urgent tone of voice.

"What happened?" Eve demanded. "Is Anthony all right?"

"Anthony is fine. Your brother took him for his classes. It's your sister-in-law I'm worried about."

"Why? What happened?" Eve demanded again, frantic.

"Miss Corrine had a baby boy yesterday and Gloria hasn't come down from her room since."

"You mean she hasn't visited her sister and the baby yet?"

"No, she hasn't. She called the school and excused herself for the day and," Mrs. Olsen's voice trailed off, "I'm afraid she may have started drinking again. I don't know what to do. I thought you could call on her. You reached her once..."

"I'll be right there."

She broke her record driving time as her patience disintegrated into a thousand pieces.

Mrs. Olson was waiting for her in the foyer.

"She's still in her bedroom. I'm so worried things will go back to the way they were before."

"If I have to drag her, she will come with me to visit her sister and the baby," Eve said, throwing her bag on a chair and charging upstairs. She stopped at the door only for a moment to take a deep breath. God only knew what was on the other side of that door. She opened it.

"My hearing must be going, because I definitely didn't hear you knock," Gloria said.

Eve felt her chest expanding as her anger mounted. She glowered at her sister-in-law and eyed the bottle sitting on the nightstand beside a glass generously filled with, Eve estimated, the amount missing from the bottle.

"Your hearing is fine. I didn't knock," Eve replied. "I heard about Corrine and her new baby so I came to visit them, but I don't know which hospital they're at. I figured you must know, so I stopped here first. Care to join me?"

Aside from her startled look when Eve entered the room, Gloria sat as motionless as a statue, in an armchair. Still dressed in her nightgown. She was looking at Eve's feet, which were adorned in bedroom slippers.

"I left home in a hurry. What's your excuse for still being in a nightgown at this hour of the day? Forgot your sister just had a baby? Tell me one thing: Did you ever stop drinking or have you been lying to Garry and me? What pathetic excuse do you have now?" Eve asked, all fired up. "Be my guest and tell me. Maybe it's so good that it will put me to shame for interrupting you."

For a moment, the room was utterly quiet.

"I don't want to see Corrine and her baby. And you can't make me do it."

"Why? Tell me why you can't see your sister's little baby. Your *sister's baby*, for Christ's sake. Spare me the part about the old feud and the unresolved issues.

"I don't want to see Corrine's baby," Gloria said, lips tight, emphasizing each word. *"Anyone's* baby, if you want to know exactly. I hate to see Corrine cooing over her baby when mine is buried. I can't share her happiness. And I don't need you to tell me how I should behave. I feel the way I do. And right now, I want to be left alone in my room. Is that a crime in your 'virtuous' opinion?"

Eve lost her last shred of patience.

"You have such a nerve to insult me right now. I was an 'angel' when you needed a shoulder to cry on and now you mock my concern?" Eve said, striding to the nightstand to grab the glass and bottle. She walked to the bathroom where she poured the liquor down the drain.

"You have no right to pour my—"

"And you have no right to act like an egotistical, hardhearted brat!" Eve shouted back. "It's all about you and your needs and feelings. How about others?"

Gloria was speechless.

"If that's your attitude towards an innocent baby, then I'll know what to expect from you in seven months. And by God, there's no way I'm letting you get close enough to take a look at my baby, because I would know that your act would be a sham."

"Your baby? Seven months? What baby?"

Because the urge to cry was so great, Eva waited at least a minute before speaking. She had always imagined she would tell Gloria and Garry about the baby when the three of them were having a quiet moment.

"I guess it was bound to come out. I'm two months pregnant."

"What happened? Why haven't you said anything since you arrived?" Gloria asked.

Eve's face fell.

"Oh my God," Gloria said, "nobody knows about it, not even Garry—"

"Not even the baby's father," Eve said.

Gloria got up and embraced her sister-in-law.

"Oh, darling. I'm so sorry you've had to suffer through this alone. Who is this man who hurt you so bad?"

Eve briefed Gloria and was thankful her sister-in-law did not make any judgemental comments.

"Now you see why I can't afford to include him in the picture?"

Gloria nodded. "That man is an idiot. Let him have his brainless, wealthy wife, and you the baby. And don't worry about a thing. We'll help you," she said. "So this is the real reason you didn't want to return to Canada."

Eve nodded. "It breaks my heart though to see Anthony suffering the consequences of my negligence, but we can't go back to Canada. Not when I know I could lose the baby."

After a short shopping spree for baby Aiden, the two women went to the hospital to see Corinne. Gloria was in much better spirits by the time they arrived. Corinne, in turn, was impressed by her sister's enthusiasm over her infant son, but knew that her attitude was in part, if not all, prompted by Eve's intercession.

After she drove Gloria home, Eve returned to Bluehay, but only for a short while, as it turned out.

"Eve, I'm sorry to have to tell you this, but Dwaine bit Anthony on the arm," Gloria's voice announced on Eve's answering machine. "Suzanne called with the news shortly after you left. She's at the children's hospital with Anthony. He is okay but she wanted to make sure a doctor checked his arm. I'm leaving right now to pick him up."

Unlike her hasty morning departure when Mrs. Olson had called, Eve took a moment to think clearly. She did not want to leave the house until she could come up with a decision she could live with. Anthony was hurt. She wouldn't be able to forgive herself if she failed to protect him from now on.

"Enough is enough," she muttered. She stopped in mid-stride, grabbed the phone book, and looked up an address.

At the door, she stopped long enough to put on a pair of comfortable shoes and place Gloria's elegant ones, which she had borrowed earlier, in a plastic bag.

Eve waited for nearly twenty minutes under curious glances at the welcome desk of AllChem Industries. Upon her arrival, the receptionist asked who she was there to meet.

"I'd like to speak to Mr. Kid please," Eve said.

"Mr. Kid is not in his office," the receptionist said, "I saw him pass by an hour ago, but he could be anywhere in the plant. Perhaps I could take your phone number—"

"Brian!" Eve said, as he came through the door at that precise moment.

"Eve, what a surprise!"

"Could I talk to you for a moment? It's very important."

"Yes, of course. Is everything all right?"

"Yes," Eve replied, and then shook her head. "No, actually. Can we go somewhere and talk? After you're done working, of course."

"Don't worry. I can leave now. I just need to return the lab keys."

They took the elevator to the main floor in silence, where he left the keys at the security desk.

"For Anthony's sake, I need to return to Canada. Could we discuss the offer of marriage you made the other day?" Eve asked, as soon as they were out in the parking lot.

There was much deliberating around her brother's table that evening. Garry was doubtful that this union — as he called it– was the only viable option. He did a lot of pacing and offered lots of options which, when analyzed, didn't seem to provide the answers they needed.

Gloria expressed regret for not having a good solution.

Once the decision was made, and the marriage took place, not much changed. Eve continued to reside at Bluehay by herself and

Brian lived in his apartment in Sydney. That was a "work-related" explanation for those who wondered about their living arrangements.

Anthony was taught at home in the morning by his auntie Gloria, and was significantly less stressed when told that they were going to return to Canada.

A few days later, Eve found a box hidden under his bed. In the box, among other things, he kept a page from a wall calendar. He was keeping tabs of the days before they left Australia. On the departure date, he drew a plane with unequal wings. Another date of importance that he marked down was "Mommy's reunion" — five days before the return date to Canada.

Eve decided to share her news with Alexia in person, though she knew it would be uncomfortable. She invited her for lunch at the Supreme Arena Restaurant, which prompted her friend to ask what the occasion was. Eve said only that it was a surprise. She felt bad about not being open with Alexia, but thought that the fewer people who knew about her situation the better.

When they met at the restaurant, Eve felt even worse, especially, that she needed to put up a happy face about marrying Brian, though she felt the opposite. Sometimes the feeling of guilt for involving Brian was overwhelming.

"Did you win the lottery or something? I never get to come here unless it's a really special occasion."

"I—*we*...couldn't keep the surprise from you."

"We? Who is *we*?"

"Brian and I. We got married on Tuesday."

*"Really?"*

Those words, coupled with a solid stare, said more than Eve could imagine. "Sorry if I can't give you news of a more exciting nature. I'll start playing the lottery—"

*"Stop!* Why don't you tell me the *truth?* Back up a bit and tell me about your life, the pregnancy, especially."

Eve felt everything come to a halt. She was certain Brian wouldn't tell on her. *But how else—?*

"Really, Eve! Do you think you could keep that from me? I've been pregnant five times, and gave birth four times, remember? When I first saw you, I thought maybe it was the whole ordeal with Jessie. But after the second time, I realized that it was more than that. I knew you wouldn't give up onion rings unless they made you queasy. But hey, I'm not upset about you deciding to keep the secret. I'll be very upset though — and I mean *utterly enraged* — if I hear that Brian doesn't know about this baby and you're trying to pass it off as his. I totally sympathize with you for getting knocked up by some dung-head, correct me if I'm out of line, but I'd hate to see you make Brian the father of a baby he didn't know about."

"All right, put the whip aside," Eve said, pressing on her temples. "Brian knows I'm pregnant. The whole affair is too complicated to explain over lunch. Marriage was his idea."

Alexia's glance rested on the entrance. "Got it. But you have to promise you'll fill in the blanks later on. Chin high and cheer up. Here comes your knight in shining armour."

September rolled uneventfully into October. Anthony crossed out each passing day on his makeshift calendar and grew more and more excited about his upcoming return to Canada. He would frequently ask Eve what day they were leaving, and she would dutifully tell him how many days were left.

Anthony, her dear son. Her fatherless son. Eve had a responsibility to give him the life he deserved. She tried not to think of her marriage to Brian as her last option, the last resort to fix the wrong in her life.

The few times she allowed herself to think of the immediate future, she experienced anxiety. The alumni reunion was fast approaching, but Eve didn't look forward to taking part. If Alexia hadn't insisted, she would already be back in Edmonton. Deep down, Eve knew why she wanted to return: to have a chance to see Adam. She knew it was crazy thinking, but she couldn't help it.

She daydreamed about situations where she would bump into Adam: at the gas station, cinema, or grocery store. The last one was even absurd — Adam was not the type to be out shopping like ordinary people. But daydreams are okay, aren't they? *Wrong!* her inner voice screamed out. They can be very dangerous. Regardless, she couldn't seem to control them and by the end of each daydream, she and Adam were once again becoming intimate. Only, at that point, she decided to take control and make the little voice inside her shout, *"I don't love you! I don't love you!"*

Delaying her departure had one small advantage. It meant postponing an explanation to Crista and Mike. She pleaded with God to make Crista less astute or observant than Alexia, because she had decided she wouldn't divulge her secret. Brian had agreed with her. "The fewer people who know the truth the better." She suspected that this also protected his ego. Her plan was to tell Crista that she slept with Brian very soon after the funeral, they found themselves pregnant, and did the honest thing. Then she would deliver "prematurely" as a result of a concocted story based on health concerns and her previous pregnancy history. Piece of cake.

"I wish I could close my eyes and open them tomorrow," Eve said. She examined her face in the mirror she had taken out of her beaded clutch purse. She was sitting on Brian's masculine and rather uncomfortable couch, dressed in a lovely evening gown that Alexia had helped her choose. Back at her brother's house earlier, when she was dressing for the banquet, she felt a light flutter in her lower abdomen. Instinctively, she had cupped her stomach, which prompted another flutter. She was sure it must be the baby's first kicks. She was excited. It was as if the baby was greeting her. Now those feelings were replaced by melancholy. *This baby will never know its dad. Never...*

"Not feeling well? We can skip this you know." Brian walked out of his bedroom, fumbling with the French cuff-links Eve had bought him.

"Let me help you with those," Eve said. "Look how handsome you are!" Eve admired him at arm's length.

Brian asked again if she felt all right.

"I'm just tired, that's all. Don't worry. Besides, I'm not willing to let Alexia skin me alive for not showing up," Eve said, trying to be cheerful.

Brian helped Eve into his car. On the passenger seat, Eve sat brooding. She fingered the diamonds at her throat. It was her only connection to Adam. She wasn't sure why she had decided to keep the necklace when she returned everything else he had given her.

The banquet was in full swing by the time they arrived. Brian took the opportunity to get her up on the dance floor, knowing it was one of the few occasions where he could hold her close.

Eve was determined to be on her best behaviour as the 'new wife'. Many of her former classmates had learned of her first husband's death but just a few knew about Eve's new marital status.

"Are you all right in there?" Alexia had followed Eve to the ladies' room. Eve had locked herself up in a stall for the past ten minutes with her back propped against the door, doing nothing but mulling over the last dance. Their last and unfinished dance. It was the song Adam and she danced to on the evening of his sister and brother-in-law's anniversary: Celine Dion's "Love Doesn't Ask Why." It was her favourite song, and his too, or so he had claimed on the dance floor. The DJ had announced that it was a special request for a special person. The song started, and that did it! She had to leave.

That was when Brian signalled Alexia to follow her friend to the ladies' room.

"I'm all right. I felt sick, but I don't think I'm going to throw up," Eve said.

When Eve came out, she looked almost like her old herself, even though underneath the façade her worry weighed her down. She felt certain now that the song was dedicated to her personally, even though the DJ had been vague. Could Adam be there, lurking in the corners, watching her? Earlier, she thought she saw someone resembling Adam from behind, but she'd said nothing because she noticed how Brian enjoyed himself and didn't want to distress him with her bizarre imagination. For that reason, he would be quick to convince her that it would be unlikely for Adam to show up right *here*. Furthermore, her mind was preoccupied with a thought. She had talked to Adam about an upcoming alumni reunion in Australia, but had she mentioned the specific venue? Most probably she did.

It was close to midnight when Brian dropped Eve off at her brother's home. She felt more mentally drained than physically tired. She tossed and turned for a few hours, wondering and worrying about bumping into Adam. Unable to sleep, she left Sydney before anyone woke up, leaving a short note on the dining room table: "Went to Bluehay."

She thought of calling Brian to let him know about her hasty departure. She knew she had been deceitful at the reunion. While in his arms, she thought only of Adam. When she finally called Brian's apartment, there was no answer. At eleven o'clock, she called her brother's house and found out that Brian was there, "having a ball with Anthony and Garry." He told her that he wouldn't have missed having fun with her son, and before he hung up, advised her not to work so hard. Good advice, of course, if it hadn't made her feel guilty. How could she have behaved so poorly? She had gotten into the habit of doing whatever suited her while someone else took care of her son.

It was in that mood that she fell asleep on the bench swing, in the backyard.

A dull, stifled sound woke her, but she didn't open her eyes at first. She shifted her body slightly and decided that the sound was a product of her tired mind or part of a dream.

Then a clear, purposeful throat-clearing made her spring up. She froze instantly, with one hand over her heart.

"Adam?" *This is not a dream*. Her next impulse was to run into the safety of the house, but Adam anticipated her move and blocked her way. He caught her wrist roughly.

"You are not going anywhere right now." The intensity in his eyes was new to her. "Not until you answer my questions. I'm fed up with getting air-sick on your account!" he thundered.

Eve struggled to free her hand.

"One question. Do you love me?"

Eve's mouth dropped open. "How dare you!"

"Did you ever?

All of a sudden, Eve seemed to gain bravery. She confronted his stare with a glower of her own. "Let go of my arm. You're hurting me."

"You're hurting yourself, if you delay answering my question."

"I did once. But I don't anymore. Now take your hands off me and leave," Eve said, by now more angry than scared.

He freed her arm slowly. And then surprised her by grabbing and kissing her but not like he ever had before. He had never kissed her in such an overpowering and engulfing way. How she ended up lying on the grass, she couldn't remember. But there she was, kissing him back without a worry on her mind.

When she opened her eyes, Adam was studying her. The look in his eyes told her that she had made a huge mistake. It was obvious that he had put her through a test.

*He had won.*

"You can't claim you don't love me anymore and kiss me like that, Eve," Adam sneered.

Eve got to her feet. She felt indignation rising up from the realization of having been tricked. She felt his hand on her stomach.

"I know your secret, Eve. It was bound to come out. How could you think that I would never know?" Adam asked. "Shocked?" He lifted her chin so she could make eye contact with him. "Tell me that you loved this man before you got pregnant with his baby, and I'll leave you alone and put our past behind me."

In that moment, Eve felt her anxiety dissipate.

*She had won.*

He only thought he knew her secret, but he didn't. Not the real one. It dawned on her how right Brian was. What if she hadn't married him? Adam showed up just as Brian said he would.

Eve started towards the house. Adam followed.

She needed to act with bravery.

"Please leave."

"As soon as you answer my question."

"Brian and I love each other—"

"Brian. You married Brian." He spat out the words.

"Yes. I married Brian, because we love each other and have much in common. The love between my husband and me is real."

"Yeah, yeah," Adam said. "Why can't you convince me of that then?" He now looked her directly in the eye. "Satisfy my curiosity. How many men have you kissed like that since you got married?" He sneered again. "If a married woman kisses another man this passionately, she either doesn't love her man or she's a bitch. Which one are you?"

The sound of her palm slapping his face startled them both.

Adam grabbed Eve by her forearms just as she was about to deliver the second slap.

"Enough. I hope your conscience is at ease, but I doubt it," Adam said, and left without another word.

Eve remained rooted. No tears of relief or anger fell. All she could think about was her victory: The baby was hers. *To keep.*

The screeching sound of car tires brought her to her senses. Then the sound of angry voices came from the front of the house. She followed Adam's steps. As she turned the corner to the front yard, she recognized Brian's voice.

"What the hell did you come here for?"

By the time Eve reached the front of the house, Adam and Brian were wrestling on the pavement.

"Stop it. Both of you."

Brian, who was ahead a few punches, according to Adam's bloody face, didn't seem to hear her. His rage was out of control. He was punching Adam mercilessly.

"Brian, stop it! Let him go or he won't be able to drive away."

Her pleas fell on deaf ears.

Eve had to do something. Anything. She started pulling at Brian with all her strength, only to take a plunge in the process and fall in a heap, one leg caught beneath her. Her intervention, as ineffective as it was, gave Adam the chance to get up and escape. For one fleeting moment, their eyes locked. His face was smeared with blood. That image and the intense, raw abhorrence in Adam's eyes would haunt Eve forever, she thought.

"You son of bitch, you slashed my lip," Adam said.

"That's nothing compared to what I'll do next time you set foot here or in Sydney. I'll kill you with my bare hands. Do you hear me?" Brian helped Eve off the ground.

"Don't flatter yourselves that I'm interested in another visit. What for? To screw your wife? If I wanted that I could have had *her* in the backyard. She kissed me the way she's probably never kissed you. But unfaithful bitches like her don't turn me on." Just as he was ready to speed away, he shouted. "If I were you, I'd have a paternity test done once the brat comes out."

Though she was shaken by the heated incident, Eve put on a brave face. She busied herself with cleaning Brian's scrapes. Fortunately, his injuries were too superficial to merit a trip to a medical facility. In her mind, the whole episode rolled like a horrifying movie: Adam, with his pitiful, bloody face, hastily retreating in his rented car, a cloud of dust swallowing him...

As she tended to Brian, she asked him how he knew that was Adam.

"Alexia called your brother's house a couple of hours ago. One of your classmates, Richard Wood, called her husband, John, about the boat they have for sale. John was in the shower, so Richard and Alexia exchanged opinions about the banquet. He mentioned that while he was having a smoke outside, a man approached him and inquired about you. From what Richard said, it sounded like the guy was after details about your personal life. When Richard mentioned that the guy was not one of our Aussie classmates, Alexia didn't waste any time," Brian explained. "When I think about it, I had the feeling we were being watched last night."

Eve's heart skipped a beat, but she didn't let it show. "Look in the mirror. You look almost as good as new." All she could think was that Adam came looking for her and found her. And the worst part was that she took some satisfaction in seeing him, all the ugliness of the encounter aside.

"He must have followed you this morning. I don't think he would have known how to get here on his own. Thank God I came in time," Brian said.

In the mirror, their eyes locked for a full second.

"To tell you the truth, I don't know why Adam showed up. Maybe he was on one of his business trips," Eve lied, knowing that Carstone had no business in Australia. "I don't know and I don't care. What I *do* know is that Adam doesn't suspect the baby is his."

As if he didn't register what Eve said, Brian added, "I can't fathom what he came here for. What does he want? I mean, this is a guy that you've done your best to hide from, and he still managed to show up on your doorstep. His snooping around and stopping here really disturbs me Eve, and I'm not trying to scare you. I wonder if, once you're back in Edmonton, you wouldn't need to alert the authorities."

"Brian, let's not make a federal case out of this yet."

"*Yet?* We should have had him apprehended by our authorities on assault charges. I'm sorry we let him off the hook so easily."

Eve rolled her eyes. "Assault charges? Adam is more injured than you!"

After they shared a simple meal of ham, cheese, fresh vegetables, and fruit, Eve went upstairs. She wondered if Brian felt as if he had caught her playing hooky at Bluehay, because there was no evidence that she went there to make good use of an "irresistible inspiration."

Brian decided to spend the rest of the day and night there, in case the uninvited guest returned. Eve agreed, though she doubted Adam would come back. She tried to sleep, but the day's events kept her awake. She couldn't help but question Adam's erratic, immature behaviour. Maybe his wife was right; he must have some mental health issues. What else could explain his presence at the restaurant the night before? It occurred to her that her suspicions had been right: He had requested that song for her. He had been watching her all night long, collecting details about her life and whereabouts.

She shuddered.

When she awoke, it was dark outside and moonlight was pouring into her room. The house was so quiet it was eerie. Where was Brian? Obviously he was not in the house or she would have heard the TV. Brian was an avid sports fan, and whenever he was there, she allowed him to indulge his pastime.

She got up to see if he was downstairs. She bent over the rail and saw him sitting at the table with a bottle of brandy in front of him. He was whispering into the phone. *Damn. Why didn't I throw that bottle away?* Eve thought. She had seen the bottle before — most probably left behind after Gloria and Garry's last visit there — but didn't remember exactly how much was in it. In all fairness, she couldn't blame Brian if he imbibed. Under the circumstances, he probably needed the drink.

She went back to her room with a new concern: Brian versus alcohol. Would Brian go back to alcohol over this incident with Adam? *Adam.* Just thinking of him, she felt her eyes filling with tears. His bloody face contorted with anger and abhorrence came back to her mind, over and over again. But she was sure he was gone, no doubt about that.

Her thoughts returned to Brian. He hadn't consumed any alcohol the previous night. Alexia mentioned to her that she knew he was over that old, ugly vice. *Is his mind fighting with the vice right this moment?* Eve wondered.

Though she was still awake a few hours later, she pretended to be sleeping when she heard the wooden stairs squeak under Brian's heavy feet. She imagined his breathing affected by liquor, ascending one step at a time. At the top of the stairs, he stopped, as if he were deciding which way to go.

When the ray of light from the hallway widened, as the door opened, she lay still, pretending to be asleep. Not even in the darkness, after Brian left, did Eve dare to open her eyes. The last time he had checked on her she had also pretended to be asleep. That was a week ago, when he brought Anthony to Bluehay for the weekend and had spent the night there. That time he had pulled the coverlet onto her and kissed her on the forehead.

She tossed and turned in her sleep. In her dream, she was running for her life but too slowly. She woke up, and the first thing she realized was that she was shaking. That was just before she felt the presence of a dull and throbbing pain in her lower abdomen. She was scrunched up in fetal position, groaning. *My God*, she thought, *this is not good.* She called out to Brian, but her voice was weak. She tried to speak louder but to no avail. She thought of calling Gloria and Garry, but even though the phone was within reach, she couldn't stretch her arm without experiencing a stabbing pain. She took a deep breath and tried to think.

She was not alone.

She must reach Brian for help.

She got off the bed slowly and crawled out of the room holding her stomach with one hand. At the top of the staircase, she called out to Brian. Her voice was that of a newborn kitten. She would need to descend the stairs, she thought, as tears of pain washed down her cheeks. She got down one step and had to sit down. From that position, she could see Brian. He was in the same spot she saw him last, only now with his head on the table, fast asleep. The glass of liquor was still in front of him, untouched. Between cramps, she deliberated. Her voice wouldn't wake him. If only she could find a breakable object within her reach to throw down…

Slowly she got up and looked around; and then she knew she was in deep trouble, as she felt blood trickling down her legs.

She had to get to the phone.

Garry picked up after two rings.

"Eve? What happened?"

"I'm in pain. I think I'm losing the baby," she said, her sobs uncontrollable by now. "Send an ambulance, please. I don't want to lose my baby."

"You'll be all right, darling. Calm down, you won't lose the baby," Garry tried to sound reassuring.

Eve could hear him talking to Gloria.

"Darling, call an ambulance on the cell phone and give directions to Bluehay. Eve is in pain." To his sister, he said, "Please stay calm. Where is Brian? He called earlier from there."

"He fell asleep and I can't climb down the stairs to wake him," Eve said, trying to take deep breaths.

"Eve, listen to me. Gloria is calling an ambulance right now."

"The ambulance is on the way," Gloria conveyed. "They asked if Eve is bleeding."

Garry asked her.

"Yes," she said.

He repeated her reply.

"Eve? Listen to me. I'll hang up now and dial your number. Don't pick it up. Let it ring until Brian wakes up."

It worked.

Thereafter, Eve couldn't remember much.

Brian carrying her downstairs, holding her...the arrival of the ambulance...the ride to the hospital...Gloria and Garry's worried faces...

It was as if it all happened in another time, dimension, or space. To someone else.

Dr. Lang, who was on call when Eve's ambulance arrived, had Eve wheeled into the ultrasound room with Brian following close behind.

Eve didn't like the silence that settled over the dark room.

Finally, Dr. Lang asked, "Do you have other children?"

"Yes. I have a seven-year-old son."

"Any other pregnancies? Besides this one and the one with your son?"

"With my first pregnancy, I carried twins that I miscarried at three months. Two years ago, I gave birth to a premature boy who survived two weeks."

"Doctor, is the baby all right?" Brian asked.

The doctor was performing the ultrasound and looking intently on the screen. He didn't answer right away. He asked Eve, "Have you had any ultrasounds during this pregnancy?"

"No. I didn't. I was afraid—" Eve's voice broke off, tears welling in her eyes.

The doctor quickly glanced at her chart. "That explains the single-foetus error."

"Dr. Lang, the last baby had Down Syndrome," Brian started. "My wife postponed having an ultrasound as long as she could this time around, afraid that history would repeat itself."

"Dr. Lang, what do you mean by 'single-foetus error'?" Eve asked.

"You're having twins."

Two hours later, the doctor came into Eve's room with promising news. The ultrasound report was normal. The bleeding did no harm.

"The bleeding in itself didn't endanger the babies," Dr. Lang said. "Twenty percent of multiple foetuses encounter the same situation at about the same stage of pregnancy."

She was carrying twins.

Every time she thought about it, she felt a wave of anxiety engulfing her. The doctor's orders were to avoid emotional stress, but she couldn't help feeling mixed, powerful emotions. Twins! She felt enormous relief that the babies were fine and also enormous gratitude towards Brian.

When Brian and Eve were alone again, it seemed as if a new bond had formed between them. It was as if she finally realized she could count on him.

"I threw you neck deep into this, didn't I? I'm so sorry, Brian."

"Yeah, you did. Double time," he teased her. "Hey, but as I recall, I invited myself in. And I'm not sorry. Let's just concentrate on you getting back on your feet and put the worries behind us."

Eve stayed in the hospital for three weeks. Garry contacted Dr. Summer in Edmonton and his office faxed Eve's medical history to the doctors in Sydney, who were preparing to do a cervical cerclage, a procedure to help prevent miscarriage and premature birth.

The day before Eve was discharged, Garry brought her a message from the Malones. They said that Eve's house was ready for their return. He wasn't happy that she was leaving Australia. If she stayed in Sydney, he could protect his sister and her children; back in Edmonton, he would be powerless. He had been petrified to learn about Adam's visit. Though he had originally considered Eve's marriage to Brian a needless manoeuvre, he knew now that it had been a wise decision.

# Eight

Edmonton international airport wasn't particularly crowded. Mike, Crista, and Brandon strolled by the busier gates where passengers were coming and going in clusters. Finally, the electronic board showed that Eve's flight had arrived.

Crista clasped her hands on the wheelchair's handles. "They would have called us if anything happened, right? I mean, there wouldn't be any reason for them not to get on the flight, would there?"

"Waiting for someone?" A familiar voice came from behind, startling Mike and Crista, and then suddenly there was a chorus of voices.

"Eve!"

"Anthony!"

"Garry?"

"Hello!"

"Here you are, Mrs. Nelson," the flight attendant wheeled Eve over.

"Thank you so much, I'm in good hands now," Eve said.

"We were expecting a new face," Crista said, as they waited for the baggage to arrive, the excitement of the reconnection still in her voice. "But we're happy to see you again, Garry."

"Brian will come as soon as he can. An immigration glitch changed our plans at the last moment," Eve said.

"Honey, did you notice how elusive Eve was about her new hubby?" Crista said that night, as they were preparing for bed. "You ask her something straightforward about him and she just gives you a vague answer."

Mike nodded.

"I mean, for Pete's sake, how hard could it be for an Australian to enter Canada? I thought we were all part of the Commonwealth, which made travelling between the two countries easier," Crista reasoned.

"This guy is not simply on vacation, honey. He would have to enter with different status, I suppose," Mike offered. "I don't know how immigration law works."

Whatever doubts Mike and Crista had, they were soon set aside to enjoy their friend's return. They decided to celebrate "all the occasions they missed" in one seating, and took Eve and Garry out to a Greek restaurant. Eve wanted to delay the celebration but needed to convince her friends she was not handicapped by her pregnancy.

The atmosphere in the restaurant was pleasant, the food delicious, and the in-house pastries, which Eve very much craved, were scrumptious.

"I hope your hubby will be here soon, so we all can enjoy a few good meals together," Crista said.

Eve was in a good mood. "Brian will love this place. He loves lamb."

Garry's eyes moved between Crista and Mike. "Brian will be here in no time. But until then, I am so very grateful for your friendship with my sister. It was hard for Gloria and me to see Eve off again, but I've always believed it's best for people to follow their own paths in life, and I respect my sister's wish to call Edmonton home." Garry added, "It was Brian who suggested setting up home here. They were going to settle in our — their — homeland but Brian thought my nephew might be happier here. He's a great man, and I'm sure you will find him as pleasant, amiable, and dear as you did William."

"What was with that gibberish about Brian?" Eve asked later. "I already told them he's a good guy. He had an option to back out, but he didn't. He won't take off once he's here, if that's what you're afraid of."

"Darling, don't misunderstand my intentions. I wasn't trying to reinforce Brian's reliability. I just happen to think that Mike and Crista are a bit sceptical about your marriage. I think it would have been better if Brian was the one to bring you here himself." Garry looked troubled. "Have you considered telling your friends the truth? Instead of being suspicious, they could be understanding and supportive."

*"No!"* Eve shook her head. "I know Mike would carry my secret to the grave, but Crista would sing it to the mountains. And not because she would be inconsiderate, but because she hates Adam for what he did to me. She would do anything to avenge me. But don't worry. Once Brian is here, everything will be all right. He knows his part and how to fit in."

Personal and work-related matters called Garry home. He returned to Sydney after a week. Before he left, he convinced Eve to hire a part-time housekeeper to ease her daily routine. A retired RN, Mrs. Shapiro was Italian, pleasant, and most eager to help. "I've been at home for eight months, and I was going through the 'retirement blues,'" she told them. "I am just not cut out to stay home and do nothing."

Eve came to appreciate the help as soon as Mrs. Shapiro started. She drove Anthony to school daily and went grocery shopping twice a week. She was also not shy to take initiatives on her own about various household chores.

Anthony felt at home back in Edmonton. His old peers fussed over him for a day or two, and then claimed him again as one of their own. One of his classmates said that he talked "with a weird accent", but others defended him and the comment was soon forgotten.

With Mike's intervention, Anthony was able to make the peewee hockey team again exactly one week after his return. Eve noticed he was anxious and restless, almost desperate to get back on the ice. When Crista drove him home after his first practice, she declared that he was "all pooped out." Although it was to be expected that he'd be tired as he was out of practice, there was a deeper disappointment etched on his face. *What could it be now?* she wondered.

The source of his despondency, however, was of a different nature, as Eve learned later on when they were alone.

"Ryan doesn't come to practice anymore."

"Oh? Is that right?" Eve asked.

"He moved to Calgary."

"Well, I'm sure you'll make new friends. You already have friends at school and many others on your hockey team. Brandon is delighted to have you back."

"I know I have lots of friends, Mommy, but I've been thinking. Do you think Adam would still come to the games sometimes, even though Ryan moved away?"

So much for hoping that the boy had finally accepted having people pop in and out of his life, Eve thought.

"Darling, I told you that Adam is no longer part of our life — yours or mine. He was there before for Ryan, because his parents couldn't bring him themselves. Ryan is gone and so is his uncle. Do you understand?"

The boy nodded. "I know Adam won't be back," Anthony said softly.

In spite of herself, Eve found herself asking, "What do you mean, darling?"

"I know that he broke up with you and doesn't want to see you."

"Anthony!"

"It's true. You must've gotten him really mad or else he would have come to visit me while we were living at Uncle Garry's. He was my best friend," Anthony said, his voice a bit shaky. "He would still be my friend. He would come to the games for me. He would, if you let him, but—"

"No buts, darling. There are rules that sometimes you may not like, but you must obey them. Like in hockey."

"Mom, why can't Adam come to watch my games until Brian comes?"

"Anthony, you must understand. That's not possible. Besides, I can't just go ask Adam to do this."

"Why not?"

"Because…because he wanted out of our friendship. And I didn't get him upset," Eve found herself explaining. "Maybe somehow he got himself upset or changed his mind about us. You must understand that Brian is my husband now, just like your daddy was. So you and I have to be fair to Brian. Give him a chance to learn to be your daddy now. He is your protector—"

"What is a protactor, Mommy?"

"A *protector* is a person who cares for someone and keeps them safe," Eve said, mildly annoyed. She sensed his eager inclination to argue that Adam — based on his promise of always being his friend — could be that person. She deftly revised her "definition" to leave no room for disagreement. It seemed to work as her son nodded his understanding.

Crista was not one to be so easily satisfied. For two weeks, she kept an eye on Eve, waiting for her to slip. She was on guard for any mention of Adam. She made a promise to her husband that she wouldn't broach the subject, yet she wanted to know if Eve had truly put Adam and the whole ugly experience caused by his deceit behind her. Mostly, she wanted to know if the wound was healed. If her feet really were on rock-hard ground, as she was trying to convince everyone.

They were on the phone on a daily basis. Finally, one day Eve asked about Adam.

"Have you seen Adam at all? After I left, I mean," Eve said, already regretting the question.

"No. I haven't. Neither has Mike. But I wish I had. I'd have given him a piece of my mind. Have you?" Crista queried back.

"Have I what?"

"Seen Adam? Since you've been back, I mean."

If the question hadn't been time-specific, Eve would have had to lie. She didn't want to remember any particulars of their encounter in Australia, let alone reveal it to her concerned friend.

"No, I haven't seen or heard from Adam. Didn't you say that the second time he called your house, Mike told him I was married? Why would he try to contact me after that?"

"You're right. He wouldn't dare disturb you. He's probably on a short leash," Crista said, laughing at her own quip.

Eve pretended to agree.

"Let's hope so," Eve said, and decided to change the subject. "Did I mention to you that Nina Murray has four orders for me?" If the buyer can wait till I have my babies, I can make a fortune."

"Really? Good for you, *Mama*. I want to hear more about it tonight, but right now I gotta go. My other phone is ringing."

Eve was puffing as she struggled into her slacks. Last week they were comfortable enough, and now they were tight. But she was thankful that, at twenty-eight weeks, she was flourishing. Two weeks before, Dr. Summer had declared himself satisfied with her health. "It will be a major milestone when you reach twenty-eight weeks," he said, then added, "After that, each week is a bonus."

"Do you mean it's possible I'll have my babies at seven months?" Eve had said, looking concerned.

"No, no. All I'm saying is that, *if* that happens, it will be okay. It would mean, of course, a couple of months in the NICU. I wish I could assure you they will be born after at least thirty-eight weeks, but I'm not the one in 'charge' of granting wishes."

Recalling the conversation, Eve hugged her belly tenderly. *You are all right, my darlings.*

She could hear Mrs. Shapiro on the phone with someone.

It turned out to be Brian. Eve was surprised, yet not completely. He remembered her having the "milestone" appointment.

"I wanted to wish you good luck," he said, when Mrs. Shapiro passed the phone to Eve.

"Ah, thank you. You are a darling."

"I booked the ticket for two weeks from today, but the time isn't going fast enough," Brian said.

"So you *will* be here for the big day?"

"Yes. I want to be there in time to hand out the cigars, you know. Gloria said that twins come earlier sometimes," Brian said.

"Brian!" Eve scolded him. "Nothing is going to happen this time. I promise you." She started laughing. "You bought cigars?"

"Yes. Lots." *More than I have friends there to share them with,* he added silently.

She shook her head but felt a rush of empathy for him. She thought, *What a good old friend, as always, ready to lend a hand.*

"I'll call tonight to tell you what the doctor said. But I must go now; I see Mrs. Shapiro has let Crista in already. She has promoted herself to my personal driver."

Crista was driving with obvious care. Eve commented on it.

"Extra caution for the precious cargo on board," Crista explained. "But hey, my driving has improved! Get this — no fines in the past eight months, to my darling husband's wonder and contentment. He believes that *something* in my body is *finally* starting to function at a normal pace," Crista said, and grinned, glancing at Eve for a moment.

When they were close to the university, they drove in silence. It seemed as if all the traffic in the city was headed to the same destination.

Crista asked, "Was that your honey-bunny Brian on the phone when I came in?"

"Yes. He's checking on me — on us — constantly," Eve said.

"Did you tell him that I practically moved in so I can chase the herd of men from your doorstep with a — what's the name of it — cricket bat?"

Eve made a face. "He knew about the appointment today, that's all. By the way, great news, he's coming sooner than we thought. In two weeks, actually. Which reminds me, I have to rearrange some furniture, and I need Mike and another pair of strong arms to help out."

They were stopped at a red light. Crista glanced at Eve and winked mischievously.

"Why don't you wait until Brian comes? I'm sure he has something else strong besides a pair of good arms."

Eve rolled her eyes. "The light is green already. The point is, I need to have this done before Brian comes. I'm not talking about the babies' room but *his*. You know I don't have a bed upstairs in the master bedroom. I need to buy one."

"Hold it. Hold it. Stop right there," Crista demanded. Of course she knew there was no bed in the master bedroom upstairs. She and Mike helped Eve move it into a spare bedroom downstairs after William died. "Why in the world do you need *another* bed? Let's move the one from downstairs back up."

"Crista! Don't you get it? I can't have…I can't make love. I had a cervical cerclage, remember? He's a man for Christ's sake. It would torture him. It's the doc's recommendation."

Eve's ultrasound had been booked at the University of Alberta Hospital, where Dr. Summer could be present for the test. She waited in the little cubical dressing room, which reminded her of the room at the HYS Centre where she had waited for Anthony's X-ray the day she realized she was pregnant. This time the signage on the wall did not elicit any trepidation. That feeling from seven months ago had turned into a unique love for her babies.

Eve adjusted her body, full bladder and all, on the narrow bed. The dim room came to life with the pictures from the monitor that represented the tiny lives under examination.

The sonographer brought in a second chair for Dr. Summer, who was now watching the flickering screen with interest. He didn't do this every day, Eve thought. Or else he wouldn't bother Julia, the sonographer, with questions that she herself would have asked, if she didn't have to hold her breath on request or worry about her bladder bursting at any moment. The doctor and the sonographer exchanged comments in medical jargon. Some things Dr. Summer explained to Eve in plain language: "We calculate the baby's weight by the length of the bones."

Eve could hardly concentrate, as she needed to go to the washroom badly. She moaned instead, loud enough to attract a compassionate look.

"Two more minutes, Mrs. Nelson," said the sympathetic sonographer.

Eve nodded, but wondered how long two minutes lasts in the medical world. She tried to think of something positive. From the tone of the conversation between the doctor and the sonographer, she presumed everything was fine. If only she could empty her bladder…

An excited exchange between the two medical professionals caught Eve's attention.

"What is it?" she asked.

"I'm not sure if you want to know," Dr. Summer started.

"Is it the gender?" she asked. "You know what they are, don't you?"

The doctor's nod and grin could mean only one thing.

"I'm having girls. Don't tell me any different. Your grin gives you away."

"Okay. If you officially want to know, then yes. Or at least one is. I sensed that you had changed your mind since last time. One is a girl for sure, but the other baby isn't letting us take a peek. If you could wait a little longer—"

"No more. Just knowing that one of them is a girl is good enough for me. My bladder is about to explode!" Eve said with a grimace.

The news elated Crista. "Lunch on me. That's, of course, if you can entertain yourself window shopping until the dentist is done with me."

A half hour later, Eve was shopping for little dresses at *Jack and Jill* children's store in the Edmonton Centre Mall.

As soon as Eve entered the store, a woman about her age welcomed her. Before Eve realized it, she was in love with all the perfect little things the salesperson displayed for her perusal. While she considered what to buy, the saleswoman learned that Eve was carrying at least one baby girl.

Shortly after, she was ready to leave with two large bags and the saleswoman's promise that she could return one set of merchandise if the other "angel" turned out to be a boy.

She stepped out of the store and looked around. Even though she had been to the washroom twice since the ultrasound, she needed to go again. The crowd had increased considerably with the lunch hour approaching, and Eve waited for the wave of people to thin out a little to find the nearest washroom.

And then, coming down the escalator, she saw *him.*

Turning on her heels, she walked briskly away from the escalator, her heart pounding. Part of her wondered if that indeed was Adam or just a person who looked a lot like him. She tried to study the picture in her head. Must be Adam. She was certain now, as she realized that Cassidy was also with him. And, that *he* saw her too.

It took several minutes for Eve to put a couple of reasonable thoughts together. Inadvertently, she had started walking in the opposite direction to the restaurant where she was to meet Crista. The thought of turning around and running into Adam threw her into a panic. She didn't dare glance over her shoulder either.

However, she had to take care of more urgent matters first, so she stepped inside the Casa Zaranda Restaurant to use the bathroom. Judging by the table settings and the spacious room between them, she knew it was not the kind of restaurant where Crista and she would celebrate. The manicured maître d' who approached her confirmed as much.

"May I help you, ma'am? Do you have a reservation?"

"I would like to use the ladies' room, if you don't mind...and I would appreciate a glass of water, please."

He agreed with a curt nod.

Eve put her bags on a chair at an empty table and hurried to the ladies' room. Once there, she took her time as she found immunity and comfort within the bathroom. She tried to occupy her mind with something other than the obvious. The thought of the baby girl newly identified filled her heart with bliss. Unfortunately, the thoughts of her immediate situation rushed to the forefront. Could it be possible that Adam followed her? Was he still angry? Was his facial expression one of pleasant surprise when he saw her? And, most importantly, and equally infuriating, was she glad to see him again?

*God, if only I could be at peace.*

Feeling calmer and more poised, she went to the sink to wash her hands and check her makeup. After deciding that she looked satisfactory, she left the bathroom with more confidence and bravado than when she came in. These feelings were fleeting, though.

From a few feet away, she watched Adam inquiring about her shopping bags.

The waiter must have looked over Adam's shoulder or else Adam wouldn't have turned around. As he did, a look of surprise crossed his face.

For a few seconds everything froze. Eve was balancing on her left foot rather than on both. Adam was half-turned with his right hand extended to dismiss the maître d', who had come to offer his services. While everyone else continued their business, Eve and Adam remained motionless.

"Thank you for the water," Eve finally said to the waiter. To Adam, more confident than she felt, she said, "I don't need a scene from you."

"I'm not here to create a scene. I saw you coming in and seized the opportunity to apologize to you," Adam said, coming closer.

*Saw me coming in? Try followed me.*

Eve glanced at her watch. Crista would be looking for her, or worse, could show up looking for her *here*. Envisioning her friend's reaction wasn't an appealing thought.

"Are you in a terrible rush? Can we talk for a few minutes, please?"

"I…I'm meeting someone soon."

"Your husband?"

"No."

"I only need a few minutes of your time. If you agree, we could sit down."

To her surprise and annoyance, Eve agreed. Why did it seem the most appropriate thing to do?

They sat down and Eve claimed her glass of water. She didn't need it, but it gave her something to do with her hands.

He came right out with it. "I sincerely apologize for the disturbance I caused at your cottage. I had no right to intrude on your life," Adam said, holding her gaze. "I had no excuse since, I admit, I already knew you were married. Before I went to Sydney, I didn't know you were also pregnant."

Eve found herself half-listening. She couldn't believe they were so close, sitting at the same table. It was like a dream. Without realizing, she was studying his face. He looked handsome but a different handsomeness than she was used to. Her gaze stopped on his mouth, on his upper lip, where a tender, pinkish scar was fading away. Her mind played with the thought of caressing his face, touching his scar...

"Did you have stitches there?" She didn't mean to ask, but to her shock, the question was out.

Adam laughed.

"No. Some special tape held it together," he lied. "I deserved it though, as I recall. When did you come back to Edmonton?"

"Two months ago. Anthony and I."

"Oh? How about your husband?"

"He's coming in two weeks." She glanced at her watch again. At this point, she didn't care if she stood up Crista.

"Is it someone I know you're having lunch with?"

Eve took a small sip at her water and said, "I'm meeting Crista for lunch at Pettra's Restaurant. We plan to celebrate—" She stopped and corrected herself. "To have lunch. That's all."

"And what do two good old friends celebrate over lunch?"

"I had an ultrasound this morning and learned that I'm having a baby girl. At least one of them is."

Adam's face bloomed with a bright smile, too spontaneous not to be sincere. "That's wonderful news." In the next moment, his brows came together in wonderment. "What do you mean at least *one* of them is?"

"I'm having twins. They could only see the gender of one, hence the shopping spree," Eve said, hinting at the shopping bags. "I got everything in pairs of soft pink, white, and lilac, with the promise of being able to exchange the second pair if the other baby turns out to be a boy."

She was talking nonsense and nonstop. The effect that her unexpected companion had on her was mutual. It seemed to her that he was interested in any word she uttered. She felt elated.

"Twins, well!" Adam noted with a wide grin. "I presume the father is enormously pleased with his *double* accomplishment."

Adam's comment gave Eve a jolt. She didn't want to give anything away, but she felt guilty. Recently, she had watched a program on the rights of a man to know if he is to become a father. The pro arguments were very strong.

She sounded confident when she replied, "Brian is overjoyed."

"Are you having lunch with us today, Mr. Carry?" the waiter asked, approaching their table with deference.

"Lunch?" Adam asked Eve, his eyes pleading.

"Um…all right," Eve agreed somewhat uncertain. She would need to find a good excuse for standing up Crista.

The waiter took their order and retreated. Eve went to the bathroom, claiming the call of nature.

Imagining Adam and her face to face, having lunch, was so far-fetched. A wave of anxiety engulfed her. What was she thinking by accepting the invitation? What if he wanted to contact her again? What if his wife walked in on them? Eve's heart started pounding. God, why didn't she think of that before?

Eve returned to the table, doing her best to disguise her apprehension. The food was already on the table.

Adam asked about Anthony. She chatted about his difficulty in adjusting to Australian life. She also talked about the tragedy of her niece's death, a subject that elicited much sympathy from Adam. To onlookers, they could have been two old friends.

"Anthony is a great child with a mind of his own. I'm sorry he had a rough time in Australia, especially after he had just lost a loved one," Adam said. "How are your brother and his wife coping?"

Eve sighed. "It was devastating at first, but as time went on, it became more bearable," Eve said. "Losing a child is no picnic, for sure."

Adam sighed. "I can only imagine."

*Oh, my God, he has lost children he isn't even aware of,* Eve thought. *He lost his children to me.* All this time she had considered herself a victor, when in fact she was a thief.

She startled when Adam said, "Do you mind if I ask you something?"

She nodded.

"Would it be possible to see Anthony sometimes?" Adam asked. "I mean, I promised him once to be his friend, and I'd hate for him to be disappointed. I don't want to intrude on his life," Adam continued. "I just wondered if I could come and cheer him on at his hockey games sometimes—"

"You know I can't let that happen. Adults shouldn't play games with a child's mind. We both know he adores you," Eve said. "Stirring up his feelings won't do him any good. He's hardly had enough time to know and adjust to his stepfather, so for you to come into his life again is the last thing he needs."

"I understand," Adam said, a flicker of disappointment crossing his face. He fished a business card from his jacket and placed it on the table close to Eve's hand. "Just in case you change your mind or need a helping hand. With Anthony, I mean."

For a few moments, both were preoccupied with their private thoughts.

Eve finally cleared her throat. "How are things for you and your family?"

"Well, not too well, really. Especially with my father—"

"I meant—" Eve started but stopped abruptly.

She saw Cassidy coming towards them with an inhospitable look etched across her face. Eve wished that she could make herself invisible or crawl under the table. Adam followed the direction of her gaze.

"There you are," Cassidy addressed her brother, who looked displeased by her sudden appearance. "Hello, Eve," she addressed Eve with a short glance.

"Should we all take a break or wait until you finish your lunch?" Cassidy said, and this time Eve felt the icy tone of voice was directed at her.

"Cass, you decide *whatever* you want. I'll be there when I get there," Adam said.

"All right, Adam," Cassidy said, and her eyes rested for a moment on Adam's business card. "I can wait, but I can't make promises for the others."

"I know, I know. Do you know that Eve is having twins?" Adam said, changing the subject.

"Really?" Cassidy said, and the doctor in her showed a sincere interest.

"Yes, and one of them is a baby girl," Adam supplied.

"That's nice to hear. When is the due date?"

"In about sixteen weeks, if they're not in a rush," Eve said.

"Yes indeed, they do that sometimes," Cassidy agreed.

After Cassidy left, Adam and Eve were silent for a while.

"Ah, you were asking about my family," Adam said and sighed. "My father is in hospital. He had another heart attack."

"Oh, no."

"Yes. He is recovering, slowly though. Luckily, it was a minor one. He's trying to convince his doctor that he is hardy and ready to go home. But home for him means the office, or so we all suspect. He seems to forget that he was there before and that history repeats itself even more viciously sometimes. That's the reason I'm in town, actually—"

Eve was no longer listening. Her mind had stopped on the word "town," which meant he was no longer residing in Edmonton. She realized that she was disappointed. She had returned to Canada hoping to see him occasionally. What a shattering and childish plan that was! His business card was still on the table, but she didn't dare look closely at it.

"You have to excuse me," Eve said, when she realized that he had finished his father's medical report. "I hear nature calling again," she lied.

"Sure," Adam said, and got up to help her but she was already on her way.

"What the fuck do you think you're doing?"

Adam jumped out of his chair.

"Crista. Unhappy to see you, too. Have you given someone a heart attack yet?"

"No, but I wish I could give you a hard smack over that empty head of yours," Crista said. "On your fucking spree again, eh? Before

Eve comes back out, give me a good reason why you're fucking with her mind right now. I've been watching you for the past ten minutes and that's exactly what you're doing."

Fortunately, to Adam's enormous relief, Crista had some good sense left in her. She didn't seem to want to cause a scene. In one swift move, she grabbed the business card from the table.

"You and I will have a little chat later. Now do Eve a favour and end this charade. Don't give me an opportunity to come back and embarrass her. You have five minutes starting now," she added, squarely tapping on her watch before she disappeared.

Adam didn't doubt Crista's threat. The woman's quirkiness could cause more grief than it was worth. He wrestled with the idea of replacing the business card that Crista had taken, but realized that by not picking it up when he placed it there, Eve made it clear that she was not interested in using it.

He was standing when Eve returned to the table. She looked a bit flushed.

"Are you all right?"

"Oh, yes. A bit tired, though. I'm afraid I missed my midday nap."

As Adam escorted Eve out of the restaurant, he couldn't ignore the depressing feeling that it was probably the last time they would be that close or talking to each other.

He handed her the shopping bags, not knowing what to say next.

He was caught by surprise when Eve said, "Adam, please don't try to get in touch with me. Don't make this any harder on me. I'm committed to keeping my marriage intact." She waited until he nodded his silent promise, then walked away.

"I said that you have doubled your requirements since I last checked. All I'm asking is if you would consent to adjust them to a degree," Helen White said. She had been Adam's business lawyer for the last five years. She looked older than her forty-five years, ruder than in her twenties, and shrewder than in her thirties. And, for the moment, she was very much annoyed with her client. In the past five minutes, Adam had asked her twice to repeat herself. She had postponed two important appointments this afternoon to accommodate Adam's urgent matter. The least she expected was his attention.

The work plan she had drawn up for him was clear and precise. At this point, she failed to comprehend why Adam felt the need to introduce changes. Of course, ideally, Alicia's lawyer and she would cooperate and move towards a common goal. She kept reminding Adam that there is no perfect answer. If Adam wanted a separate 'silver tower' located in Calgary, he should work his butt off to get it arranged. She had run out of fresh ideas.

Adam argued that he would only stay involved with Carstone until his father recovered and returned to work. Then they could empower a committee with the leadership. Helen countered that he was not being realistic, because that "may not happen so soon." It was her idea that Cassidy be present at this meeting. In fact, the two women had had a few private teleconferences in the past three days and had agreed that Cassidy could be influential over Adam. Adam wanted to relinquish his rights as inheritor of the Carstone Corporation, which was a suicidal move, something a sister and a good lawyer couldn't allow to happen.

Adam was tapping his pen on the large table absent-mindedly. He was not aware that he might be seen as being childish. If he resumed his position at the corporation, the worst thing that could happen would be his moving back to Edmonton and putting his current job on hold. But for how long? He needed to know.

"As long as it takes, dammit. Don't you see? You must step up to the plate, like it or not. Father will be gone someday," Cassidy said.

"No way. I have been at his mercy long enough—"

"Okay," Cassidy said, ready to compromise in spite of Helen's hard look. "If father's health is seriously impaired or he dies, then you sell his share, and go on and build as many skyscrapers as you please. Can't you just try to work with Alicia for a bit longer?"

Adam felt trapped. He started pacing the room, shaking his head in disbelief. His life had been turned upside down so many times because of other people's needs and wishes. Everything he wanted to do with his life seemed impossible for him to grasp.

His cell phone ringing interrupted his thoughts and pacing.

Those waiting at the table couldn't believe he would be so inconsiderate as to leave his cell phone on, when they all made such an effort to meet and find a solution to his problem.

"Adam speaking—"

"Let's talk about morals. You seem to be in need of some lessons in this area," Crista rudely suggested.

Adam's face contorted with fury. "Save the advice for yourself, because I don't have time to waste. Whatever you have to say, I am not interested," Adam said through his tight lips. "Now, goodbye!"

"Don't you dare cut me off, Carry! I will pester you until you find the time to listen to me, I promise."

"I knew you would be a pest ever since you grabbed the business card from the table. What do you want?"

"Leave Eve alone. If you ever come near her again, I will personally meet your fool of a wife and tell her about your rendezvous lunch."

"What the hell are you talking about?" Adam fired back.

"I'm not in the mood for your questions, Carry. This is a warning. And let me add that, if your wife ever decides to pay Eve another visit to beg her to leave you alone, I will make sure Eve protects her own interests first."

Adam pressed the phone closer to his ear. "What are you talking about? Wait a minute! Who paid a visit to whom?" Adam asked, his attention completely focused on the conversation now.

Crista's sarcastic laughter filled Adam's ear. "Oh, come on. You want me to believe that you never knew that your wife, Cruella, had a tête-à-tête with Eve-the-naive?"

"Actually, all I know for sure is that you have a vivid imagination. Why should I believe your tale?"

Crista was fuming. "Carry, you are so full of shit that you don't know the difference between a *tale* and the *reality* itself! I'm telling you, your wife went to see Eve at her house. I'm not bullshitting you."

"When was that? And how come I don't know about it?" Adam demanded.

"Simple. You weren't supposed to know about it, that's why! Here is the story. Do you remember the morning you left Eve in 'wonderland?' Well, a few hours later, your darling wife, Alicia, showed up and exposed your mental health issues, and that you were using Eve before you went back to your consort."

Cold sweat ran down Adam's spine.

"I believe what you're saying is the truth, but it isn't the *whole* truth. There are some facts that would shock you if you knew. I can show you some evidence," Adam said. "How about meeting me back at the restaurant?"

"I can be there in no time," Crista agreed. "But Carry, don't waste my time. This had better be good. No bull. Okay?"

Crista was at the table when Adam arrived.

"I hope they didn't give you a hard time before they gave you a table."

"I think you're worried about the wrong person, Carry. What is it that you think I'll be so impressed by?" She extended her hand.

Adam took an envelope from his briefcase and extracted a couple of pages, held together with a paper clip. Placing them on the table in front of her, he suggested that she take a glance at "reality."

"What is it?" Crista asked. When Adam didn't answer, she took a better look, "Your divorce papers?"

"Exactly. Fortunately, I had them with me," he said. "Check the date."

Crista took a closer look at the papers, and her mouth fell open.

"You've been divorced all this time? Why the heck did your wife — ex-wife — come to Eve with that story? And why the hell did you take her to Europe that day? Don't deny that, I talked to your secretary. Obviously, you *forgot* to mention that to Eve. She thought you went back to China. When Alicia spoke to Eve, she was very convincing. Eve was certain she was an innocent victim of your reckless conduct."

Adam nodded, as he saw the episode playing out before his eyes. *Act by act. Scene by scene.*

"Alicia knew every detail about you and Eve," Crista continued. "Especially about the ring you gave Eve the night before. That detail alone broke the spell you cast on her. Alicia claimed it was *her* engagement ring."

"That's such BS. If she knew the key details about the ring, it was probably because she'd seen the receipt. I bought the ring the week before I gave it to Eve. On my way back from the airport, I stopped by my place and checked for the divorce papers and left some things at home, the ring receipt included. The bitch must have gotten into my room," Adam said, and shook his head in disbelief.

A long moment passed. "Remember what you told me once, about my chances to make things right with Eve?"

"How about you remind me," Crista suggested, because she wanted to know where this was going. She knew that something was coming to life.

"Well, you told me to have the divorce papers, a ring, and a date. Do those words ring a bell?"

"Ah!"

"I knew I should have received the divorce papers before I came to see Eve," Adam started. "Alicia gave them to me in China. My guess is that she didn't want me to have them when I saw Eve, to prove that I was divorced."

"Interesting. Alicia said you two were going to Russia to adopt a baby, not back to China," Crista said.

"Russia? To adopt a baby? Hell, no, nothing could be further from the truth," Adam said. "I was so sure I had outsmarted Alicia, by pretending I didn't know she had snuck into Eve's home—"

"What do you mean she 'snuck' into Eve's home?" Crista's shock was evident.

"Alicia was in the house the day before, while Eve was out. How she entered the house, I'm not certain. One possibility is that she duplicated the key Eve gave me. My guess is that Alicia waited for Eve to leave the house, went in, did what she needed to do, and then rushed out to the airport. I know for sure she was in the house, because when I arrived at Eve's house that evening, I detected Alicia's favourite fragrance."

"Man, do you know how stupid that sounds? She broke into Eve's house? For Christ's sake, why? And how the hell did you keep quiet about that?"

"I didn't want to scare Eve."

For a moment, Crista was thoughtful. "You could have told me," she said. "Or better yet, Mike. Damn. I told Eve to set her alarm every time she leaves the house. Thank God she changed the door locks soon after that, since you still had a key."

"Believe me, I had one hell of a night trying to figure out the best approach. I decided that I could take the matter into my own hands without alarming anyone, especially Eve. With her safety in mind, I decided to keep Alicia as far away from her as possible."

"By taking her with you…" Crista concluded.

"I took her with me to China pretending that I needed her help to finalize the business." Adam sighed. "No wonder she was behaving so well. She had already done the damage," Adam reflected. "And to think that, all this time, I couldn't blame anything on Alicia... I shouldn't have ignored her spiteful nature. And her previous threats, for that matter."

"You know what aggravated me the most? Just how easily you gave up. If I were you, I would have gone to the ends of the earth to win Eve back."

*To the ends of the earth*, and back. Adam thought about his trip to Sydney and the scuffle with Eve's husband. He had the scar to prove it. He realized Eve hadn't shared the details of that disturbing occurrence to her friends. No use to tell Crista now.

"I called Eve that day, but she didn't answer. I didn't worry about it then. Nor the next day nor the ones that followed. I thought about the situation with her niece and reasoned that Eve must have left the country unexpectedly. We didn't communicate much when I was away on business, and I didn't expect her to contact me, for that matter. I respected her too much to demand her attention in such a stressful time in her life. If I only knew..." Adam sighed. "When I came back, and my mother gave me the things that Eve left with her, my life turned upside down."

"If only Mike and I knew some of this then," Crista said.

"No wonder Eve sought comfort in another man. And so soon. I understand perfectly now."

"Yes," Crista agreed. *And it's all wrong when you still love each other.* She knew this was true from what she had witnessed in this very room just a couple of hours earlier. *Now it's too late.*

"He'll be back soon," Cassidy kept saying. She was outraged but couldn't afford to lose control. If anyone left before a decision was reached, it meant another day would go to waste. If it was her choice, she wouldn't be here at all, but Adam only accepted his responsibility with Carstone if she sat on the board of directors. Like she wanted any part of it. So what if he had to lead side by side with Alicia? Business is business.

*And to add more fuel to the fire, that woman comes back to mess up his mind,* Cassidy thought with exasperation. Nothing good is going to come out of this, Cassidy knew. Love is sometimes a bitch you can't win against.

Two hours had passed since Adam left and there was no sign of him, though he'd said he would come back soon. She was about to recommend that they reschedule the meeting when Adam walked in with two long, bloody scratches on the left side of his face and neck.

Cassidy's annoyance gave way to fear and then to anger.

"What the hell happened to you? I've thoroughly had it with you, Adam. I won't be surprised if you end up in some ditch with your brains blown out because of that woman—"

"What woman?" Adam snapped back. "You don't know what you're talking about," he said, pointing to the bloody scratches with a shaky finger. "See this? This is Alicia's signature, which by the way, is going to change all the plans now on the table," Adam said, throwing the box of Kleenex, which Cassidy passed to him.

Helen White was on her feet in an instant. "No way, Adam. I won't allow this to happen at your whim."

Adam was adamant. "Yes you will. You're paid to listen to me and make changes as I require. And you will do it right now, because I don't want to waste another day. I won't work with Alicia. Not now, not ever. Especially after today. Aren't you curious to know why? Because I don't want to rot in jail for killing that bitch, and by God, I mean it. I would surely kill her." Adam emphasized each word. "I hereby authorize Blaine to act on my behalf and that's final. Now put your heads together and come up with another draft."

Cassidy drove back to Calgary later that day, with Adam in the passenger seat. He was clearly too distraught to focus on the road. They talked for a while, or he talked and she listened. Cassidy was shocked. Alicia had succeeded in generating a scheme that victimized two innocent people.

Cassidy was deeply concerned about the consequences Alicia's actions would have. Adam's biggest regret, he said, was that he hadn't found Alicia alone so he could kill her. The conviction in his voice gave her chills, and as long as she lived, she wouldn't forget the cold, crazy look in his eyes when he said it. She made a mental note to call Helen and tell her they must find a way to keep Adam away from Carstone — away from Alicia — as he requested.

The sad thing was that, even though the truth had come to light, no one could change anything. After today's episode at the restaurant, Cassidy clearly knew that life would never be the same for her brother.

After Adam had shared his story, he sat silently on the seat beside her with his eyes closed. Cassidy prayed he would fall asleep. She prayed history wouldn't repeat itself this time around and he wouldn't react like he had over six months ago when he returned from China…

After Adam returned from China, Janet had many reasons to be worried about her son. When she gave him the package Eve left at her home, she was the first one to witness the anger of a man going out of his mind. Janet realized that Adam took Eve's rejection to heart. Week after week, her worry grew to the point of making her sick. She never told anyone in plain words, but she feared Adam was going to end his life over this breakup. She knew he needed help, and there was no one better equipped with insights on how to overcome this difficult phase than her daughter.

"Darling, I haven't heard from Adam in three days. I haven't been able to reach him on his phone. I fear for his sanity. His life," Janet told Cassidy.

The property Adam had shared with Alicia was on the market, so he had taken a furnished apartment. Janet offered to help unpack his belongings, but he rebuffed her and requested space and privacy.

Janet conferred with Cassidy, but she too advised her mother, "Give him time to think things through."

Cassidy didn't tell her mother that she was also checking on him. She had received a call from Garth, who shared his concern for Adam's well-being. "He's hit bottom, Cass. No doubt about that. We all need to keep tabs on him for a while."

At first, Cassidy kept tabs on Adam with an easygoing nature, but when she realized Adam's condition, she held nothing back. "You're drinking again."

He told her that it was his choice as to how he was coping with his situation. She felt hopeless but decided to give him more time.

It was her mother's frantic call one day that really shook her up.

"I know something has happened, dear," Janet said. "Don't ask me how I know, but I have this dreadful feeling. He has not set foot in the office for over a week and doesn't answer the phone. I don't have his keys and the complex manager doesn't return my messages."

"Okay, Mom. Stop right there. I'm sure he's fine. There is no use worrying yourself sick. I have some business in Edmonton this afternoon. I'll stop and see him."

"Stop by and pick me up," Janet pleaded.

Cassidy asked her receptionist to cancel all her afternoon appointments. Fifteen minutes later, she was on the road. Her thoughts were filled with an overwhelming stream of horrible images of her brother. Just the week before, there was news coverage of a man who hung himself in response to his wife's love affair with her boss. *God, please don't let anything happen to my brother.*

She had her own issue to reckon with. She had visions of her son being snatched away and given to his biological mother. Yet, envisioning her brother dead, made her own fear unsubstantiated.

The manager of the apartment building was waiting for them at the front entrance. He had the good sense not to be inquisitive and retreated as soon as he opened Adam's door.

Not knowing how the apartment was laid out, Cassidy followed her nose. A pungent odour became stronger as they came closer to a bathroom. They passed the living room, which looked — even with the blinds pulled down — as though it had never been used. Cassidy opened the first door they came upon and switched on the light. It was another bathroom, nice and clean, except for the floor, which was covered with pieces of broken beer bottle.

Cassidy's intuition proved right. The next room was Adam's bedroom.

*He must be in there, alive or—* She stopped and took a deep breath, irritated with her dark thoughts. If he had been dead for several days, there would be an unmistakable smell of decay by now. Her mother pushed her slightly. She pushed the door open so hard that it hit the wall and came back half way, almost hitting her in the face. She was so stunned that she remained rooted in the doorway, right hand over her nose.

Behind her, she heard Janet asking in a weak voice, "Is he, all right, dear?"

"Yes," Cassidy said, as she strode across the room to open the window. Of course, she knew he was in a drunken stupor from the second she laid eyes on him, but health-wise, he was all right. She was too disgusted for words and couldn't remember ever being consumed by such intense anger. She made a slight gesture with her hand to assure her mother that his condition was not life threatening.

Adam was lying on his back on an unmade and unclean bed, with one leg hanging off the side. He was breathing soundlessly. The stubble on his face was at least a week old. His fly was open, probably to save the effort of opening it on his next trip to the bathroom, where he had missed the target. His shirt was open and his white undershirt was lifted up, leaving his stomach uncovered. Various stains covered his undershirt, revealing what he had recently eaten and drunk. Empty bottles of beer and hard liquor were scattered everywhere.

To top it off, the whole room looked like an "art gallery" disaster. At least eight relatively large canvas paintings were strewn about the room, all bearing the same signature: *J. Angel.*

Janet was cleaning up the kitchen, and Cassidy was disinfecting the bathroom for what seemed like the tenth time, when Adam finally woke up. He cleared his throat to announce his appearance in the hallway. For a long moment, no one moved or said anything.

Adam glanced around and immediately stiffened. A few cardboard boxes were piled up at the door. So were the canvasses. And lots of garbage…

He opened his mouth to protest, but his sister was quicker.

"God, you're so self-centred. You don't seem to care whose lives you impact. You don't give a damn if Mother had to miss her physiotherapy appointment to stand up here cleaning the shit in your kitchen. Or if I break my neck driving like a lunatic from Calgary to check on you, because you haven't answered Mother's calls and she's too scared to come here by herself. We thought you were *dead*. Do you hear me?"

Cassidy's words cut like a knife. The realization of the damage he had done was quickly sobering him up. He was not surprised by his sister's treatment; she had a right to be angry. What he hadn't realized until now was the deep effect his conduct had on his loved ones.

"I'll get myself together."

"When did you reach that decision? Was it before or after you emptied all those bottles?" Cassidy asked, pointing to the plastic bag filled with empties. "I'm curious to know."

"I'm equally curious to know when you decided to run my life for me," Adam retorted.

Janet couldn't handle the tension any more. "Adam darling, Cass and I want what's best for you. Right now, you're too consumed with what's happened to think straight. You need help, and who else is there to care more for you than us? Please, listen to your sister. She can help you."

"Well then, go on, sis. Tell me what you have decided is best for me."

"You have two choices. You either check yourself into a rehab clinic or you come with me to Calgary."

At the end of a long pregnant moment, Adam sighed.

He chose the second option.

Adam's family proved to be a major pillar of strength for him. Brad and Cassidy were supportive when Adam announced that he joined Murphy-Bird Structural Enterprise. Although it was not an extremely well-known construction company, it gave Adam a chance to work through his fears of inadequacy and gain confidence of belonging in that field. It also gave him a chance to satisfy his longing to fit into the real world and stand on his own feet.

At first, he put in long hours — mainly because it was asked of him, but also because he didn't feel confident enough that he would use his free time constructively.

There was only one other time when Adam gave his sister a reason to be worried about him. It was the day she found a succinct message on her machine: "Left for Sydney. Don't worry. I'll be back in two to three days." Clear, concise, and to the point. Alarming, nonetheless.

She consulted with her husband, whose opinions she highly appreciated, to help her understand Adam's motivation. She needed a male view of the male mind. Brad felt that Adam needed to do something to find closure. He needed to see Eve, and free himself, so he could carry on with his life.

Cassidy hoped Brad was right.

*And what a closure that was,* Cassidy mused. It came in the form of a black eye, badly bruised knuckles, two broken ribs, and a deep cut on his upper lip that took five stitches and a good plastic surgeon to close up. Adam was left with a scar on his upper lip as a bitter memory.

Yet despite the injuries, the experience was cathartic for Adam. He started slowly to regain his old confidence, to be himself again. Cassidy finally was able to relax. She deemed that her brother's head was above water, at last.

About the same time, something else helped Adam solidify his new lease on life. Cassidy and Brad brought their son to live with them in Calgary. It was a tactical move. "The child needs to live with his parents," Judge Parson advised firmly, and asked them to make the arrangements as soon as possible. His rationale was to prevent the biological mother from stating that her son didn't even live under the same room as the adoptive parents. It was a huge bonus that Ryan and Adam truly adored each other.

This move however, caused a huge argument between the Johnsons and the grandparents, especially Janet. Cassidy justified the relocation by saying that Ryan needed his parents, and that having Janet at his beck and call meant too much strain on her. Her mother was not getting any younger and her sore, injured leg would benefit from less strenuous activity. Janet argued that the move was unnecessary. Cassidy almost lost patience with her mother. Neither of her parents had been aware of their legal battle to keep their son. It was bad enough that Ryan didn't take the relocation well. He grumbled about changing schools and parting with his hockey teammates.

Cassidy glanced at Adam. They were halfway to Calgary. He still had his eyes closed, but she suspected he was awake.

When Cassidy saw Eve and Adam today at the same table, enjoying each other's company, she knew that love was there: in Adam's whole being, and more disquieting than that, in Eve's eyes. Her brother talked to Eve enthusiastically, as if they were connected somehow. It made Cassidy worry. It had crossed her mind what could happen once Eve learned — and she was bound to — that Adam was single and available. The outcome was easy to foresee: Adam would forget his "resolve", Eve would turn to him, and meanwhile both of them would be ignoring the fact that her new husband wouldn't just sit there unbothered, watching his new family disintegrate.

Her troubled thoughts were interrupted by the ring of her cell phone.

"Missed me today?" Brad asked.

"Sure. One extra lawyer brain would have helped the meeting."

Brad laughed. "You'll never guess my news."

"Okay. You win. Out with it!"

"Dorothy Whalebone just paid me a visit."

For a moment, Cassidy was silent. "Is that who I think it is?"

"Yes. We met briefly today, but we'll see her again tomorrow. Just the four of us: you, me, her, and her husband," Brad explained. "The good news is that her intention is not as we initially believed; she actually wants to help us. I already contacted Leon Hill and Judge Parson for advice. We agreed to make a deal with her. There is a lot more to it, but I'll tell you later. The fact is she is ready to withdraw her claim."

"Meaning?"

"Meaning — we keep our son, and she'll get some money."

"I don't care about the money as long as we keep Ryan. What prompted her to go for the money now, instead of asking for it from the beginning? Are you sure she's not up to something?"

"Darling, let me worry about that. That's my line of work. You'll see, the last piece of the puzzle just fell into place. And we should take care so it stays in place. No surprises later on. I have to go now," Brad said, hanging up.

"There is always good news after bad," Adam said, and Cassidy looked to her right, startled. She smiled at her brother's open, genuine, yet remarkably sad smile.

Eve was reclined on her favourite chair. It became customary that this time of day was hers alone, private and tranquil. For thirty minutes, she indulged in sweet daydreams. Mrs. Shapiro had gone home and Brian had gone to pick up Anthony from school. Thankfully, her babies were coming to term.

It was warm for Edmonton, a sign if not of full spring, then at least a defeated winter. In the backyard, close to the house, Eve had seen small reddish sprouts the day before. She loved her tulips. The yellow ones, especially. What a time to bring new lives into this world! One year from now, her little ones would be taking their first steps. She smiled. With her eyes closed, she envisioned the little ones pulling at those lovely tulips.

After a moment, she sighed. Who was she trying to fool? She was trying so hard to force pleasant thoughts to the forefront of her mind and ignore the endless, suffocating ones. Ever since she saw Adam, she just couldn't stop thinking of him, even more so now that she was about to bring *his* children into the world. She knew that she wasn't being fair. She had denied Adam's right to fatherhood. She was doing exactly what she would have condemned in others.

Sometimes she felt as if the guilt was almost choking her, and in those moments, she felt a great deal of anxiety. She thought of confiding in Crista, of coming out with the whole truth, but she quickly reconsidered. Crista was such a fiery person and had railed against Adam since the break-up. Eve realized that she could not succumb to such sentimental thoughts. She couldn't risk what was most precious to her: her children.

Unaware of the exact stage of Eve's pregnancy, Crista didn't comment, one day before over the phone, on Eve's desire to come along to support the boys at their championship hockey game.

However, when Crista and Mike went to pick up Eve and Brian, they were taken aback by the way Eve looked. She seemed enormous and completely exhausted. It was as if she was going to give birth to those babies at any moment.

Crista inquired, "Sure you want to come along? Because we are recording the game, you know."

"Of course I want to come," Eve said.

On Brian's cue, Crista didn't say anything else. She sensed that there had been a discussion on the same subject before they showed up. Was Brian worried that Eve wanted to go for a completely different reason? Recently the children announced that Ryan had moved back to Edmonton. Maybe he suspected that Adam would be at the game. Crista and Mike had discussed the same possibility. With his nephew back on the team, Adam would want to support him, and no one could stop him from being there. Mike felt that Adam would have the sense not to approach Eve, especially with Brian close by.

The teams were on the rink warming up, hopes and expectations mingling with their nervous excitement. Crista kept the entrance under close surveillance. Five minutes before the game started, she saw Adam come in with Ryan's father, and noted that they positioned themselves a few rows behind their group.

About ten minutes into the game, Eve asked Brian to bring a blanket from the car. Crista took the opportunity to look back and acknowledge Adam's presence with a wink.

On the ice, both teams were battling fiercely. The score was still 0-0. Both teams got a power play, but neither could score. And then, with five minutes left to play in the first period, the opposing team, the *Blue Pucks,* scored.

The *Oil Patch* immediately played offensively, but they couldn't seem to get the puck to the other end. Their coach decided to send out a player to convey a new plan of attack.

The players got the message. Through an admirable and dexterous move, "little Stuart" managed to get control of the puck. This was his famous move, where he took advantage of his small size and great speed, taking the puck down to the other team's goal line. With two opponents bearing down on him, he paused long enough to fake a shot on goal, and then flicked the puck to Ryan, who was standing at the top of the crease. Ryan glided between two players and shot the puck into the top right corner of the net before the *Blues* knew what hit them.

The crowd went wild, as did the players. Everybody was standing. Disengaging himself from his teammates' congratulatory embrace, Ryan took the opportunity to search for his own supporters.

"Dad! Uncle Adam!" he shouted in the direction of Section E.

Eve instinctively turned to look. As she did, her right foot slipped between the concrete step and the wooden bench, causing her to lose her balance and fall. It happened so fast that even Crista, who was the closest person to Eve, could not have prevented it. She froze. Everyone else seemed to react but her. Only after she saw Adam, scooping Eve up in his arms, did she finally come out of her trance. Mike was suddenly there.

"I'll take it from here, Adam," he said, handing over the video recorder to Crista. He'd been sitting at the end of the row so he wouldn't obstruct anyone's view, and though he saw Eve fall, he couldn't get there sooner than Adam. The man seemed to fly, throwing himself down the seats and skipping down the rows. "Brian will be here any second, Adam. Stay back please," Mike advised, as Adam transferred Eve into Mike's arms. "And call *911. Now!*"

The ambulance arrived quickly. The medical team assessed Eve's condition and drove off to the closest hospital. Mike and Crista followed in their car.

The female paramedic questioned Eve about her fall, pregnancy, and due date, while attending to the scrape on her right leg. The paramedic frowned at the large bruise on Eve's lower abdomen. She assured them they would arrive at the Royal Alexandra Hospital within a few minutes, where the babies' heart rates would be closely monitored.

Brian asked the paramedic to correct the information provided earlier, while Mike and Crista were present, regarding the stage of Eve's pregnancy, and told her that she was scheduled for a C-section on Monday. The paramedic said that she would look into it once they arrived at the hospital.

On the gurney, Eve shuddered in pain. She closed her eyes, breathed in sharply, and clenched her jaw for a few seconds and then relaxed. Brian missed the cue.

At the hospital things moved fast. Eve was wheeled right away to the Women's Centre for an ultrasound. Eve's doctor was notified and was on his way. A young obstetrics resident took charge. While a sonographer prepared Eve for the ultrasound, he busied himself with Eve's file.

Brian became impatient. "Doctor, half an hour has passed since my wife fell. Nothing has been done except for cleaning the scrape on her leg. I want another doctor to examine my wife."

"I'm sorry, sir, but all doctors are in the OR right now," the resident replied. "I can put in a request, but Dr. Summer will be here by then."

"My wife is carrying twins and had a cervical cerclage a few months into her pregnancy. I request that someone more experienced take charge of my wife's care."

The resident looked astonished.

"Mr. Nelson—"

"Kid. My name is Brian Kid."

"Mr. Kid, I appreciate your concern, but I have experience in obstetrics. I have this under control. Both babies' heartbeats are present and normal. The mother's vitals are also fine, so it's likely that the fall didn't cause any distress aside from the lesion on the leg and bruise on the lower abdomen. At this time, there is nothing more to be done. At thirty-two weeks, it is not recommended that we do a pelvic examination due to the history—"

"Thirty-two weeks? Are you blind? Look in the chart!" Brian shouted.

The doctor paled as he turned the pages. On the last page, under "observation," he found the correction Brian had asked the paramedic to make. He opened his mouth to say something, but a sharp cry coming from the ultrasound room made him jump.

"Doctor, her water broke. She's having spontaneous contractions," a voice shouted.

Just then, Dr. Summer rushed in. After one look at his patient, he moved into action.

"Let's move her to 48, people. We deliver right away. Brenda, call NICU for the twins and page Dr. Andrew to come to the OR. We need help and don't have time to waste. Also, get the father into scrubs ASAP!" the doctor ordered.

Dr. Summer pushed Eve's stretcher from one side, the resident from the other.

"Meyy, you realize what's going on here with that bruise on the lower abdomen, don't you?" Dr. Summer asked the young doctor. "We might deal with a hematoma," Dr. Summer explained. "We need to act quickly." He knew very well that, in medicine, mistakes happen, but in many instances time was their worst enemy.

Brian was struggling to keep up with the doctors when he heard his name being called. He looked back but didn't stop.

"Brian, I want you to wait here until someone comes to get you," Dr. Summer said. "Eve will have anaesthesia now. You can't be present, but please stay close by. It is *extremely* important that I can reach you."

Before the stretcher passed through the double doors of the restricted area, Brian bent and kissed Eve's forehead. "It's going to be all right, darling." It was then that he noticed how pale Eve looked.

"What happened?" Crista asked, approaching Brian. "Why is Eve so white?"

"Why did they take her to the OR?" Mike asked.

At that moment, he turned to face Eve's concerned friends. And then, his face contorted with fury.

"Why is *he* here?" he shouted at Crista and Mike, looking in Adam's direction.

Brian started towards him and Mike stepped in between them. "Listen, Brian, he was at the game; he saw Eve falling. He's concerned—"

"He feels bad about Eve's fall," Crista interjected. "Wait a minute. Do you know each other?"

Brian ignored her.

"I don't want you here; do you hear me? I told you to stay away from Eve!" Brian shouted.

"Okay, buddy. Let's all be cool," Mike said, positioning his body between the two men. "Let's be civilized."

Crista and Mike pulled at Brian's arms in an attempt to gain distance from Adam, at the same time making desperate signals to Adam to disappear.

All of a sudden, Brian pulled himself free and started towards Adam.

"And why exactly are you feeling bad about this?" he demanded.

Mike caught up to Brian and took him aside, hoping Crista would take the hint and remove Adam from the vicinity.

Crista pointed Adam in the opposite direction.

Mike tried to calm Brian down, "Look, Adam feels bad because Eve is hurt. While you went to fetch the blanket, Ryan scored for his team and he waved at his uncle and called his name. We all looked in that direction, because we didn't think he would be there. At that moment, Eve's foot slipped and she fell. He saw the accident. He feels guilty like crap," Mike said.

"*You* don't understand. Guilty or not, I don't want him here. Is that clear?" Brian said through clenched teeth.

Just then the OR doors swung open and a doctor wearing a surgical mask called his name, holding the door for Brian as he entered.

"How is my wife, doctor?"

The doctor pulled his masked down and cleared his throat, the furrows on his forehead deepening.

"I'm Dr. Novak. Dr. Summer asked me to talk to you. Your wife spontaneously delivered one of the babies — a girl of about six pounds — before we finished preparing her for the anaesthesia. Something went wrong when your wife fell. I don't have time to go through the details, but the bottom line is that the first baby was affected during the fall. We don't know yet to what extent. We do know that there is a severe contusion on the baby's head. Unfortunately, your wife has lost consciousness and we must deliver the other baby by C-section. Dr. Summer is doing that as we speak. Our biggest concern is for the other baby, because it may be in danger of oxygen deprivation. In this situation, as a backup precaution, we need plasma from the parents."

"What are you saying doctor? Because, if I follow you correctly, you're suggesting that you need the biological father's involvement. Is that it?"

The doctor nodded. "Dr. Summer told me about the complicated situation between the parents, but this is not about their predicament.

This is a life and death situation. One of the babies could die. I'm afraid we need the biological father's assistance *right away.*"

"Are you sure there's no other solution? Because I can donate—"

The doctor shook his head. "I am sorry."

At the other end of the hallway, Adam was talking animatedly on his cell phone. He stopped the conversation when he noticed Brian wrestling with Crista and Mike. He seemed so distraught. Adam assumed that something must have happened to Eve. A numb feeling engulfed him and before he knew it, his feet carried him towards the group.

"Where is he? I want to see him," Brian kept saying, as he struggled to get free. "You don't understand! *Let me go!*"

"Brian, don't worry. He won't bother you, again. He's gone," Mike said, doing his best to block the view of the other end of corridor.

"Is everything okay?" Crista asked. "Tell us what the doctor said. Was that Eve's baby they took in the incubator?"

"No. Yes. It was the first baby Eve gave birth to. Something is definitely very wrong," Brian said. "I *must* talk to Carry. People *listen* to me. I *need* to talk to him—"

"I'm here."

"Adam, I told you to go away," Crista said.

Adam kept walking closer.

"I need you to hear me out," Brian said in earnest. "I wish I never needed to tell you this, but I must. One of the babies' lives is in danger. It needs *your* help."

*"His?"* Why?" Mike asked.

"The doctor thinks that plasma may be needed to save the baby's life."

"Brian, you lost me," Mike said. "How in the world can *Adam* help the baby by donating *his* plasma—?"

"Because he's the *father!"*

Adam laughed. "Yeah, right."

"Listen Adam, please just go away, man," Mike begged, and then turned to Brian. "What are you talking about? Is this a joke?"

"Do you think I'm joking when an innocent life is at stake?" Brian yelled.

"Brian, are you serious?" Crista asked, stunned.

"I'm telling you, I am not the father of those babies." He pointed to Adam, almost touching his face. *"He is!"*

"Isn't it a bit too late to run from your responsibilities?" Adam asked, and turned to leave.

With a quick move, Brian pulled Adam's arm forcefully. The jolt brought the two men face to face, barely a foot apart.

"That's a question for you, you son of a bitch! *You* got Eve pregnant! Don't pretend that you can't fathom why she had to run away from you!"

"I don't know what you're up to, Kid. All I know is that I am incapable of impregnating Eve, because I can't have children."

"Yeah, right," Brian snorted. "You're a liar. You might have a long list of problems, but being sterile? Well, that's not one of them."

"As far as I'm concerned, this conversation has gone too far. I couldn't father Eve's babies, regardless of how much I would have wanted to," Adam said, and realized he was not helping the situation by sticking around. "Crista, Mike, I'll catch up with you later."

"Wait, I'm not finished! You are the *father* of those babies and only *you* can help! Believe me, I would rather help them myself, but I simply can't!"

"Let me reiterate, I can't have children. And in case you have your math mixed up, I wasn't with Eve…what…seven months ago? So there you have it."

"You're right. You were not with Eve seven months ago. How about eight and a half months ago? Yeah, let's talk math. Let's draw the line. Is that so bizarre of a coincidence that Eve's pregnancy reached thirty-eight weeks yesterday?"

"Thirty-eight weeks?" Crista repeated.

For a moment, nobody even breathed.

Crista was the first one to speak. "Oh my God. *Oh my God!* No wonder Eve was so big! How idiotic of me to believe she was that huge because she was carrying twins!" *Poor Eve, Adam was...and she doesn't know...and Brian...*"Oh my God!"

There was no reason for Cassidy to babysit her father any longer. His blood pressure had lowered to a satisfactory level. She prescribed a nap, to which he obediently agreed. Janet, on the other hand, found a temporary diversion giving ineffectual directions to her housekeeper.

"Mom, Dad is sleeping. I'm going to catch up with my family," she said, before she left her parents' house in a hurry.

An hour later, Cassidy was still searching for Adam. He had called her, asking her to come to the hospital. "Eve fell down and she doesn't look good," he'd said. She advised him to back off as Eve was in good hands. The prospect of him being in close proximity to Eve's husband gave Cassidy chills.

The closest Cassidy came to learning of her brother's whereabouts was through Crista, whom she found in the visitor's lounge at the Women's Centre.

"Adam went to the Red Cross to donate plasma," Crista volunteered.

She would have said more, but Cassidy vanished too quickly.

Crista started laughing. Brian stared at her.

"It's funny, you know? Of all people, *I* have to tell you the 'big secret.'"

"What are you talking about?"

"Adam Carry is divorced," she said. "He was, in fact, divorced many months ago, just as he told Eve. Eve and he were victims of the fabrications of the cruel, sad excuse for a woman he was married to. She was an actress, a very good one. I didn't know that until recently. Eve probably told you how things happened with her and Adam. Until a couple of months ago, I believed that was the truth, too."

By the time Crista stopped talking, Brian was speechless, his pain visible.

He didn't question his position, even though it was now more complicated than ever. Months ago, he had stepped in. It seemed like the appropriate thing to do. He wondered though, how Eve could have given up on Adam without confronting him, if she loved him so much.

"By running away, Eve fed into the manipulation," he said.

"Exactly," Crista said. "But she couldn't help it. She's a decent human being who can't measure up to someone so vile. Besides, she was afraid she would lose her babies—"

"Mr. Kid?" a voice called from the door.

Brian stood up. "Is my wife awake?"

The nurse smiled. "I don't know about that, sir. I'm from Neonatal Intensive Care. I came to tell you that it's all right to come and see your babies."

Cassidy would have slapped Adam's face if it could wipe off his foolish smile. "Are you out of your mind?" Cassidy's voice came out in a strained whisper. Out of the corner of her eye, she saw a man approaching. She recognized Mike Malone, but her fury blinded her and stole her ability to be discreet.

"Who the hell came up with this idea?" she demanded.

"The doctor," Adam grinned. "I have a feeling she doesn't know yet," he told Mike, who was now by his side.

"Know what? How juvenile you act?"

Adam turned to Mike, "I told you she doesn't know."

"Cut the crap, Adam," Cassidy said.

"I guess no one took the time to give you the news. To congratulate you on becoming an auntie," Adam said. "Cass, I'm a father. Do you understand? A *father*. Eve was carrying my babies. *My* babies. I know they're mine, okay? I thought I could never—"

"That's impossible. What, do you think some miracle happened today and made you a father? I don't think so."

"That was my first reaction too," Adam tried again to explain. "But it's the truth. Think about it, Cass. The babies were born at thirty-eight weeks and that's good enough evidence for me to be assured they are mine. Thirty-eight weeks ago I was with Eve."

"Oh, my God!" Cassidy said, her face flashed from the rush of adrenaline. "I've seen them. They are full-term size for twins. I've read their file, but it didn't cross my mind to put the two together."

"What do you mean you've *seen them?* You've seen the twin? How is *it?* What is *it?*"

"Same as the first. Except she's in perfect health. And that's a miracle. She's about six pounds, with a loud mouth — I mean — a great voice and promising beauty."

"I have two daughters! I have *two* daughters, Cass! I can't believe it!"

"This is wonderful news!" Mike proclaimed.

"Oh, Adam, I was so furious. Now I'm shocked, but in a good way. I thought the results of the fertility test came back and you were sterile. I'm sure you said…oh, my Lord!"

"*Alicia!*" brother and sister said at the same time.

# Nine

On their way back from the Red Cross Centre, heading to the Royal Alexandra Hospital, Cassidy briefed her brother on the health of the babies.

"There is evidence of head trauma: a contusion to Twin A's head that occurred when Eve fell. It's too soon to predict how or if it will affect the neurophysiology. The baby is having a computed tomography, which is an imaging procedure to diagnose any physical and neurological abnormalities. If the baby's skull is only superficially affected, there will likely be a complete recovery with only a minor scar," Cassidy said.

"The second baby girl has made up for the first one. She got a high score on the Apgar scale, which is a measure of the baby's physical condition in the first minutes after birth. A medical professional checks the heart rate, skin colouration, respiration, muscle tone, and response to stimuli. Twin B could have been taken to a normal nursery, but went to NICU instead with her twin sister, more as a favour to the family to visit them both at the same time, than anything else," Cassidy concluded.

"Cass, have you seen Eve?"

"No," Cassidy said. She could have seen her, but chose not to.

Adam remained silent.

"Adam, I know you must be disappointed. I intended to see her. I really did, as a doctor if not as an acquaintance. But when Crista told me you went to the Blood Centre, I snapped. If I had only known the truth—" Cassidy said.

"If *I* only had known the truth..."

"I did inquire about Eve though," Cassidy said. She was not sure how to break the news. "Remember how you told me on the phone that Eve was very pale?"

"I said as *white* as the sheet she was covered with."

"Exactly," Cassidy said. The last thing she wanted was to alarm Adam. She believed he truly loved Eve. "Her paleness is a result of renal ischemia, which is a kidney malfunctioning because the blood flow into the kidneys is somewhat reduced. The fall Eve sustained caused great pressure on the kidneys, affecting their normal activity," Cassidy explained. She decided to leave out the worst case scenario: renal failure.

"That's temporary, isn't it?" Adam asked.

Cassidy felt her brother's tension.

"I'm not very knowledgeable in matters of the renal system in adults. I suspect it will take some time for her to recuperate. Eve is young and healthy enough to pull through."

Adam sighed.

To pull him from his negative thoughts, Cassidy suggested they call their mother.

"She'll be over the moon about the babies."

Janet was not one to worry easily. Over the years, she had been complimented on her patience. However, there were times like this when she couldn't help herself. She could feel a headache coming on. When the phone rang, she jumped from the sofa.

"Where are you, dear?" she asked Cassidy. "You said you were going to meet Brad and Ryan. Brad called and said he couldn't reach you. I've called you three times. And Adam doesn't answer his phone either."

"Mom, take it easy. I'm fine and so is Adam. He's here with me. Is Father still napping?"

"Yes, he is. Where are you? Why isn't Adam with Brad and Ryan? They left together for the game."

"Listen, Mother. I'm driving and don't want to be on the phone for long. Remember when I told you Eve was pregnant? She had two little girls two hours ago. Those two little angels are *your* granddaughters."

"Cass darling, how is it possible?"

"That's bullshit!" George's voice thundered into the phone. "That bitch may be able to fool Adam, but she can't fool me! She's after our money! I told you that before! I'm telling you now! I'm calling my lawyer right now!"

Adam and Cassidy found Crista alone in the visitor's room. She didn't look happy.

Cassidy said, "Your husband just went to pick up Anthony and Brandon from my place."

"I know. I just spoke with him."

"Any word about Eve? Where's Brian?" Adam inquired.

"Brian was called in for a conference about Eve's condition. I'm afraid something terrible has happened or else her doctor wouldn't look so sombre."

Adam was already at the door with his sister close behind.

"Adam, wait here. You won't get far, but I will," Cassidy said, pointing to her white coat, which she had grabbed from the staff lounge next door.

"Here comes Brian," Crista announced in a hoarse voice.

Judging from the look on Brian's face, he wasn't bringing good news. He didn't even make a fuss about Adam's presence. If anything, he reacted to the sight of the woman in a white coat.

"Brian, this is Adam's sister, Cassidy Johnson. She's a paediatrician. Tell us what's going on," Crista insisted.

"Let's all sit down," he advised with a sigh. "Nothing we can do but wait and see, the doctor said."

The room was small and cluttered. Several empty coffee cups had missed the garbage can. A strong smell of stale Chinese food lingered in the air. The medical professionals assembled paid no attention to the messy surroundings as they were listening carefully to Dr. Weil.

They took notes or listened, refraining from any questions or comments, as per Dr. Weil's instructions. This was not a Q & A session.

"You see, ladies and gentlemen," Dr. Weil continued, "this case doesn't follow the rules. In all cases when foetuses suffer trauma caused by an external impact, we see the hematoma form at the rupture point between the placenta and the uterus. This is observed, unfortunately, after the delivery, when, as the statistics show, the damage is already done. Time is the most decisive factor. The hematoma was present in this case too, yet the result was unusual. In sixty-six per cent of recorded cases, the foetus was stillborn. Like I said, time is the deciding factor. In twenty-one per cent of cases, the mother died. Several factors are responsible for this: gangrene of the uterus, glomerulonephritis, septicemia, and cardiac and pulmonary arrest. And finally, the rest — a small number — are happy endings where both mother and baby survive and recover without any major health problems. This is what I hope to see happen in this case."

"Dr. Weil, have you considered consulting with other specialists around the country who have dealt with similar cases?" Cassidy challenged.

Dr. Weil lifted his eyes only a degree from the materials he was gathering. He scanned the room and noticed the mature, female doctor.

"Dr. Johnson?"

"I'm here on behalf of the patient's family. The twins are my nieces. The well-being of their mother is of personal interest and concern to me," Cassidy said. The few people who were still in the room stopped and watched. No one crossed the line with Dr. Weil. "Also, I came across some material on the subject you discussed. Just recently there was a case in Toronto that can be a useful reference to your patient's course of treatment. I can offer my assistance if you like—"

"That won't be necessary. *I* have everything under control."

Cassidy couldn't ignore the doctor's condescending manner. She waited for the last audience member to leave and approached Dr. Weil. He was talking with Dr. Summer in a low voice.

"And I think the patient's family has the right to choose another doctor. Or hospital, for that matter."

"*Ms.* Johnson, *I'm* the head of Obstetrics," he fired back. "Besides, *I* must agree with the request, and *that* happens only *if* the representing doctor is acting incompetently."

With that said, he left the room.

"God, what arrogance! *Head of the department!* And all that bull about doing his best. Why didn't he mention the risk of kidney failure? Does he need gangrene and cardiac arrest to realize his patient needs urgent consideration and expertise of the best specialists?"

"Good to see you, Dr. Johnson. Long time no see," Dr. Summer said approaching Cassidy. You're right about Dr. Weil. But as much as I hate to admit it, he has power. Nonetheless, he is a good, capable doctor — one of the best we've got — you know that. Let's be smart and work together," Dr. Summer winked. "Did I hear correctly, you're related to the babies' father? His sister?"

"Yes."

"Okay. All our forces should focus on the mom's health. I'd appreciate your opinion and suggestions. Please forward them to me rather than to Dr. Weil and I'll make sure he covers any insights you offer," Dr. Summer said and wrote down his cell phone number. "After all, I'm still Eve's primary doctor."

Cassidy and Adam were visiting the babies when they saw George and Janet in a dynamic conversation with a security guard. They couldn't hear the exchange, but it was clear from George's body language that he was being patronizing.

"I hope the guard calls for help to throw him out," Adam said under his breath.

To say they were surprised to see their parents was an understatement. When Janet called Cassidy and told her that George was coming to the hospital, no one took it seriously. Cassidy expected Janet had more sense than to let him out of the house, considering his health.

"One foot in the grave and the thought of losing money brings him out," Adam said, utterly disgusted.

"Well, are you surprised? You know our dear daddy," Cassidy said, as they walked towards the sliding glass door separating them from their parents.

"Father, what on earth are you making a scene here for? This is a hospital. An intensive care unit," Adam hissed, once he and Cassidy were on the other side of the glass door. "Mother, how could you let him come?"

"Since when have you known your father to take orders from anyone?" Janet whispered. "Thank God he changed his mind about calling Paul Greene. I had to work extremely hard to convince him those babies are yours. I just hope to God it's the truth. Now all he wants is to see the wee ones with his own eyes. That's all."

Adam looked around. The silence was calming.

Cassidy had somehow managed to placate everyone. She even talked Brian into allowing her parents to visit their granddaughters. She knew if George could see the babies, it would help make peace. But George wanted more. Within minutes, he was in a rocking chair with Twin B, the easiest to be picked up, in the crook of his right arm. Once the baby was settled, Cassidy placed Twin A in his other arm.

"And this is your first-born granddaughter," Cassidy said, after she arranged the IV line and other wires connected to the baby. She commented on the little girl's head injury in a way that sounded as if it was just a minor, superficial abrasion.

While he sat there, she examined him. She knew she had taken a chance with her father's heart when she let him in, because it was such an intense, emotional experience. Yet, at the same time, she thought he might benefit from it.

"They are so small."

"No, Dad. They're actually a good size for twins. One weighs 6.1 pounds and the other close to six. Aren't they beautiful?"

"Oh, yes. I can see Adam's face in theirs. And they probably have something from their mother. I never met her, but she is probably beautiful."

"Probably?"

Everybody laughed.

"Grandpa, do you want a picture with your precious granddaughters?" the nurse in charge of Twin B asked, a Polaroid camera ready in her hands.

He stopped rocking, a proud, heart-warming smile on his face.

Getting a second chance at life sometimes depends on each drop of intravenous solution into the pool called *life.*

Twenty-four hours had passed since Eve lay in intensive care, working hard on that second chance. She was in stable condition but still in an induced sleep.

Her kidneys were working again, but the urinalysis indicated erratic results. The doctor said it had to get worse before it got better. And worse it got.

At noon the following day, her temperature reached 39.5°C, which alarmed both her doctors and loved ones. Everyone waited close to intensive care, unit 49.

A new battery of tests was ordered, one of which showed that Eve was anaemic. Promptly, a blood-line was inserted.

Adam called Cassidy, who had returned to Calgary just hours before, and updated her on the new situation. In return, she called Dr. Summer, who assured her that they — meaning Dr. Weil and himself — were already in collaboration, via video conference, with Dr. Staniluk, the renowned urologist from Toronto, just as she suggested earlier.

Another twenty-four hours passed. Eve's body temperature remained at 39°C.

Meanwhile, on their third day of life, the twins had a new visitor: their uncle Garry. When Crista called with the news, he arranged the earliest flight possible. It seemed an eternity before he finally stepped out of the restricted area at Edmonton International and saw Mike. At Garry's earnest request, Mike drove him directly to the hospital.

At the hospital, Garry met Brian, who took him in to see Eve. Seeing his sister buried under tubes and hooked to various machines shook him to the core. He asked that the doctors consider him a prospective kidney donor, if it came to that.

With Twin B in the crook of his right arm, Garry was wiping away a tear when he noticed Brian's gaze over his right shoulder. He half turned, guessing who had just come in. He heard Brian saying, "Garry, this is Adam Carry." And to Adam, "Adam this is Eve's brother, Garry Davis."

Both men smiled and nodded their heads in acknowledgement, understandably a little uncomfortable, but they didn't shake hands as the baby was between them.

"My nieces — your daughters — are enchantingly beautiful," Garry said.

"I'm certain they got that from their mother," Adam said.

"I don't know what's going to happen, Mother," Cassidy said, annoyed. They were having lunch in a rather crowded cafeteria in the sub-basement of the hospital. Cassidy disapproved of her parents' monopolizing the twins and surrounding them with expensive gifts, seeming to ignore the fact that the babies also belonged to their mother's side. It was as if they — Grandma and Grandpa Carry — were trying to usher out the other party. Janet asked Cassidy if she thought Eve would divorce *that* man and marry Adam.

"Mother! Don't even go there. It's not our business," Cassidy snapped. "The little ones will always be related to us, no matter where and with whom they live. Isn't that enough to make your heart soar?"

Janet lowered her eyes.

"Oh, Mom. It's impossible to be mad at you," Cassidy said, squeezing her mother's hand across the table.

Janet's blue eyes rested on her daughter's face thoughtfully.

"What is it, Mom?" she asked.

Janet sighed, "Darling, we *know* about Ryan."

Cassidy's mouth dropped open. "How? From whom?

"Cass, darling. Your father has his ways. You know that. Your father and Judge Parson are old friends. Thank God he learned about the saga after it was resolved. I don't know if he would have survived otherwise. You know how much he loves Ryan."

After a full minute of silence, Cassidy asked, "How much do you know about our nightmare? And why didn't you ever mention it to me?"

"I personally don't know all the details, dear, but I'd like to, if you would confide in me. And for the second part of the question, we kept it to ourselves to protect you. Your father decided — and I agreed with him — that it would have hurt you to know that we knew about your family problems. You scratch through his steel veneer and find a mushy, good-hearted soul deep down. That's your father."

The younger woman shook her head. "It was so awful. I still get goosebumps thinking about it. Any other hurdle Brad and I ever encountered before seems nothing compared to this. And to think that, even as we speak, the problem wouldn't be resolved if it weren't for the wisdom of the woman who gave birth to Ryan..." Cassidy took a sip of her coffee.

"The fact is that no one could have guessed, let alone comprehended, what was behind this entire process of 'child hunting.' If we knew, the pain would have been easier to bear.

"It started with a letter from the birth mother's lawyer, informing us that she wanted Ryan back. Brad didn't tell me at first, but it got to a point where he realized there was only a 50/50 chance of us keeping Ryan. We were prepared to throw in a large sum of money, but at the last minute, Judge Parson advised against it. He said that her lawyer could have suspected our intention and had it recorded as evidence of coercion. Besides, Ryan is close to the age when he can decide who he wants to live with. Of course, you may think, 'That's fine because he will chose us, of course.' Wrong. In some cases, children feel they have been betrayed and often cross the floor to their biological parent. Not all of them, but we couldn't risk it. The biological mother held more cards than we did."

Cassidy studied her mother, who was wiping tears from her eyes.

"Remember when Adam was in Edmonton the last time? When Dad was in the hospital and wanted Adam to officially take control?

The following day, Brad and I met Dorothy and her husband. She called the meeting; we chose the ground. No lawyers, no judge, just the four of us. At first, she was rambling and in the middle of it, we got the shock of our lives. It was not *her* who wanted Ryan. It was the 'sperm donor' — as she described the man who got her pregnant — a white guy who was a police officer on her reserve back then, who actually 'gifted' her one more time, six months after the twins' birth.

"Before she knew she was pregnant again, the officer was transferred to Saskatchewan. It took some time before Dorothy got in touch with him. She pleaded with him to take financial responsibility for the new mouth to feed. He fired back 'it can't be mine', but agreed to provide her with money for an abortion. Disillusioned and frightened, she came to that conclusion herself, oblivious that she had offered him an easy way out."

"How old was she then?"

"Barely seventeen," Cassidy said.

"Oh, God."

"When the money came, she used it to satisfy her new habit: drinking. Her next problem came along quickly. She gave birth to a baby girl afflicted with foetal alcohol syndrome."

"What a waste of life."

"Yes. She admitted it too. But back then, she didn't care. She didn't have the motivation to live. She was young and very depressed, mainly because she loved that man, who in fact had just used her.

"She didn't bond with her new baby, because she was never sober. Her mother had already taken in Ryan's twin brother Matthew, along with her own full house of children. Understandably, she refused to pick up the extra burden, the afflicted baby girl. The poor thing spent her first five years of life in foster homes. After Dorothy cleaned up, she took charge of her children without any help.

"About two years ago, Ryan's biological father — who in the meantime had become an important political figure in Manitoba — lost his wife and their two children in a house fire. It was then that he 'remembered' that he had fathered a boy years before. Taking charge of his *son* seemed the 'right thing to do.' He knew about Matthew but nothing about his twin brother: our Ryan. When Dorothy returned to her mother with the healthy baby in her arms, she told everyone the twin had died.

"Strange how some people's mind work after a tragedy. He decided to 'make things right' but had the shock of his life when he found out that Dorothy didn't terminate the second pregnancy when he sent money for that purpose. And you could guess which child he was willing to claim as his own."

"Not the poor girl but Ryan's twin, the liability free child," Janet said, with deep indignation. "Such perversity!"

"Yes. And of course, he was not too shy to throw threats left and right, making the poor woman's life a living hell when she refused to give up her boy. Scared and desperate, Dorothy was forced to 'unearth' Ryan's existence. From that point on, the biological father, who seemed to like the alternative even better, took control from behind the scenes. He put a down payment on a nice house for Dorothy's family and secured her husband a well-paying job in Fort McMurray. His stratagem was to bolster their family finances to demonstrate that they were prosperous enough to sustain the claim of getting Ryan back. And then, he waited patiently in the shadows, only to gain nothing. He overlooked the possibility that Dorothy might get cold feet and eventually seek our help."

"That was a good thing she did, darling," Janet said, wiping her tears.

"A truly wonderful thing. Dorothy was stunned to learn from Brad that she didn't need to grant him anything. The guy never wanted to be pinned down before, by recognizing any of his children legally; he had no rights as a father now. His heartless attitude backfired on him.

"Dorothy was honest with us. She said that she needed — as a loan — thirty thousand dollars to pay back the amount the biological father had given them. We knew that was the truth; our sources said that they had used that amount for a down payment on their home."

"Did you—" Janet started to ask.

"Yes, we paid their house off. We made things right and got peace of mind in return."

"Yes, yes indeed," Janet said, looking sad. "I wonder, dear, how this poor soul must have felt throughout this turmoil. Like losing Ryan all over again."

"As I recall, she didn't feel that way at all. You know it astounded me how she grasped the whole circumstance. It scared her to death to think of losing any of her children, yet she said that it was more terrifying to live with the guilt of causing someone else to lose their child. *My child.* So she turned around. The least she could do was to protect the innocent. She decided that nothing should upset his happiness, just because a stranger wanted to fulfil his own happiness at any price."

By late Thursday, the doctors considered Eve out of danger. Her temperature remained at a normal level for twenty-four hours. She was sleeping peacefully on her own and required significantly fewer drugs. Some of her daily supporters tended to their fatigued bodies and got back to the normal routine of their lives.

Some, but not all.

The Malones came to the hospital less frequently, as they were taking care of Anthony and his school routine. Garry and Brian took turns and stayed days or nights, retreating to Eve's house to sleep or eat. Brian disappeared for hours at a time. Sometimes he came back freshly changed and shaven, indicating that he had gone home. He became quiet and seemed somewhat preoccupied.

Everybody wondered if Adam ever left the hospital. The same jeans, leather jacket, and the growing stubble on his face suggested he hadn't. He came and went from the nursery to visit his babies, but always returned to visitors lounge in unit 49. The past few days had taken a toll on him. His face was beginning to look pale and gaunt.

Deep in his thoughts, Adam didn't hear anyone approaching. He was startled as he recognized Brian's image in the window's reflection. Adam turned and stared.

The soft sparkle in Brian's eyes disarmed him.

"Sorry if I startled you," Brian whispered, glancing at Garry who was dozing in an armchair. "I wanted to talk to you, if you don't mind."

"Yes, of course."

"I'm sure we both could benefit from a breath of fresh air," Brian said.

At the main entrance, outside the Woman's Centre, they sat down on the concrete bench.

"Any more news on Eve?" Adam asked.

"She's coming out of it. Slowly but surely, she is finally giving us a break."

His emphasis on *us* didn't escape Adam.

"That's actually what I wanted to talk to you about," Brian started. "Her doctor decided that she could go to a regular unit tomorrow. It will only be a matter of hours before she is fully awake and responsive."

Adam was dismayed. Did Brian want him to vanish when Eve was back to her old self?

"Eve called your name," Brian said.

Adam's chin lifted up in disbelief.

Brian laughed. "No, she is not delirious any longer, if that's what you're thinking. She sleeps peacefully but from time to time cries out a few words. I doubt she'll remember most of it when she fully wakes."

Adam looked Brian hard in the eyes.

Brian held the stare. "If I told you we could shake hands and part as friends tonight, would you believe me?"

"It all depends," Adam said and stood up.

"I'm leaving tomorrow. Permanently. There is no need for me to hang around here. Eve loves *you*. I knew that before I married her. As for your feelings for her, well...one would have to be blind not to see that she's the light of your life."

Adam looked stunned. "But what about you? I mean—"

"I'm keeping a promise. I prayed to God for Eve's recovery in exchange for my stepping out of her life. He did His job, so I'll do mine. Once upon a time, Eve and I loved each other dearly, but I made the mistake of taking her feelings for granted. So I've lost her. We met again, but it was too late. She loved you this time — made no secret of it. There was nothing I could do to change that. The love we shared this time was of a different sort."

"Where do you go from here?"

"Detroit, most likely. I've gotten in touch with some of my Aussie mates who live there." Brian stood. "I have a favour to ask. Can you help Eve handle the divorce?"

"Yes," Adam promised, still reeling from shock.

Brian extended his right hand. "Friends?" he asked.

Adam laughed and nodded. "For sure."

"I leave precious cargo in your charge, mate. Take care of them," Brian said. "Eve is going to be awake soon and will need you. I'll be on guard for a couple of more hours. Call a taxi and go get some rest. I won't go inside until I see you on your way."

When the lights of a cab turning into the parking lot brightened their faces, the two men shook hands again and said their goodbyes.

Halfway towards the sliding door, Brian turned and called, "Hey, Adam! Do Eve a favour. Lose the beard!"

Adam laughed. "Will do!"

Eve woke to the sound of a crying baby. Her motherly instincts made her want to jump out of bed, but the pain stopped her. One hand over her stomach, she manoeuvred her body into a sitting position, and then rolled her legs down the edge of the bed, just as the occupational therapist had instructed.

It was easier this time, Eve sighed with relief. Just then, the door opened and a nurse entered sporting a wide smile.

"You're up again, Mrs. Nelson. That's very good, but don't overdo it. We're here to help, just give us a buzz. As for the precious little ones, I can take them back to the nursery after you feed them. You need your rest," the nurse said and helped Eve to the rocking chair, supporting her as she sat down.

Taking the extra pillows from the windowsill, the nurse noticed a small, exquisite, white floral arrangement behind them. A small envelope was protruding from its middle. "What beautiful flowers!"

"What flowers?" Eve asked lifting her head.

After both babies were fed and asleep in their bassinets, Eve picked up the envelope. She unfolded the paper and her face relaxed as she read:

*My dearest Eve,*

*While you may think that I "snuck out" on you, I assure you it was done at the best of times and with good intentions. I left you in good hands: Adam's.*

*Darling, do not fret reading this missive. Adam was divorced just as he told you back then. Evil blinded you both but in the end it was overpowered and crushed by the purity of true love.*

*Last night I had a momentous talk with Adam. Yet, one thing I left out so you can enlighten him yourself.*

*Be happy my dearest, and don't be hard on yourself about me. I'm the soldier that returns home proudly wearing the medal for a tender mission accomplished (if they ever come up with that one!). I am doing what I need and want to do. You and I shared something special that's going to stay always in our hearts.*

*With all my love,*

*Brian*

It was time to go home. After four days in that room and six in the intensive care unit, Eve was ready. She marvelled as she looked about the room, now full of flowers and dear memories of the last few days.

Like the memories of Adam's first visit…

Her light sleep had been interrupted by the squeaky wheels of the hospital baby cart. In her wildest dreams, she never could have imagined Adam pushing the bassinet with the twins in it.

"I was hoping to be the first one to introduce my daughters to you—" Adam started and smiled apologetically. "But I overslept."

"Tell me that when *I'm* awake," Eve said.

They embraced for the longest time with tears pouring down their faces.

"You just don't like to be wet during supper, is that it, Victoria darling?" Eve was cooing over the crying baby, applying soft, warm kisses on her tiny fingers and toes, when Adam came in.

"Dr. Hasinoff will be here in about an hour to discharge our little princesses," Adam said. He rushed in to take over the job of changing the diaper, and then moved on to do the same with little Janet.

Eve was amazed at Adam's ability to fall into fatherhood. When he was done changing little Janet's diaper, Eve finally asked.

"Darling, how is it you never knew that you *could* father a child?

For a moment, a shadow crossed Adam's face. "You recall how I told you I received the news while I was on business in Halifax?"

Eve nodded.

"Well, that was a hoax, a doctored piece of paper. But at the time it seemed credible, to someone like me, who was busy, confused, and overwhelmed by feelings of inadequacy. In retrospect, Cassidy said a specialist would never confirm infertility from only one assessment, no matter how sophisticated the test was. I regret that I never showed her that letter.

Eve was touched. "I'm so very sorry, darling. You didn't deserve that."

Adam laughed. "But I got what I deserve and what is rightfully mine in the end. Didn't I?"

"You certainly did, with double bragging rights."

They were silent for a moment. Both Mom and Dad were revelling over their creations: one on her shoulder working on a burp and the other in his arms waiting to be fed. Waiting for another burp, Eve spoke her mind again, "Your parents are quite a couple. One only needs to spend a bit of time with your mother to fall in love with her. It's a privilege for us to name one of our daughters after her. I was a bit nervous to meet your father, though. I imagined him to be a real dragon, flames coming out of his nostrils and all."

Adam was amused by her description. "He was all of that and more, but then he metamorphosed. He's so different — no, opposite — of how he used to be. He's so loving and dedicated to his new granddaughters that one would think that his own life depended on guarding them. Funny how he's finding this side of himself towards the end of his life. On second thought, it's better late than never."

An impish look crossed Eve's face.

"What's so funny?"

"Yesterday, when you practically chased your parents out of the room, your father asked you if you had asked me something. What was that all about?"

Adam adopted a casual tone. "Ah, that? It was nothing."

"Really?"

"Really," Adam said averting eye contact.

"You know, I have a very convincing way of forcing your hand into confessing that 'nothing'. You might be surprised, but it's a pretty effective way."

Adam played along. Bending over the babies, he kissed her and said, "You're bragging."

"I'm not. I won't feed your daughters until you tell me what ensued yesterday between you two Carry men."

Adam protested. "That's blackmailing a poor father!"

"So, what's it going to be?" Eve pretended to frown. "Putting your daughters back on formula, or—?"

"Okay, okay," he settled, kissing her. "No need to hurt the innocent." They exchanged the babies so little Janet could be fed. "I blamed my parents for letting me sleep in on Friday, when I should have been here first thing in the morning to ask you to be my wife," Adam said. "But I couldn't have done it anyways because I sent back that ring. Dad realized I was serious about asking you to marry me and asked Mom to pass me her ring so I could make my offer to you—" He stopped. "Why are you laughing? I mean, please do. My parents have been acting like school kids lately."

"No, no," Eve said, through her gales of laughter. "It's not them. It's you, Mr. Adam Carry. You're blushing and looking quite vulnerable. A picture I quite enjoy seeing. But I wonder why your dad was so insistent that you should give me a ring," Eve said.

"Well, probably he wanted to make sure I would catch you between husbands, beautiful *Miss Scarlet O'Hara.*"

"Oh, *Rhett Butler*, but you do give a damn."

# Epilogue

It was a good business decision. One he could live — and die — with. And most importantly, one he made by himself. He knew it would shock everyone, but it gave him immeasurable pleasure and peace of mind. He looked in his old notebook and dialled a number he had never thought he would dial for this reason. Without delay, he was transferred to the right person.

"David Tomlinson speaking," a thunderous voice announced.

"David. It's George Carry. How do you feel about buying my ownership in Carstone?"

"George Carry?" A short pause followed. "George, are you serious?"

"Answer my question. Do you want to buy it?"

"George, my man, of course I want to buy it. However, I just can't believe I'm hearing right. In the forty plus years we've known each other, we have always wanted what the other one had. And now this? Lord! If we were not declared enemies, at least we were open rivals and now you make this proposition. No need to waste time on questions, George. Let's meet and talk numbers."

The room was filled with smoke and champagne. Although, at first, David Tomlinson was afraid the offer might be a hoax, he was wealthy enough to pour away a river of champagne.

Nine men in their impeccable three-piece business suits sat around the table. An urgent call from their executives had brought them here.

They were bewildered, asking themselves an obvious question: Why were WestPump's people sitting at the same table with Carstone's? It seemed unimaginable, sharing a cheerful moment with champagne and Cuban cigars.

"Welcome everyone," George Carry started. "Gentlemen, I know this comes as a complete surprise to you, but your boss and I invited you here to witness the union of our corporations. I am calling it a union, because I am selling my shares with a special stipulation that pays careful consideration to my employees: It gives them continuity under new management.

"As you all know, I survived my second heart attack. My decision to sell came mainly due to my health issues but also because I finally realized that my son has no interest in the oil industry. I have come to respect and appreciate his aspirations and interests."

For a moment, George watched the astounded faces. Then he continued, "As you see, David and I didn't invite our legal representatives. We had a cordial, candid meeting just before you were called in. We decided that it would be appropriate to let our most loyal friends — as David and I like to think of you, valuable people here — know about our plan first, because you've helped our corporations achieve an enviable place in the industry. There are going to be changes, as anyone can imagine, but they will be easily managed under David's leadership."

Under the thick smoke, a Polaroid picture was being passed from hand to hand. With much conversation and celebration taking place, the slamming of a door went unnoticed.

"What the hell is going on in here?"

The room went deadly quiet. Only the last puffs of smoke danced lazily in the air. Suddenly someone snickered, and another followed. A man cleared his throat and there were a few gasps. Before George could get a hold of his Cuban cigar, Alicia snatched it from his mouth.

"You old fool. Why don't you put a gun to your head? It would be less painful to die that way."

George allowed himself to weigh her opinion for a moment and snatched back his cigar.

"'Old fox' suits me better. And by the way, didn't J.P. tell you not to disturb this meeting? I'm in the middle of a business transaction here."

"What the hell are you talking about? What kind of business transaction and why wasn't I invited?" Alicia demanded.

"Well, actually, I've just sold all my company shares to David. He will be taking over for me, because I have decided to retire and spend time with the newest additions to my family," George said, noticing Alicia glancing at the Polaroid he was holding in his hand. "Oh, and I'd like to introduce you to my granddaughters — Adam's babies."

"That's all a bunch of bull. It can't be the fucking truth." Alicia looked possessed.

"Accept the truth, Alicia. I was greedy and stupid and blinded by your sick mind, but now I'm free from your poison and want to enjoy my life."

Alicia made a hasty exit, a trail of obscenities behind.

Eve read the precious letter again. She kissed the page with the familiar writing as she would kiss the hand that wrote it. With all the busy tasks in his life, Garry found time to write her a letter. The second one in the last four weeks. His words made her feel special. He apologized again for leaving so soon but knew that she would thrive in Adam's care. He also wrote that he was happy at the way things had turned out.

The second letter was from Brian. Her dearest friend Brian. He wanted her to know that he found supportive friends in Detroit, and through them, acquired a job in his profession. She should not worry about him. He promised that he would visit them someday.

Adam went to Calgary to finish training his replacement; there was only so much he could do by phone. He relinquished his rocking chair in the nursery reluctantly. Eve tried to convince him she would be okay, because she had lots of helpers.

"Fine," he had said. "One week, and I'll be back to my family."

Every time Eve entered the nursery, her heart filled with joy. She remembered the very first time she'd opened that door: the day Adam brought his new family into this rented house in the country. Adam said that they would call it home until the lady of the house found the time to give him insights on what kind of house he could design and build for their family. He had asked her to close her eyes until she was in the babies' room. When she opened them, the view surpassed her dreams. All the babies' furniture was made of white wicker!

She walked over and lightly touched the scar on Victoria's head. It looked more like a long scratch that was fading away. She'd had a CT Neuro scan and everything looked normal. She then wiped Janet's forehead of fine droplets of perspiration. "Little Janet sweats a lot and would need all her clothing changed twice a night." Adam had told her before he left for Calgary. Satisfied that both babies were asleep, Eve decided to take a nap. The night before, little Janet was cranky with colic. For the first time, Eve acknowledged that taking care of two babies was a lot of work.

During the day, Anthony, the grandparents, and everyone else who dropped in for a visit were helping her, but at night she was on her own. Little Janet woke up every hour and it took as long to get her back to sleep. Sometimes her crying woke up Victoria, who had already formed her sleep routine. If Janet had a quiet night, Victoria had the same. One of Eve's nipples was also of concern. She winced in pain as the babies sucked ravenously from it. *If Janet senior offers to stay overnight again, I will take her up on the offer at once,* she thought.

Saddened that she was celebrating the six-week milestone alone, she retired to the master bedroom and soon fell into a restful sleep.

"Adam?"

"Garth, my man! I'm on my way to Edmonton. Driving, actually. I'm done with my work in Calgary. What's up? You seemed mysterious and hesitant in your message."

"Betty and I are getting married next month. Will you be my best man?

"Man, I thought you'd never ask!"

"Thanks so much."

"Did you say next month? What's the rush?"

"It's a shotgun wedding," Garth said. "We just found out that we're pregnant. Gotta do the right thing. For the baby and Betty's little girl. Man, I'm scared and thrilled at the same time. I wanted you to be the first to know."

"Congratulations are in order, my man!" Adam grinned. "The three of you need to come over this weekend. Time to celebrate. I want to thank you for getting Eve's divorce finalized."

"No problem. But enough about that and *my* news, my friend," Garth said. "Want to hear some unparalleled news? Hot off the press? Alicia is in Hollywood—"

"What's so unparalleled about that? We all knew she went there after she cashed in her shares," Adam said, with slight irritation in his voice.

"You didn't let me finish. She's locked up in a mental institution."

*"What!"* Adam couldn't believe it. "What happened?"

"She snapped. WestPump was lucky she finalized the sale before she went over the edge."

A rush of adrenaline filled Adam's body.

A little more than an hour, he would be home with his family.

His mother saw him first. He was charging up the stairs two at a time but stopped to hug her. She was coming down the stairs with two little bottles of milk in hand.

"Adam, you didn't tell us you were on your way home. Your darling wife is sleeping. And your return is timely, since I believe your daughters," a word she knew he loved to hear, "are keeping her up at night. I wish she would have let me stay the night sometimes," Janet said, and then tilted her head toward the garden. "Grandpa took the wee ones to the garden for an alfresco bottle feed," she said, lifting up the tiny bottles. "Mike and Crista are here. They're in the garden with the boys. Make sure you go and say hi to everyone," Janet called after her son, as he started up the stairs again.

At the bedroom door, he put down his briefcase. He vowed that he would never bring work over that threshold.

Walking in quietly, he stood still by the bed for a moment, mesmerized by his wife's sleeping form.

He then went into the walk-in closet to undress. He stepped into the shower and let the water pour over his body. Moments later he gasped as he suddenly felt Eve's embrace from behind.

"Sweet Lord!" he said, as he turned to meet his wife. Finally.

Minutes later, and a trail of water on the hardwood floor, they moved to the bed, depleted, covered in water and sweat and consumed with love. With his last shred of energy, Adam pulled Eve's head onto his shoulder. She responded to his invitation by hugging his body, entwining her legs with his.

Freely, they lay there doing nothing for a long while.

Then Adam said, "You really know how to shake a man of his last wits."

"Only my husband. And only because I know his wits can take it."

"Right," Adam murmured and pulled her closer for a kiss, his mind and body still under the effects of their lovemaking.

Idly, Eve was playing with the hair on his chest. The peacefulness of the moment embracing them.

*This is the moment,* she thought. In fact, it was too right not to think of it. "I haven't done this since that night..."

Adam watched her fingers on his chest, a mixture of confusion on his face.

"No, not this. But...that," she said, moving her hand down onto his abdomen and then lower. And lower. "This was not a part of my marriage to Brian."

Adam couldn't suppress his breath of relief. "I kind of guessed. Or maybe it was just my wish that *that* was the case."

Eve supported her body on an elbow and pulled herself up to straddle him, letting the towel tumble off in the process.

"How else could it have been when only you lived in my heart?"

"God, how much I would have given to hear these words when I thought there was no more hope."

"What am I going to do next time?" George grunted.

"What do you mean, Grandpa George?" Crista asked, amused.

The old man made sure he was supporting both bottles at the right angle simultaneously, before clarifying his statement, "What I mean, dear lady, is this: What am I going to do with only two old hands, if Eve and Adam have triplets next time?"

Everybody laughed.

Soon Crista joined the boys for a ball game. They needed one more player to make two teams and Mike was in deep conversation with Grandpa George, as everyone called Carry senior these days.

Eve and Adam appeared and Mike greeted them with a loud, "Look who's here!" Then, as George made a sign to lower his voice, he added softly, "Man, I never knew anyone who could be missed that much after only being away for a few days. Nor one who comes home in sport slacks and damp hair," he whispered and winked.

"Welcome home, son."

"Good to be home, Dad."

"I hope you don't leave home so soon, son, or else you'll find your daughters six feet tall in a blink of an eye."

"Oh, God," Eve laughed. "Not six feet, please."

An hour later, when the babies attracted attention with their cries, the adults debated what to do. They looked around and called for help.

"Eve? Adam?"

They had disappeared again.